KINGSLEY L. DENNIS

THE REALITY GAME

Relations with Ourselves, the World Around Us
& the Greater Universe

THE ABE COMMENTARIES
VOL.2

THE WAY BACK HOME SERIES

BEAUTIFUL TRAITOR BOOKS

CONTENTS

PREFACE

This is the second volume in the ABE Commentaries series. In Volume One of this series, *Life in the Continuum: Explorations into Human Existence, Consciousness & Vibratory Evolution* (2022), the dialogue with the Unified Field (ABE) was broad and ranged across a set of diverse areas that included mind, body and spirit; human society and culture; science and technology; and humanity and its future. The commentaries in this second volume are based upon a set of communications, mostly from question and answer-based sessions, that we had with Abe from the end of 2018 until late June 2019 – that is, a period of 6 months. Unlike the sessions that comprised the first volume (which took place over a very intensive 4 weeks), these sessions were conducted within a more open and free-flowing timeframe.

At the beginning of these sessions, we asked Abe whether they had any further information to convey, and in which direction they wished to take the conversations. Abe answered that they would wish for the next sessions to cover the subjects of relation – 'that being to each other, to your world, to the universe.' Hence, the subjects that are covered in this book fall under the following six sections: Relations with Ourselves; The Reality Game; Relations with the World Around Us; Contact with the Greater Universe; Consciousness, Time & Energy; and Clarifying the Way Back Home. The final session on the topic of the way back home was added at the end after we had finished our questioning on the subject of relations. As usual, we asked Abe what they would wish to communicate next, and they replied that they would like to discuss further the subject of the way back home. Whilst it is not essential to have read the previous volume, it would help in providing a framework and context for where this second book in the series will take us.

NOTES

I. ON THE ABE COMMUNICATIONS

They are a series of Questions and Answers between two people – Nicola and me – and Abe. The Abe materials are positive and inspiring communications that urge us to find our way back into balance – from a 'splintered mind' into 'home resonance.' These communications are **not** a channeling but an *allowing*. This second volume of communications contains almost 200 questions and answers covering such topics as relations with ourselves, relations with the world around us and the greater universe, the nature of our reality, consciousness, time, and energy, and more. This material has been 'allowed' at this time for it is essential that humanity finds its home resonance and comes back into a harmonious relationship with itself and the world.

Nicola receives the Abe communications in a kind of 'stream of consciousness' style. That is, the words are almost entirely without punctuation and consist of continuous words rather than sentences. After I receive the communications, I read through them and do my best to format them into grammatical sentences. It appears that the sentence style can be somewhat 'archaic' at times. There are many 'but see,' 'but hear this,' 'see this,' and similar phrases. Yet these are very useful markers as they allow me to see where one sentence finishes and another one begins. There were times also when Abe seemed to say something in a way that was not the most fluid, or modern way of expression. I wondered if Abe wanted for me to 'translate' their communications into a more flowing, informal manner. Abe replied: 'If you feel extremely strongly to do so, then yes. We would also like to say that if you are on the borderline of wanting to, then we feel it should be kept as it is.'

There you have it – we were given permission to make alterations only if we felt 'extremely strongly' to do so. Otherwise, we were to leave it alone. Perhaps there is a good reason for this. Maybe, just maybe, the transmission style of Abe is also impacting us as we read – acting upon our own inner cognition? The point to repeat here is that these communications are not to be regarded as a form of 'channeling' as is commonly known. Channeling usually takes place between an entity and a human being: often this entity is a discarnate spirit, a sentient intelligence/species, or other form of non-terrestrial being. Yet, in this case, the communications are being received from the Source of Ourselves. In other words, we are in communication with the 'higher,' or non-manifested, part of our consciousness. For this reason, we were informed not to regard this as a channeling but as an *allowing*. We are 'allowing' a part of our incarnated self to communicate with the unified field of consciousness. We are, so to say, not in contact with another 'being' but with our own Being. And since each person has this ability, this contact, it is regarded as a form of 'allowing' – we only need to *allow* ourselves.

Another point to raise is that in these initial communications – or *allowances* – most of the messages were signed off with 'Love & Light.' This may seem like a cliché in many channeled or 'new age' material. Yet the reason for this became evident in our later series of communications (not in this book) when Abe shifted from 'Love & Light' to 'Allowance & Light.' The energy of 'love' then became the energy of *allowance* that is central to how all forms of consciousness relate. There will be more to say on this switch in any later volume of the Abe material. What I would like to point out here is that we should not take the phrase 'Love & Light' at face value but also recognize for how it represents the various states of existence. Love represents pure consciousness, the Source of All That Is. And Light represents the photons or building blocks of materiality. All matter is created from the density of photonic arrangement; that is, we are essentially light beings. Therefore, by signing off with the phrase 'Love & Light' Abe is in fact, to my mind, signifying the unity of no-form and form: of Pure Consciousness (Love) and of Matter (Light).

II. ON THE USE OF THE TERM 'ABE'

The name that we use and which we were given – Abe – represents 'an abbreviation of pure consciousness.' For me, that makes sense. I hope it does to the reader too. Abe has never been wholly a 'form.' As a unity, it is formless; yet it can be expressed through form. Abe is not a being, a person, a species – Abe is *Everything*. Abe exists within the source of all manifestation: the collective consciousness field from which all materiality is birthed. It is also both you and I. Abe refers to itself as the collective Source - yet prefers to use the term, Unity. Unification is a major theme of Abe's communications. In the words of Abe:

> We are but your original state of being, it is just that you do so have conditions of a body which creates different

vibratory interference in a way. For you see, we do not have a physical body and are not of a point of place only, but when in communication with you both...We want to guide you to the way back home, here and now.

III. REFERENCING

All quotations and citations in the text are taken from the Abe communications (see Part Two). No outside material is referenced. When you see a few words in speech marks 'like this' then they are the words of Abe that I am bringing into my sentences. Longer citations and quotes are referenced according to the section and question/answer from where they are located. For example, when it is written (S.2.Q10), then this refers to Section 2, Question 10. I have gone through the sections, with their questions, in a chronological order from beginning (S.1) to end (S.6). The sections can be found in Part Two of this book, if the reader wishes to look them up.

INTRODUCTION

We live in a world that is now defined by our digital connections and communications. We are witnessing a transformation across the planet into a rapidly expanding physical-digital ecosystem that operates 24/7. Planet Earth is undergoing transformation as well as an electro-terraforming. From the viewpoint of technological progress, all this would seem so wonderful. Then why so much strife, struggle, and suffering? The problem is that while we have enhanced our connections, we have simultaneously neglected our relations.

We are not communicating correctly. We are not in right relationships with ourselves, others, or the world because we do not understand the fundamentals of *how* we are connected. Just because we talk through our devices to one another does not mean that we are in a relationship or are communicating. We have not yet fully grasped our essential natures; how, in essence, we are aspects of unified consciousness existing in pinpoints of physical expression. It is impossible to separate ourselves from the greater field of consciousness (what is often referred to as Source). The isolation we sometimes feel is the unknowing of our true state and potential. We are experiencing a profound sense of alienation as our world hurtles rapidly headfirst into advancing technological systems that, at the same time, take us further and further away from what it means to be an essential human being. Our true relations have gotten out of synch, and we are all feeling this uncoupling in various and diverse ways. I have no doubt that it is because of this that Abe provided the direction for taking these conversations into themes of relationality. As the reader will soon see, Abe is communicating that humanity is not sufficiently aware of its relationships. Furthermore, if we move ahead now without first recalibrating our fundamental relations, then we are building upon sand. As individuals, many of us innately feel this disconnect, yet for the most part we push it away from ourselves – we project it externally onto a myriad of other things. But now is not the time for turning a blind eye or for allowing distractions to overtake us. On the contrary, now is the critical moment for viewing, recognizing, and acknowledging our very deficits so that we have time to make amends and recalibrate before life gets ahead of us. Humanity, as a collective species, is now ready for these important shifts and rearrangements to occur. Now is the time, for we are surely witnessing a transformational moment in the development of the human being.

The outer and inner fragmentation that humanity is experiencing is also largely due to how we are currently perceiving the nature of reality. The depth to which we understand reality corresponds to our capacity to perceive. And in this, there are many false perceptions, illusions, and delusions that we can get entangled within. Without awareness, we remain locked into a system – a 'reality game' – that does not currently serve us well. From Abe's perspective, it is as if humanity is forever chasing its tails. Reality is playing us, but we are not playing it: 'reality is only reality if you do so meet it.' The less aware we are of the nature of our reality and how it operates, the more likely we are to slumber through our lives, never questioning the Game. In fact, is reality a 'game' at all – and if so, what does this mean? These are some of the questions and queries that are brought up in this volume. Through the communications with Abe, we are being nudged to view with a critical eye some of the things we have taken for granted in our lives. Primarily, how we relate to everything around us, and the nature of those relations.

I hope the reader will gain as much insight from the conversations in this book as I did in producing my own commentaries upon the material. The more I reflected on the information provided, the more those little 'aha' moments suddenly popped up. And we each need such nudges to steer us into perceptive awakening. If there was ever a time for an awakening of the human species, then that time is certainly now.

And now I hand this material over to you, the reader.

PART ONE
THE COMMENTARIES

If you believe you are out of the game, you're still playing it.

ABE

18

SECTION ONE
Relations with Ourselves

The main theme running through this volume is that of 'relationality.' In our connections, we have what Abe refers to as *relational value*. This interconnectivity runs through all that we do and encounter here in the physical domain – 'even the smallest of things.' And it is in these relations that we can make new patterns, new pathways. In creating new pathways, we are re-wiring ourselves; and this re-wiring then gets reflected back into our external world. This notion of internal re-wiring, or re-patterning, to then reflect externally into our outer life is a major theme running through this second volume. As the sub-title shows, the theme here is of relations with ourselves, with the world around us, and with the greater universe: 'These are but the states that need to be addressed, that need to be aligned, and do indeed need to be looked at in depth - is this of understanding?' (S.1.Q2) By Abe specifically providing these themes, it gives us a message that humanity is not sufficiently aware of its relationships – both with itself and the wider universe. Yet, as in all new things, 'this will take time to take root.'

The message here is that if we, humanity, start to build forth – i.e., make advances – without getting our footings right now, then we shall be building upon 'un-solid ground.' In other words, we need to get our foundations correct before going further. Abe discussed this also in Volume 1 in terms of going forward from a splintered mind. People inherently feel this innate connection between themselves and others, whether it be a person or an object, event, or experience: 'They feel it when they watch a sunrise or in the eyes of a lover; they feel this on a deeper level, but they do so put it outside of themselves.' (S.1.Q3) By placing it away from ourselves, we deny us new pathways of connection and this affects frequency resonance. This is one of the issues of the intellect, or over-intellectualization. The intellect tries to rationalize and categorize experiences, and this loses out to the greater integral feeling that comes from opening up to our inner senses; that is, of combining the intellect with the heart-brain. New internal pathways can be formed quicker when the intellect-mind is in resonance with the heart-brain. This creates a greater balance and dynamic within the individual and forms a more coherent, and distinct, frequency resonance. As we build these resonant pathways within us, so will they also affect our outer realities: 'and you will not only feel these new pathways internally forming but also see them being built in your reality. This is the path of unity - is this of understanding now?' (S.1.Q3)

If we are not 'synced up' then we will not be allowing this unity to form and to be a part of our reality. An imbalance shall remain within us, and this will manifest in various ways as dissonance within our outer lives. The bottom line is that we are as separated as we feel ourselves to be. If we cannot shake off these feelings or beliefs of our own separation – 'for if your mind still carries this notion' – then we shall not be able to attract the new resonant pathways. We shall remain within our energetic bubble of dissonance. These then become our limiting patterns that define our lives. In this, there is a sense of waste for we can always be so much more than we imagine: 'It is such a shame for you can, and always have, the option to be much more, to let in so much more, if you allow yourselves to be but cracked open.' (S.1.Q4) There are external shifts occurring that are nudging us into recognizing our current state and the need for change. One of our limitations is that we crowd ourselves too much; like trying to stuff all our house belongings into one suitcase when we travel. We need to create a space. On this matter, Abe is quite blunt: 'If we would like to put this entirely bluntly, it would be this - create a space, create a void, and then allow for things to come together, to build themselves up, for it will be in this void that emergence will happen.' (S.1.Q4) For there to be change within and between people, it is necessary for *people* to change. It is this that can trigger relational patterns and create shifts. As always, Abe tells us that what we wish to be seen without 'has to be firstly seen within, and when seen within then shines without. Like we said, a multiplying and unity - a wave, a pattern.' (S.1.Q4) And such things can only be seen when there is a pause moment, a halt for reflection.

Such relationality is part of a mutual arising; it cannot ever be isolated to just one side. For whatever we create and establish within ourselves will always resonate out into our relations – we cannot keep it within us no more than a stream flows in one spot. Abe says that this needed space, this void moment, has arrived – humanity has entered into a dip, a rest period. Abe made the following comment at the end of 2018: 'The multiplying stage is peaked - you are now in the dip; the rest is unity. This is all we would like to say for it will all become evident.' (S.1.Q5) As any perceptive reader will know, humanity entered into a global slowdown, or halt, in early 2020.

Whilst within this slowdown period it is beneficial to consider consciousness and the human conscious experience.

Abe communicates that there are 'levels of consciousness but only one flow of consciousness.' A little explanation is then given:

> Consciousness is not an interaction with things, it is not separate - it is an arising. There is just this one flow which is us and which is you, and everything else that you can think of, even something that looks like it cannot be conscious, is at some level. Now, hear this, many other things are operating and flowing with pure conscious experience. More so than what you are, for it does not slice and dice it up; it does not get wrapped up in other vibratory patterns that are so constricting. (S.1.Q5)

Humans have evolved, of this there is no doubt; yet, in our evolution we have come to a material state where we separate things. Through our so-called advanced thinking we have come to view consciousness as a phenomenon that emerges from the material (in this case, the human brain). Yet consciousness is an arising from itself as Source and emerges into manifestation through the physical aspect of itself (e.g., as in human bodies). To recognize this allows for us to step back into unification, and away from our perspective of separation. At present, Abe informs us that there are five levels of conscious experience within the unity of consciousness flow. These are identified as: i) uninterrupted consciousness (unitary consciousness); ii) vibratory essence of self (vibratory signature); iii) unconscious (autopilot); iv) sensory vibratory essence (sensory feedback); and v) conscious experience (mental filtering). These levels are vibratory patterns within an underlying unified frequency (the one flow of unitary consciousness). At the fundamental level we have what Abe calls the 'uninterrupted consciousness.' This can be said to be pure, or unified, consciousness. What we may also refer to as Source Consciousness. At the next level we have the 'vibratory essence of self.' This is our qualitative self, and from this state we experience life. The next, third level, is that of the unconscious – the 'vibratory essence of unconscious behaviour of programming.' People drop into this state of consciousness when we slip out of conscious awareness. This is casually referred to as the 'autopilot' mode. The next level from this, we are told, is that of the 'sensory vibratory essence.' This relates to our interaction with the external world; our senses and the feedback that these senses relay to us. It is an interactional form of consciousness that constantly provides our body-mind with environmental responses. And the final level is that of conscious experience; this is not to be confused with our general definition of the 'mind.' It is similar, yet not a singular experience as how we tend to view the mind. Taken together, these five levels of conscious experience all flow within the vibratory pattern of a unified consciousness. Multiple patterns of conscious experience all flow within the one pure consciousness; for in truth, 'there is nothing that is outside of this stream.' These differing aspects of conscious experience all make up the human integral life experience.

The human being tends to remain tightly wrapped within several of these vibratory patterns – like being smothered by a tight overcoat – without perceiving the integrated whole. Thus, life is perceived as a separateness. We are advised not to consider these consciousness levels as being with a hierarchy; i.e., as one being 'higher' or 'better' than the other. Rather, they are varied expressions of a whole. It may be cosy to be tightly wrapped up within the overcoat, but the time has come to take this off and to open up conscious perception. This is not so difficult; only that humanity makes it much more difficult than it actually is. The uninterrupted flow of consciousness is never amiss or absent, but because of its being shut out it is almost unrecognisable; and this is not allowing a conscious resonance to be established. The human being needs to resonate with the flow of consciousness. Abe then provided the following diagram which is a representation of the wholeness of relation and the integrated levels of consciousness.

This symbolic integrated wholeness includes the five states of consciousness as well as three other states: the *you, us,* and *both*. In other words, it seems to suggest the trinity of 'I', 'Thou,' and the I/Thou together as trinity/unity. The 'dots of the eight points are all aligned, all synced up neural pathways.' (S.1.Q5) This symbolic 8-point integrated unity thus embodies all degrees and states of consciousness (Five) alongside the trinity of Source (i) and Vibrational signature (ii) as a whole unity (3). This is the trinity of Source = Energy + Manifestation, which is a unity.

Yet, as Abe repeatedly states, we confine these levels as within the Russian Doll. We limit our experience to one, or two, of these levels. These levels are not to be classified as 'lower' or 'below' but rather as limiting aspects of the whole. For example, if we function mainly through the unconscious coupled with the sensory vibratory essence then our lives are lived mostly on autopilot based on feedback responses we gain from our environmental contexts. Such a state can be applied to many people in their life experience, unfortunately. And yet, at all times, a person is still within the flow of pure Source consciousness. These aspects of consciousness are only 'parts' if we limit our perception and experience to them. They are all aspects of the unified consciousness that we cannot be separated from, even when we are unaware of it: 'For in this you will be able to see that all of these parts were never parts but one whole expressing, never apart from it, never anywhere to get to - just an opening up and a letting go.' (S.1.Q5) These levels that we tend to limit ourselves within are like an overcoat, says Abe. And there will come a time when 'the heat will get so intense that you will have no other choice but to remove the overcoat.' We will be compelled to drop the layers of separation and unify with pure consciousness. It is comfortable to exist within a limited perception, yet this comfort pulls us back from the greater perception of our wholeness. It is we who make life more difficult for ourselves, and always have.

Again, Abe refers to the necessity for resonance. This is another major theme in these communications (as discussed in Volume 1). For pure consciousness to flow within our world, we have to resonate with it. If we are not at the appropriate frequency, then there will be no merging – like oil and water coming together. The Source consciousness is always present, of course, yet it can be almost indiscernible to us if we are not vibrationally aligned with it. This overcoat that needs to be taken off, according to Abe, represents our blockages. These blockages have mainly been produced through our conditioning and social programming. This is all part of the 'illusion' of our reality. Humans, for the most part, are perceptually blinded. We have gotten caught up in the fractals – the 'fractured splintering' – rather than the integral relations: 'You have but long forgotten the relation, the correlation, the unity of such parts.' (S.1.Q5) We have been splitting life into smaller and smaller bits and have now forgotten the whole picture. This is like the story of the boy who dissected a fly; he took off the wings, the legs, etc., until he finally asked, 'where is the fly'?

Part of the problem also comes from our use of language. Human language is good for explaining things that are in parts, the physical components, but not so good when it comes to explaining or representing aspects of a unified experience. That is why many experiences, states (transcendental states) leave us at a loss for words. And whilst we focus on the elements of existence, such as speaking of universes and dimensions, we neglect (or forget) that there is an underlying reality of unity to all of this. As Abe says, 'Dimensions are just differing states of conscious experience.' (S.1.Q6) The more we come to understand this, the more awareness we express, then the more possibility there is for different vibrational pathways to be formed. Humanity is undergoing a rewiring – a resetting. And this is necessary for there to be an alignment between species and planetary frequencies. One method that has been utilized for this 'rewiring' of humanity has been through the use of symbolism. Symbolism has been used in all the major religious and spiritual paths. It has been put into architecture, gardens, drawings, art, and much more. It is a way of by-passing the over-explaining, or intellectual, style of language: 'Symbolism has always been used when language fails - do you see?' (S.1.Q7) Symbols have been used to great effect in contrary situations, such as in corporate logos. When we see a familiar logo, nothing needs to be said for we know what it represents, and more. A symbol speaks more loudly than a few words ever could. Geometry is another use of symbolic patterns, and very few people realize how such patterns of space, shape, and size have a resonant vibratory affect upon our states. Such patterns can resonate with the totality of our consciousness – all five levels. What many people do not realize is that they are operating through one, two, maybe three conscious states but rarely all five. We may be in the chariot, but we are not steering the horse. As the mystic-philosopher G.I. Gurdjieff was famously known for saying, we have a multitude of 'I's' within us, and we are never sure which 'I' is driving us at any particular time. That is, we are not psychologically unified. As Abe puts it, that which we have always been chasing or rejecting is just a part of us. Importantly, such realizations can never be forced upon people. They must come to their own recognition, otherwise it becomes a part of external control: 'You are only ever right when it is right for you; everything else is but to be left alone - do you so see this? For it is never about a following of other but a knowing of self that what is truth.' (S.1.Q8)

Everything comes back to us, to the individual. Each person needs to find their *way back home*. No individual journey can be walked by another person: your shoes cannot be rented out. We are each faced by those things that are a reflection of ourselves. Our splintered nature is a reflection of our original unity. Until a person recognizes – until a person *feels* – their dissonance within self, they will not resonate with the unity. This lack of recognition is created by the conditions of the world. The world distracts us: 'It creates noise so that you cannot feel, it links you up to something else. You are wired up to the system, constantly gaming, playing - you are but a reflection of a system.' (S.1.Q9) It is okay to go away from the noise for some time, to seek a retreat, yet the real work has to be done from within the noise of the world: 'This is well and good, but you need to walk in the noise again and show people that silence is here too, in your very own being.' (S.1.Q9) The answers will no longer be found from dwelling in a cave. There is no solution if the silence cannot be found from within. The 'quiet in the noise' is a state of resonance. As Abe informs us, it is not about 'shouting from the rooftops' but 'aligning yourself first and foremost.' Our individual resonance is not a proclamation, an announcement – it is a state of being. Abe puts it best when they say: 'When you have but walked this path of realization yourselves, you are a beacon of truth and it is but always your truth, and those who so feel it will be drawn to you.' (S.1.Q9)

Traditions have often talked of the 'Fall' of humanity as if it were a great tragedy. Many systems treat it as some kind of sin, a blame upon the human race. And yet a *fall away* also suggests a regathering – a return. And such a return places the responsibility upon the individual being to gain back their inherent power. We are, then, to 'wake up and shake off this hierarchical dew and begin to see the interconnectedness of your own being, this unity, slowly piecing yourself back together.' (S.1.Q10) It is time for people to claim back their own power and to get themselves out of the 'rabbit hole.' And what exactly is this rabbit hole: 'You see, the rabbit hole, in the context of which we speak, are these layers of conditioning; of the falsities that have limited your conscious experiences, have kept you trapped and splintered.' (S.1.Q10) Whether it is the layers of the overcoat, or the spiral of the rabbit hole, both represent the levels of social conditioning that have been placed upon the person whilst in this physical reality. What we now need to do is to 'resurface.'

This is the journey that so many of us now find ourselves upon. It is quite literally an awakening; or, as Abe puts it, like coming out of a dark tunnel and being blinded by the light and the sounds and smells. And this will require adjustment and grounding. This is what Abe means when they say that we need to be rooted. It is when we place ourselves too much on the outside, onto externals, that we lose this grounding, this rooting. The rooting must take place within. Yet humans have, by and large, been conditioned to find security by outsourcing this onto others and 'on the placement of things.' The upward journey out of the rabbit hole, to use this analogy, will require that we listen to and trust ourselves. No one can make the journey for us. At each step we will be faced with questions; how shall we respond? As Abe says: 'you may even run back in this cave once you feel the bright light of perception. For some, it may seem too exposed, too raw, and they do so like the comfort of the darkened cave. Or will you love yourselves enough to give yourself time - to adjust time, to feel time to be?' (S.1.Q11) Change too is infectious. People can change when they sense others changing – the energy of change is contagious. Yet we each must be the change for ourselves without waiting for others to make the move before us. Everything has a knock-on effect. Life is always seeking balance, within and without. Our own change should not be seen as a sacred or holy thing, otherwise we separate it off from us – we view it as a thing distinct from our everyday lives. On the contrary: 'The whole point of grounding this energy right now is that you do so bring it into the noise of your own life.' (S.1.Q11) As Abe says, our own change should not be something we slip on and off like a pair of shoes. It is something that shines through us and is effused into our lives; it is all we do even when we are not thinking about it. Also, importantly, we are told to 'lighten up' about it!

It may not assist us if we try to keep things repressed. At some point or another they will need to come out – to be faced and made peace with. Life will show us where we are blocked, where things are stagnant. Once we are aware of such a thing, then the process for its removal has already begun. We should not try to store it or arrange it, otherwise we may end up putting ourselves under lock and key: 'Allow life to show you who you are, who you all are, and see the unity in your being. There are no steps, for no two people are the same. For that is the beauty of life.' (S.1.Q12) Each person is uniquely interconnected; there are so many variations for each thing. Everything intermingles and synchs up. We need to allow life to show us this without us trying to impose our own limitations upon life. Life meets us at the place we are coming from – from where we are vibrating at.

Some people will simply not resonate the same as where you are at. A person who perceives one truth will not resonate with another who does not perceive. Resonation can be an effortless connection; it can be unrestricted and authentic. It is often the social norms, rituals and conditions that make such connections so complex. The base line, so to speak, is about syncing back up to who we truly are – to find our home state, the home resonance. As Abe puts it: 'Only, but only, when you do so piece yourself back together to unify and pick up all those pieces will you be able to step forward.' (S.1.Q14) The stage where we are at is about our individual conscious experience. And from this, humanity's collective evolvement at a conscious level. We are hindered when we remain too heavily connected to a world of division and dissonance; this connection does us a great disservice. It would do us well to 'cut the cords' to many of these draining external connections:

> The meaning of so 'cutting the cords' are these very many parts of consciousness, like little tentacles, that do so place themselves upon people, situations, establishments, religion - all being outside of yourselves. Drop them, for now they may very well sync back up again. (S.1.Q15)

30

We have so many tentacles – energetic chords – attached to external sources that take us out of ourselves. In this, we create so many 'lock-ons' that produce stagnant pathways. By dropping such connections, we can re-synch and develop more resonant vibrational alignments.

Without realizing, we get locked-in to our own false sense of self. We wrap our social personalities around us as a comforting layer. We then stuff these layers with our beliefs, opinions, and everything else we accumulate upon our journey. Now it is a time for unwrapping and unwinding ourselves out of the rabbit hole. Our notion of 'self' has become dependent upon the outer, and from this becomes ever more illusionary and further away from the essence. At essence, the self is whole and unconditioned. It then becomes coloured by the inks of the outer life. By cutting our cords, we are not severing ourselves from life; rather, we are stepping back from false or dissonant attachments. It is like a meditation when we lose our sense of the stagnant 'I.'

Another attachment that we often get confused about is the sense of belonging. A person often feels the need to belong to something other, whether it be a group, organization, or religion, etc. And in this need what we are experiencing is a 'longing to be.' Yet this search 'to be' gets placed outside of us and projected onto an external 'other.' Many people have a need to feel acceptance; to be told that everything is okay. In this, people find themselves moving from one group or person to another, endlessly seeking this confirmation of self. This, says Abe, is a form of trickery, of deceit. We just long 'to be' and we don't need this to be confirmed by an outside source, but we have been conditioned to think that this is so. We are caught up so much in our cultural programs, layers of social conditioning, that we even get our own 'belonging' entangled in these outer events: 'You are wanting this gathering to reassure you, to back you up

- that this way is of truth. That is why there are so, so many groups; we would not to be able to decide to whom we belong - can you?' (S.1.Q18) Our belonging is to ourselves, for if we are never home, then where are we? What we often don't see, for it is clouded to our sight, is that we already belong. Our external seeking often ends up like the 'dog-chasing-tail scenario.' In this, we end up creating our own separations:

> Can you see how you do as humans go around and around? You separate and then you have to but search from what you think you are separated from - like the times you lose your glasses and then you realize they were but on your head, and you laugh for you had been searching for something in which you already have. (S.1.Q18)

And that's the point: we search for something we already have. And until this is seen then we shall continue to chase our tails. As Abe says, it may be fun for a while 'but it does soon become tiresome.'

Whatever takes our attention externally is often a mirror of our internal state – both aspects are relational. Our connections and connectivity can be externally extensive, yet they only function in relation to how we are internally connected. It is, as Abe says, a mutual arising. There are needs and requirements from both sides, internally and externally, yet there is no 'I was here first.' The outer events we experience are related to how we are, our state of being, and we cannot have one without the other. When we make, or connect up with, an outer resonance then this rewires us internally to form new pathways – new brain patterns. This then affects how we perceive and respond to external events and stimuli – and this goes on. It is this mutual arising back and forth, a participatory play, that forms our relational interaction with the world: 'a resonance is sparked to create new pathways within, and you see it creates this without - and then you see it without. It is but confirmation of your inner.' (S.1.Q20) Our thinking patterns are like fractal relations; they are parts of an integral picture. Sometimes they do not relate coherently, and we think ourselves into a dark place only to later realize it was a product of our false, or imaginary, thinking. The basic situation is that we have de-aligned ourselves from a vast communicative web. Communication requires coherency. Just as our bodies have their own form of communication. The cells communicate amongst themselves; if not, we would have no immune system – no functioning physical body! Similarly, humans are like cells within a vast cosmic body; yet we have dropped the line of communication. As Abe says, we have splintered, segregated ourselves from a vast network and we need to 'mend the line:' 'when this is but unified, your vibrational communicative web will become more and more vast; more and more getting online with this cosmic consciousness - linking back up.' (S.1.Q21) This, we are told, is evolution; yet we have been splintered apart from this communicative unity and this cannot any longer work for us. In this way, humanity has stagnated.

A critical aspect of the human situation is perception. Perception, when focused, highlights an area of reality: 'For whatever you do so shine the light of perception upon, is highlighted.' (S.1.Q22) Yet the crucial matter is being in unification and balance. If the focus (perception) is shaky, the thing illuminated by the light (perception) will not be clear. Abe consistently urges us to find our foundations – our grounding. As everyone knows, you don't build a house on sand (as the adage goes). If we are not 'wired up correctly,' then we cannot see clearly. Realities exist according to the level of perception that brings them into awareness. It has been known that people can experience a 'reality slip' when one reality appears to have caused an intrusion, or disturbance, into our consensus reality. If this occurs, then it does so upon a vibrational level. All realities are a dance of vibration, an interweaving of frequencies. Existence is this endless fractalizing of unity – 'this forever dividing of but one thing.' However, at some point, Abe informs us, we have to make our way back to unity – and this is our 'Way Back Home.'

We again come back to the theme of creating separation through our stereotypes. There is also much talk about masculine and feminine energies as if they are completely distinct categories. Especially in certain 'spiritualist' circles there is mention of the 'Divine Feminine' and 'Divine Masculine.' Yet we need to be careful here for there is the tendency to slip into separations when the truth is that all these energies are contained within us:

> For you see, you but all have these within - it can be but no other way. It is about the fine balance. It is but likened to that of what you call brain states. You have but separated this too into a masculine side and a feminine side, and really there is no such thing. It is of division, and these are but qualities that you have but given an identity. That is all, nothing more, and all a part of unity. It is time to wake up to this knowing if you do so want to go forward. (S.1.Q24)

If we take ourselves out of this balance, into identities of separation, then we misalign from our vibrational harmony. When people talk about 'raising frequency' what they are often referring to is a realignment of frequency. After all, if there is a 5th dimensional state, then it will not be something outside of us but related to our inner state. It is a question of gathering our frequencies unto us, not chasing after them.

People speak often about their 'gut feelings' and 'gut instinct;' and many people now realize that the gut is classed as a second brain. In truth, the whole body can be classed as a 'brain' for it is a receiver. Parts of the body have their own pathways of communication; they have their own relational networks. When, for instance, the gut receives a knowing or understanding about a situation, this then gets sent as a vibrational pathway to the head-brain that then decodes and interprets this vibrational pathway. The human body is a whole system of vibrational communication, just as our external world acts through networks of communication. Within the human brain, however, we have neural pathways that can be rewired both through conscious experience as well as unconscious. Until we allow for new resonance, new neural pathways, we will remain stuck in old patterns, and thus old ways of thinking. Everything is in relation: 'You see, all these things are but interlocking, relational to one another. You know this of your bodily parts - they are only effective as a whole system, only resonation as a whole system.' (S.1.Q25) If we are synched up internally, then this vibrational state gets projected into our external relations and interactions – there is a mutual resonance. As Abe puts it: 'For you see, you are but pure potentiality until you do so create the pathways within - and then so without.' (S.1.Q25)

As we are now, humanity does not have the full story. We have many different and varied stories – our spells and enchantments – yet we have splintered meanings. We have only plucked at aspects of reality, at the fractal pieces, and from this we create our mythic stories. Yet real meaning only comes from the whole, and not the pieces. This is what has been referred to many times by the famous Elephant in the Dark story, as each contender only feels one bodily part of the elephant and never the whole. It is time now to go beyond these splintered parts and to perceive the grander aspect of reality.

SECTION TWO
The Reality Game

It seems a contradiction that as a species we are more externally connected than ever before and yet there is an epidemic of loneliness in the world. How is it that we can be so highly interconnected externally yet so separated internally? This contradictory state, it seems, is in relation to our self, and how we perceive and feel ourselves to be. If we see ourselves as 'a lonely island of me' then this causes a deep feeling of separation and fragmentation, whether we are consciously aware of this or not. This inner fragmentation is then projected outwards and into our external relations. Abe advises us to lighten up a little too: 'you just need to but lighten up a little. To lighten the load of this constant bashing of doing life and allow it to do you for a while.' (S.2.Q1) Rather than continually imposing ourselves onto life – this 'constant bashing' – we could benefit from allowing life to come through us. This continual imposition onto life also seems to have had the effect of closing down our heart space, for we are in an active, forcing vibration rather than in a receptive state. Often unknowingly, we become in fear of life – a suspicion of others and even of love! The result of this is that we become 'cold and stranded upon this island of me.' In this, we have given ourselves away. Abe has a more direct, yet effective, way of putting this: 'You have but allowed to sell your parts to the devil and bought them back from the snakes.' (S.2.Q1) By being in this state, we cut ourselves off from others. We close ourselves down, constrict our vibrations, and ultimately close down the heart vibration. And this becomes all too often the reality we end up experiencing.

It can be said, with some truth, that humanity as a whole has lost its connection to Greater Reality. Abe confirms this and adds that we have lost ourselves to so many things, and now it is our responsibility to find our way back into connection and balance. Even people who aim to do good in the world, and are doing good deeds in the world, need to come back to this first principle of resonation. It is from this primary resonance that we shall gain our genuine strength: 'true strength will come from gathering your parts first, for you will have good groundings to stand your ground and but help others. If so, this foundation is strong - is in resonation.' (S.2.Q2) If we are in a resonant unity within, then we shall automatically align externally for we always align with that in which we resonate with. As Abe puts it: 'Find your own light before lighting others.' If we keep chasing after an external reality, then we can be easily lead on a false chase by the pied piper. We can, as they say, be lead along on a merry dance. Reality as we know it is, in one sense, an illusion – yet we have also been tricking ourselves. We have been plugging ourselves into our own illusion and feeding into the same system that constrains us. This situation is relational and not just one-way. If we continue to blame this situation upon the 'other' then we enforce this state of separation and entrapment: 'if you do so see that there are but others who control this game, this illusion, you will see to it that you are but always trapped.' (S.2.Q3) By giving strength to the 'other' we create the illusion of our separation and weakness. Of course, there will always be those people content with their life situation, and not wanting to 'get out of their seats

38

of comfort,' and that is fine. No one can be forced to act or perceive in a specific way. Each person is responsible for becoming their own resonant frequency. Yet it also has to be said that a person only has real control over those things they are wakeful to and are aware of. Unawareness leads to control being placed over oneself.

Without awareness, we remain locked into a system – a 'reality game' – that does not serve us. From Abe's perspective, it is as if humanity is forever chasing its tails. Reality is playing us, but we are not playing it: 'reality is only reality if you do so meet it. You have to meet it; you have to but keep playing and participating for anything to be upheld as a reality - your reality.' (S.2.Q5) The system itself knows how to play and manipulate the game by using fear to entrap us. Humans have the creative potential to build new worlds, new realities, yet we remain restrained and contained within the limited confines of a reality that has been programmed into us. The Abe messages are here to serve as a nudge to help awaken us: 'We are here to act as an alarm going off; to say – "this is not what life is;" "this is not what I have to be;" "this is not MY reality."' (S.2.Q5) Yet the individual must make the first move and align within. It is all about our 'own resonation of being.' If we are unable to find this resonance within ourselves then we remain in a kind of tug-of-war in our relations with reality. We remain within the illusion that we ourselves perpetuate. We are unable to reclaim ourselves because we remain chained to a splintered and 'outdated system' that 'sells you back your parts and never in full.' We are never whole for we have become enchanted by the external desires that control our drives and passions. We neglect our own inherent power for the power of money and status, and other worldly objects. It is time, says Abe, for a 'break in the clouds.' This illusory reality that keeps us spellbound needs to be broken away from. We are now to break the chain, and this is a vibrational chain. We need to shift ourselves into a different space, and into new vibrational pathways and alignments: 'You but so have to break that chain. How it is done so is with a space, a break in the line of connection.' (S.2.Q6)

Humanity has remained slumbering for so long. It was often the case that only the most blatant, forceful events and impacts would serve as triggering 'alarms' to wake us up, such as disasters and large cultural events. These were required since human culture 'was anaesthetized and was but kept in this unconscious cycle' (S.2.Q7) Yet now, it is not the nature of the events that are important but their energy – the vibrational resonance. Many people are feeling this shift so much more strongly; it is a question of 'whether you learn to jump with it or not.' Many things can awaken us; it need not be catastrophic. As Abe says, it could be the 'tiny whisper that does so catch you.' Such a small trigger can allow the heart to open and the light resonance to enter. And when there are catastrophic events at the ground level, there are also many more extraordinary things happening 'below the surface.' Abe assures us that there is indeed this break in the clouds now where people are beginning to awaken. At the same time, however, people can easily slip back once again into the 'falsity of the illusion of the illusion.'

There can be no 'breaking of the chain' unless people choose to do so of their own free will. We have to seek to break from our conscious reality 'whilst still wide awake.' This gathering of space away from the reality illusion is what Abe likens to words on a page: 'it is very hard to write a letter if you do not have the space in-between. It is the space that really shows the meaning. Words are filled-in all your day, every waking moment. Sometimes it is the break that does so speak louder.' (S.2.Q9) When we allow a space, we are allowing a certain letting go. We

40

are often too quick to rush in and try to fill up the space, to fill the gaps. It can be this space that allows the true connections to form: 'This space then allows you to see that you are but connected - you are but unity - you just don't need to talk about it; you don't need to fill it.' (S.2.Q9) It is a new mutual meeting space.

Humanity collectively needs a new meeting space for it has resided too long within its state of vibrational anesthetic. Over generations, and many of our years, we have been mesmerized by the illusory world-picture that kept us cut-off from a true source of knowledge. When one dose of the anesthetic wears off, we administer ourselves another dose, even when we are unaware of this. It has been a state of unconscious numbness: 'you have but unconsciously taken this shot - vibrationally hooking up and plugging in, resonating, lining up, and therefore participating. What we say, and this is with great love, is it is but time to stop; to have a break, to see, to feel, to stop numbing and dumbing yourselves down.' (S.2.Q10) We are unable to *feel* a genuine resonance, or vibrational state, if we are too numb. In such an energetic state, we are even unconscious to our own being. And this is how the illusion of our reality works, by keeping us numbed and dumbed down. It is time to 'feel, feel, feel again,' as Abe puts it; otherwise, we shall remain in our perceptual slumber. Our cultures have us going along in autopilot. Sometimes we get distracted, we open one of our eyes for a brief moment, and then we go back to sleep again. It is hard for individuals to be awake when so many people are asleep and 'under the spell.' In such instances, it may be that a physical catastrophe creates the space whereby we realize that things have not been working for us: 'Sometimes these catastrophes create space to see that things aren't working in the way they should. You feel again. You get out of your seats and go see what all the commotion is.' (S.2.Q11)

It needs to be recognized that whilst our human cultures are good at getting us to participate in their ways – their 'illusion of the illusion' – we should also bear in mind that for the great majority of us, we are willingly participating. And this forms our vibrational relations, and we get used to how these relations feel to us. In other words, we become comfortable and settled. It takes effort to seek out the exit doors. Many have sought and found such doors, and even exited and returned to tell the tale (as told in Plato's Cave Allegory). At the same time, our cultures can be tricky in setting up 'false exits' for us: 'your culture can put up another exit door that does so mimic the original exit door. And in this you are but caught in a sort of loop - a pattern, a cycle, if you will.' (S.2.Q12) To break this loop, this pattern, it will require that we break from a *vibrational pattern*. And this act of breaking away is not so difficult as some may envision – yet it takes a genuine desire, an authentic wish, to seek for this vibrational shift. As Abe says, it is 'like a spark but can grow to a great glow and will guide others.' As a start, we need to drop our vibrational entanglements with the illusion. Each person is vibrationally hooked up into so many connections and things – and this is the energetic entanglement that claims our awareness. Why do human cultures wish for these entanglements – this spell – to be perpetuated? Abe says the reason is to keep humanity splintered: 'It is but to keep you apart, to keep this division; for if you knew your power, they would completely crumble, would they not? We say - what would be the point of an illusion if it were not upheld and fed into?' (S.2.Q14) This division is not only within our external cultures but is also within the human psyche. People who feel themselves to be divided inside are much easier to maintain within the cultural divisions. In other words: 'they

42

are just upholding that in which you think you are, and that is one of great division of being - and you are in a loop, in a rabbit hole.' (S.2.Q14)

Even though there are people in power who uphold and maintain these illusions, a great many of them are also splintered and divided in their psyches. Ultimately, however, it is each individual themselves who upholds the illusion by participating within it. The fundamental shift has to be from within us. The ones at the top 'of the game' have no intention of quitting the illusion, for why should they lose their position? Illusory or not, this position of power suits them. There are those in this position who are aware of the nature of the game that they uphold, even if they do not understand it in its entirety – for they too are coming from a splintered mind. This division, lack of wholeness, is interwoven into our social structures and our lives. Yet a person must wish from their own inner being for a shift away from this: 'It has to be of resonation of your being, and as humans you can go around blaming people at the top as you have done for so long. But you see, it is not moving anything and therefore just causing more and more division.' (S.2.Q16) Our innate human vibratory essence is one of love and balance, and so this vibrational entanglement into division and dissonance blurs our true connection – it 'does so fog this line.'

There are various vibrational states that can exist between a splintered psyche and unified consciousness, and it may be that some of these shifts occur without knowing the paths ahead. Yet, as Abe says, you can keep stepping forth on a pathway you do not know through a faith in yourselves: 'For you can see it as clear as day that you yourself are guiding yourselves and everyone else.' (S.2.Q17) That is, to be directed really means to be guided through yourself. A person's growth is through an increase in perception, and then to allow these perceptual insights to link up to form new pathways: 'Be slow with yourselves - allow it to link up itself to allow these new neural pathways to form, to resonate, to connect, and in this it can be solidified.' (S.2.Q17) Abe suggests that we 'be slow' with ourselves; by this, meaning stepping back from the rushing and pushing we give ourselves to invest in the reality that we think of as the Real. We have invested completely into this entanglement, and do not allow for a crack in the clouds to bring a ray of light through. Our focus and attention are energetically entangled into an illusory reality that distracts us totally. We are asked to be 'gentle with yourselves' in order to allow some space, a moment of rest, so that we can regather our senses. Abe states this as an analogy of stopping for a while to repair a wheel, for instance, as it gives us a breathing space:

> You see, you can pull your heavy carriages over the rock in the path and risk your carriage being broken, breaking a wheel - giving you time to repair it, to rest. And you can but also stop and take time to remove the rock. But you do so see both of these things give space. (S.2.Q18)

This simple analogy appears to suggest that an event that we may consider as disastrous or chaotic may in fact be regarded as an opportunity to make us take a halt – a very necessary pause in our lives. And through this space we have an occasion, an opening, to reflect upon our lives and to perhaps see things in a new light. We could say that the events of the past few years, beginning from 2020 (the pandemic period), was such a time when humanity hit a metaphorical rock in the road.

New perceptions and ways of seeing the world can shine a light upon the underlying unity, yet people cannot be forced to take such views. Each individual must 'want to come forward' by their own volition, otherwise they will not be open or able to align with the resonance that such new perceptions bring. As Abe says: 'for it to solidify in your physical reality it has to be of resonation, of relation - to meet up. It is but pointless to talk flower language to a seed for there is still much growth.' (S.2.Q19) You cannot convince a seed to understand the 'flower language' for it still needs to grow in order to understand. Yet the flower continues to wait, patiently. At certain times there are circumstances that can be used to further such growth and awakening. In these moments it feels as if 'something' is breaking through the cracks in the illusion; and this can be experienced as a 'wobble.' That is, it feels as if a ripple is moving through our world, our known reality, and causing imbalance. This may be a cause of confusion for some people; for others, a nudge of awakening. Abe puts it this way: 'this may seem like utter devastation to some, like their whole world that they have but become so reliant on is crashing to the ground, for you have become accustomed to this illusion.' (S.2.Q20) Like a child frightened by their own fears of the monsters under their bed, they only need to venture to look for themselves to dissolve their fears: 'Your angst and depression and anxiety are a sign that you are clinging to but a monster in which you have to battle - allow the space in which you are but so frightened to have, and in this there will be much growth.' (S.2.Q20) There needs to be a space in which growth can enter. Each person has to create that space, otherwise they remain too full of their own self-created worries and imaginings. These too need to be let go of.

Our societies are creating their own confusions and affronts against consensus reality. We hear ongoing reports about fake news and alternative facts; many people are feeling flustered and unsure. The danger here is that such confusions may only push people further down the rabbit hole of the illusion. Some people feel attacked by these manipulations of information, and others feel a loss of control. On the whole, people do not wish to be told, or to find out for themselves, that this reality is not what they have always thought it was: 'To say that this reality that you have invested but all your life unto this point is a sham, you will have people that will lash out and try to uphold this falsity. So long as you can decipher through this mess you can sail to the shore.' (S.2.Q21) The safety of the shore will only come when we have navigated – or 'deciphered' – through 'this mess.' As Abe says, humanity is its own worst enemy and also its only saviours. This collective illusion that we know of as reality is the result of collective participation. We should not always place the blame on some exterior 'darker forces.' There are polarizing forces in play as part of the illusory reality, yet this situation that we find ourselves in is not beyond our capabilities to resolve. This is the victimhood mentality, when in fact we can – and have to – be our own saviours. And since existence is a unity, then everything has a 'knock-on effect.' Each aspect of perceptual growth and awareness is related: 'Now you are but a plant that is growing; but you are also the soil that nourishes and the gardener that tends and nurtures.' (S.2.Q23) Humanity is the plant, the soil, and the gardener. We are already a part of the unity, so it is not a question of striving to become a 'finished product as such' but rather a question of 'making your way back home consciously.' In other words, of synchronizing back into a unified resonance of vibratory wholeness.

It is not a time for looking backwards, of eulogizing past ancient civilizations as if they lived in greater harmony with the planet, and all the rest. Now is the time 'to go forward consciously with that in which you are at now.' If we remain looking backward then we can get ourselves tangled up and distracted, and maybe cause ourselves to take a step back. It is the tendency of the modern human to get so overloaded with attachments, distractions, and things that glitter and catch our eyes. Abe says that we can think of this as 'vibrational shopping,' and has a good analogy for this behaviour:

> ...collecting this and that, putting it in the trolley, adding it to the cart - round and round they go, seeing more that they seemingly need when in truth a few fine ingredients would suffice. But you see, they had but come with an empty vibration and everything seems so enticing, so they keep adding. This is but the point at which you are at - the cart is full, you are overloaded, and there is but no slight chance that you can but consume it all or use it all. (S.2.Q24)

In our earlier history, the human being arrived with an 'empty vibration' (a pure resonance) yet over time we collected vibrational embellishments – adding shopping elements to our cart – that distorted our vibrational frequency through too much external accumulation (the cart is full). We are weighed down by all the extra vibrational distortions that have become attached to us. The human vibrational essence is overloaded. But it can also be dropped; our load can be minimized. Yet we have to want this. We cannot let go of our outer clutter and external connections if we are still attached to them. Abe advises us to: 'Use what you have brought forth up to now to enhance life, not to compensate for a life not lived.' (S.2.Q24)

Since the human vibrational accumulation has taken place over much time in the physical realm, we cannot expect this decluttering to be 'an overnight process.' It may be a quicker process to be able to declutter from our physical attachments, such as by downsizing our possessions, yet most of the human cluttering is a mental-vibrational one. A person may have

47

physical possessions, yet the attachments are made mentally and emotionally. An individual will be more willing to give up such attachments when they feel the strain of them: 'there will be people more willing to leave behind the mental clutter due to tiredness of upholding these vibrational loads more so than they would initially the physical clutter.' (S.2.Q25) A physical possession can be easily let go of, yet mental/emotional vibrational attachments and accumulations are not so easy. As Abe says, the aim should be to go forth 'un-splintered, unattached or overloaded.' As a consequence of such vibrational decluttering, people will have more space for receiving new vibrational alignments, for a person's capacity to receive is based upon their vibrational clarity or openness. Everything is connected according to relational vibrations. And although humans tend to perceive the world around them as fragmented and broken down into separate parts, they all belong to an integrated whole. Our perceptions of fragmentation are a reflection of where we are at vibrationally: 'our species is splintered because of the vibrational resonance of which they are at individually.' (S.2.Q26) To be 'resonating higher' or lower is not a question of hierarchy but of growth – everything is a process, such as the seed one day that becomes a flower the next.

There have always been individuals among the population that exhibit a higher resonance, and this enables them, whether they are conscious of it or not, to act as 'alarm clocks' for others. Abe comments that the 'real disaster in the physical' is not so much of the world ending but of 'not enabling these vibrations to take root now - or rather, arise.' The real 'apocalyptic' is really the breaking down of old ways and the bringing in of new resonant alignments. By doing this, we are 'clearing societal residue' from our vibratory essences: 'It is no longer continuing to feed into it by being hooked up and invested in it. You take a step back from being consumed within it and just watch for a brief moment.' (S.2.Q26) Those vibratory essences that have been 'overridden' can now come forth to make new relational pathways. It is difficult for humans to accept that great change and shifts come about through breakdown, and what appears as destruction. That is, beginnings need a new space from which to emerge, both physically and energetically.

There is already enough damaging, and intrusive, vibrational interferences in the modern world. As any observant person will know, we live in an environment awash with digital waves and electromagnetic pollution. Yet, as Abe says, this may not affect us as much as we may think, if our resonance is aligned in the unity vibration: 'when your own resonance is of unity - of grounded true unity within - then you see there are not so many things that can so distort it; that can contaminate it in a way as to redirect it to get caught up in other resonances.' (S.2.Q27) Furthermore, we are affected by those influences that we allow to affect us. In this, we do have a conscious choice. If our vibratory resonance is grounded and not fluctuating so much, then we have more natural immunity against vibrational interference. It is a question of holding to one's truth without becoming too rigid: 'Not in such a way to stand stiff in a storm, no, for you could easily break - but like the bamboo that is so flexible to enable it to be touched but not broken.' (S.2.Q27) The problem with technological interference is that it is too one-sided and not in balance with our genuine needs. It is not a question of throwing something away if it can be brought back into balance; and there are currently many vibrational influences that can be brought into a resonant synchronization.

One of the central factors affecting human life – the life of the human being on this planet – is vibrational interference. This most often comes in the form of over-stimulation. These are caused from many and varied vibrations that build up, like an 'overload of exterior stimulation.' This can be more consistent and impactful within built-up and urban areas, and people who are more aware of resonance are generally more sensitive to these impacts. Being in Nature can be beneficial in this respect as external vibrations tend to be less 'distorted and disrupted.' This is also why there is more stress and feelings of 'hectic madness' in large built-up areas. Wherever this vibrational distortion takes place, it signifies a 'void of connection,' and this influences a person's sense of limitation. Where there is vibrational stress, a person needs to recognize this and take a conscious break from this influence: 'when you see that there is but a break, an exit, the thing is, you just need to look up, stop, and see.' (S.2.Q28) Of course, Nature can also function as a healing space for people as we have an innate and deep vibrational relation to it. Nature is our natural home – the home resonance of the planet. If we are cut off from Nature's resonance, then we only cut ourselves off: 'to cut out this is to cut out part of who you are, and in this it is not unity.' (S.2.Q28)

The current reality of the modern world has much within it to overload the human senses. There are many factors that contribute to vibrational dissonance, and this seems to be increasing, not lessening. Part of this is related to our advancing technologies, especially our digital devices and communications infrastructure. Other aspects are related to the human psyche, and its individual and collective state of vibrational emanations. Both elements are interrelated and affect one another. And these elements affect our psychological, and resonant, state of unity. Furthermore, there are also deliberate human strategies to maintain this dissonance and state of fragmentation: 'if it is used in a way as to manipulate, to control, to divide, to box up each individual inside your own conscious experience - then it has but

50

missed the point completely and will not be to your own advancement but rather to your own demise.' (S.2.Q29) Unification is about bringing things back together again, into wholeness. Human consciousness was never to be constricted, as if placed into specific labelled boxes. We have become so used to experiencing our consciousness within limited parameters. These are our restrictive thinking patterns, that then go on to form belief systems, intellectual structures, and programmed perspectives. We are living out of boxes, not within the genuine freedoms that are our legacy. We become lost by projecting ourselves onto a myriad of things: 'anything that you do so lose yourselves to, and see that this is putting yourself into something else - be it a person, a religion, work, or even a coffee machine - that you do so want, and as stupid as this does so sound, it is but truth.' (S.2.Q29) We put our 'vibrational antennas' out there and latch onto, get entangled, upon so many unnecessary things. We each need to know when it is time to release such connections and to bring home our tentacles of vibrational attachment.

Abe came forward to make a specific comment about the confusion people have with the concept of resonance. There is a popular notion that resonance is something to be 'raised' through certain actions such as positive thinking. This, says Abe, is more of a 'sugar coating' – a 'band-aid problem' they call it: 'You are masking the pain but not actually rooting out that which is embedded in your own vibration. And in this your default setting is but the same.' (S.2.Q29) By seeking out positive thinking style practices, this is like using medication to mask the pain without finding out the root cause. And in the end, it may serve as a distraction rather than a benefit. A certain unwanted vibrational pathway may be blocked through this, but no new pathways are created. There is still a resonation to the old patterns, and this just functions as a delay – but not as a remedy.

Abe is clear here that positive thought is not a bad thing, but it should not detract from the understanding that a person is, relatively speaking, 'already of high vibration.' What is needed here is not further socially created distraction practices but rather some polishing: 'But it is also good to be realistic sometimes too and see that you are already of high vibration. You just are a little but dusty – you need a vibrational clean out.' (S.2.Q29) The misunderstanding here is that people are pushing to 'raise something.' But in this, people often remain clinging 'to all the baggage, the contamination.' And this makes it still harder for people to let go, to disconnect their vibrational entanglement. Natural resonance is that which arrives with an *allowing* energy. It is a question of being receptive rather than pushing to 'raise' something. That is, we are being reminded to refine what we already are – there is no need to feel compelled to go anywhere 'higher.' As Abe puts it: 'it is but a clearing out, if you will, to connect you back up to your natural resonation. It is a wakeup to the spirit.' (S.2.Q30)

A person's vibrational resonance is relational to how they feel within. As such, it is strongly connected to our mental and emotional states. As we know (and was discussed in Vol.1 of this series), the human being is highly socially conditioned. A person is taught early on to 'hook up vibrational resonance to these structures, these patterns and pathways.' (S.2.Q31) It is time to 'drop it, bring it all back' and to give ourselves a rest in this continual entanglement. A balance of resonance should not be a flooding or an overload, but a growth where the body comes to learn to resonate with its vibratory essence. The human being's strength is not only in the body – 'it is also dependent upon how strong is your resonation, and how easily influenced and manipulated it is. For when you give but yourself away to something, when you link up, it takes a little away.' (S.2.Q33)

This is a significant point, and one that we may easily overlook. What Abe is telling us here is that the more things that we link our energy up to, the more we can be influenced. In this, we can be giving our energies away without a reciprocal exchange. This can be through linking up to other people, as well as with possessions, ideas, desires, etc. The more we send out our vibrational tentacles, the more we are liable, often unknowingly, to give a little away of ourselves each time: 'do so make sure that the things that you are linking up to are but feeding back in equal quantities, of equal resonation. If not, they will not serve you.' (S.2.Q33) A person is always growing, and yet we may forget, or not be aware of, the need for a 'spring clean' now and again. We forget to 'draw back the links,' and to reevaluate them. As Abe says: 'It is never too late to start over and over again, clearing as you go.' (S.2.Q33)

Just as we open a window to allow the spring breeze to flow in, so too do we need to *allow* these energies to flow through our lives. It is often our own complications that block or distort this flow. Just as we arrange our house the way we like it, to give us the energetic feel that makes it right for us, so too should we arrange our life, our connections and relations, in a way that harmonizes with us. We should be aware for the need, now and again, for a 'vibrational clear-out.' Humans have the advantage over other animals that we have a high degree of self-awareness. Yet because of this, we often over-complicate matters; whereby animals, on the other hand, are much more instinctive and responsive to vibrational fields. Humans should be mindful that they have the capacity to 'enable relations, to initiate them, and change the neural connections.' (S.2.Q35) At the same time, we should be aware that there is a strong resonant bond between humanity and the animal kingdom. Abe notes that humans have far too many distinct groupings of things, especially for animals:

'a dog will be loved and pampered but on the other hand a spider would be squished without second thought. And you see, this kind of mentality is abound in your societies.' (S.2.Q36) As we keep 'separating things down and down,' we further lose our connection to unity: 'break it apart, see how things work if need be, but do so remember to piece it all back together again.' (S.2.Q36) In the end, our human survival is dependent upon our connections. We cannot evolve as a species cut off from its environment, vibrationally isolated.

It seems that humanity has gone down its rabbit hole, but all alone. We have lost part of our essential connection in how we resonate to the planet, the animal kingdom, and with the ecosystem. We are in need of making our way out of this vibratory hole:

> Make your way back out firstly to self, then more outer and outer. For when you do realize the intricate web of existence that you are so encased in, you are but a part of, you will realize that one part taken out intentionally - not coming from unity - will but upset this balance. (S.2.Q37)

And we have indeed upset this balance. In the end, we are only distancing ourselves; the imbalance will cause our species the greatest upset. The planet, and its environment, can always find rebalance, for this is their natural resonance. On the other hand, humanity has forced this disequilibrium and off-kilter resonance upon themselves. As Abe says quite bluntly: 'We would like to but say this: to Unify is but key to your species survival now.' (S.2.Q38) It is essential now to 'bring it all back in – bring it all back.' The human vibrational resonance has to become one of connection and unity. It is not the case of just saying this, of saying we are all connected – but of resonating at

54

this truth. A person can lie with their words, yet they cannot but show the truth through their vibrational resonance.

When a person is truly rooted and grounded in their resonance, says Abe, this will bring them certainty in their being, and no other vibrations will be able to penetrate this. Furthermore: 'Only then can you step forth from this place of great strength and build a new world. Let the structures fall, cut your ties, and see them plummet.' (S.2.Q38) After this letting go, we are advised to wait for a time, for 'unity to grow and ground from within' before we take our steps forward once again. How we understand this 'reality game' is not about the practice or the place but what we ourselves resonate at: 'For you see, your home has a vibrational resonance - everything does. You are not to be rid of it, any of it, but sync back up.' (S.2.Q38) Everything exists within an intricate interwoven web – a 'web of communication between all things.' And this web is 'intricately intertwined.' And when the human being truly *allows* this unification of consciousness then, says Abe, all these patterns will become evident: 'For in this you will see the patterns - the connection, the relation, and the beauty. With much Love and Light – Abe.' (S.2.Q38)

SECTION THREE
Relations with the World Around Us

In this section of the Abe conversations, the theme was shifted to focus more on peoples' relationship with the world around them. Specifically, to explore how people relate to their social and cultural systems; especially now at a time when many systems are seeming dysfunctional. Also, I wanted to address themes of power, alienation, authority, attachment, identity, and more. I began this series of questions by asking why there is so much alienation experienced by people in modern life at a time when we are more highly connected through our technologies and communication devices. I wondered, why this contradiction? As always, Abe brought the focus back onto us, the human being – 'the contradiction is but within yourselves.' One of the issues involved was that people were losing the 'fine art of conversation' and the ability to conduct themselves due to greater dependence upon technologies. Because of our reliance on technologies, people were losing confidence in themselves as there is now a 'go between:' 'whenever there is something placed between yourselves, be it a gadget or even the mental wall that you create to guard yourselves, it is always a second-hand exchange.' (S.3.Q1) In this second-hand exchange we are moving away from our human default mode which is the need for genuine connection. If we want to truly connect, says Abe, then we have 'to drop any sort of middleman.' Alienation seems to be a defense mechanism that humans have built up for themselves. As such, it serves as a divide, a split, that affects us internally and is then reflected externally. Once this divide exists, we often then allow 'for this divide to be widened and fed into.' (S.3.Q1)

It is maybe because of this internal divide, this lack of confidence, that so many people willingly give their power away to external systems/agencies or forces. At the same time, dominant social power is becoming increasingly non-visible as it gets placed into bureaucracies and automated infrastructures. Our innate human power needs to be brough back to ourselves 'first and foremost.' Abe states that we need to 'bring it all back in - to then re-reach, reassess, and recalibrate.' (S.3.Q2) Recalibrate is also another term that Abe makes frequent use of. This term fits well with the theme of re-synching our vibrational frequencies. In this, we should remind ourselves that our reality is a response to how we are, and our vibrational states. The human being is the foundation of its world: 'You are the foundation in which a new world needs to be built upon - each and every one of you are a part of this foundation.' (S.3.Q2) This understanding is easily forgotten within our regular social lives. Or else, people may think that such notions as 'unity' and 'unification' are noble ideals but beyond the everyday life. Why be the 'foundation in which a new world needs to be built upon' when most people have a hard enough time dealing with the regular life they have already? The human path of development – 'a process of becoming' – is something that goes against all that we have been taught. Or rather, against all the social programming and conditioning that we are brought up within: 'Life is a division of you, and this is your current programming; but it is changing, it is developing, and develop it you must.' (S.3.Q3) Unity/unification is our default state yet we need to 'clear out the vibration' so that we can resonate once again with this state. It needs to be rooted: 'You need to give it time to be rooted, to create resonation within your brain so that these pathways can then join up, can strengthen.' (S.3.Q3) When Abe discusses the creation of new pathways, they often refer to the creation of new neural pathways in the human brain that can allow for a new resonance pattern. This is where the re-wiring should occur – in our own internal workings, not out there in the physical world. Besides, what happens within will also be reflected without: this is also part of the integration. It is about reprogramming ourselves first, before we rush off trying to reorder and reorganize the world around us. We need to take time to reassess and to question ourselves and the world we perceive. Again, Abe emphasizes that this is not something that will happen overnight: 'Like we repeat, it is a becoming and humanity will not change overnight the programming that has been embedded within you. But it is time to start to cut it back - back to the basics for that is where the truth lies.' (S.3.Q3) It is time for us to take a good, deep look at our own human programming.

Humanity has seemingly got itself embedded into a 'vicious cycle,' or loop pattern. Our socializing processes literally hypnotize us, and we create a myriad of manifestos and ideologies to keep us entertained (or transfixed). We have forgotten that unity 'can but take so many forms and still be of one thing.' Humanity gets trapped within its own rankings and system of hierarchies, and little realizes that our species is engaged in a process of becoming: 'The thing to know is that you are all a work in progress in which may never be complete. And that is the beauty of life.' (S.3.Q4) After putting on so many layers – socially, psychologically, etc. – it is now time to start stripping them back. We often refer to the life experience as the 'game of life,' yet we repeatedly miss the point in that games are meant to be played. As Abe says, 'only this game has no winners' for we are all an intrinsic part of the game itself, playing ourselves. In playing ourselves, we also should be playing our own truths. Yet most of the time we end up playing someone else's truths. We need to ground ourselves first. Otherwise, we are liable to be swung around by the events of life: 'it is fine to meddle out there in the world, but it will be swung and swayed. You will not have the strength, and indeed the capacity, to create these pathways without firstly doing so within. It is indeed so - as within, so without.' (S.3.Q5) Again, we have this emphasis upon the within-without relationship. This is part of the agreement, and there is no division here. If there is a division, then it is one that we have artificially created. Abe wryly comments that this 'within-without' relation or terminology is one that 'has been tarred with the notion of witchery or new age philosophy in which people tend to shy from.' (S.3.Q5) Yet at its core, it is a profound truth. The barriers, blockages, and the illusions that so many people have built up around them now need to be dropped. And, as Abe notes, 'some are just not ready.'

As we resonate and synch up with our natural vibrational state (our 'vibrational signature'), this allows for a greater receptivity of consciousness. This then allows for a more expansive synching up with others. Using an analogy, Abe says that humans spend so much energy (as we have been taught/conditioned) in moving the pieces around the board, when in fact we could be synching up with the pieces instead. As we shift to this, we will realize 'what a slog it was to always do it the other way around.' And we have also been too quick to give away our own power – how very human! We were taught that what constituted power lay in the things external to us, and so we projected onto this. Because of this, we tend to get 'tossed to and fro with life's circumstances.' Furthermore, just knowing about unity is not going to bring us instant happiness:

> Unity doesn't mean everything will be happily ever after – no, but it does so allow you to see the connection in things and the wholeness. It is not about life giving you constant happy gifts and continually being positive - it is really about the beauty of wholeness and that wholeness starts with you. In unity, you are given back your power for you see that things are not good and bad, but just that you withstand because your happiness is not dependent upon things outside of you. (S.3.Q5)

Power, in one aspect, is about knowing our state of being is not dependent upon the things outside of us. In this, we can form more balanced relations with the world around us – relate more open-heartedly – instead of 'resisting one experience over another.' The more we place ourselves, and our well-being, upon external things, the more we shall lose our grounding, our rooting, and be at the whim of outside forces.

Another common theme in the Abe communications is that humans tend to get in their own way far too often. This also applies to our manner of communication, especially in regard to how we rely on devices. We rely on so many gadgets to mediate our connections: 'you do so place yourselves, or more so that in which you consider to be yourselves, in-between all interactions.' (S.3.Q6) Rather than seeing physical objects, such as gadgets, as being distinct from us we should regard them as 'a physical manifestation of that in which you already hold.' What this does is once again bring the perspective, and focus, back onto the human being. This is where the Abe conversations constantly place the focus – back onto the human being. This is bringing it home. This is recognizing *the way back home.*

Unfortunately, we also have a spoken medium – language – that emphasizes and upholds the notion of division and separation. Language, we are told, 'will always be a divider.' Abe goes on to state that: 'words are dividers - it conceptualizes that in which cannot be conceptualized. But you see, it does not need to be dropped - it just needs to be seen in a new light.' (S.3.Q7) We know very well that there are experiences that just simply cannot be put into words, as is often said. In Abe's expression, language 'conceptualizes that in which cannot be conceptualized' and thus often acts as a divider. Yet language cannot be dropped – and should not be dropped – but rather 'seen in a new light.' Language can also be used to express unification, if only we shift our focus of vocabulary. But no words will have real meaning if they are not backed by an aligned resonance. We cannot "walk the talk" if we do not have a frequency alignment with the words we are using. Again, it comes back to us. The steps we take can be in relation, in unison, or they can be misaligned. We have no in-built road map: 'It is but likened to taking a step from truth each and every time; and the step appearing in unison with the foot being placed back down.' (S.3.Q8) We walk our truth with each step, one step at a time. And as we walk, we can also talk. It is about *being* and *allowing* – it is relational.

Consciousness is also very much about the act of *allowance*. The human being can manifest consciousness, yet it is not exclusive to the individual. Everything in existence is consciousness – pure consciousness is Source. This is the *Continuum* (see Vol.1) in which everything is a part of, and never apart from. We only make it more complicated for ourselves when we try to claim it: 'you as humans, you seem to claim so much and in this do so make life hard for yourselves. For then, you have to make something happen that in which happens spontaneously.' (S.3.Q9) We are always trying hard to 'make something happen' as if nothing will happen without us. We are pushing, pulling, and resisting instead of participating. People are constantly trying to change the world by forcing human action upon it. And still, the world continues to respond in ways we do not fully understand. The path of force is not a path of synchronization: 'when something is forced upon anything you but know that something is not wanting it, is resisting - it is but not resonating.' (S.3.Q10) We can only be in alignment with something when we are in sync with it. And it is hard to be in sync with anything if we are not first in sync and aligned with ourselves. This is one of humanity's fundamental issues. We are racing forward upon a trajectory of so-called "progress" without first finding our own alignments. Whatever we create will be aligned with our own state. It is the foolish person, they say, who builds their house on sand. We may go about trying to 'fix things' yet everything will spring back in relation to the state of the human being: 'And you see that, always out there, things need fixing, need aligning. But then they bounce back - they realign to that resonation and that is you. It is but an endless loop.' (S.3.Q11) We need to be the ones to break these patterns first. Otherwise, what will be the point of our actions? It is not a selfish act to look to oneself first – it is fundamental. As Abe puts it, it is of essence that we align first: 'You will not make new pathways without for you have not tended to the already established pathways within.' (S.3.Q12)

Each person's life experience is within their own seeing – the capacity to perceive – and the more a person cleans or polishes the way they see, how they view life, the more that is revealed. In other words: 'you need to clean out all that has been keeping you from seeing it.' (S.3.Q14) A person's way of seeing needs to be rooted, not changed daily – perception has to be established. A shift in resonance that brings about perception has to become a default setting. Conscious evolution, or the evolution of perceptive awareness, is about moving away from constriction and into conscious expansion. It is the cracking open of the Russian Dolls, in Abe's analogy, and moving from the smallest doll to the largest. It is about creating more space because, as we are now, humanity is 'constricted in space.' And the more space we allow ourselves, the more we crack open these constrictions, which then allows for more space to unfold. What are some of these confinements? Abe places them as such: 'These confinements, we would like to add, are that of your signatures, of bodily constrictions, and the vibratory essence that does so go with it. You are but the constrictor and also the space.' (S.3.Q15) We further confine ourselves by the hierarchies and the status symbols we use. We automatically use labels and create imaginary definitions from this. Abe gives a good, and unexpected, analogy to show how humans create barriers through such invented hierarchical systems:

> You do so put upon people for you think 'ahhh, the professor - I bet he would be an interesting chap.' But you see, it may not be true, and an old drunk at your local pub may indeed have more a true word to say that would 'wow' you. You see, you do so place these hierarchical systems between you and other people. You create barriers when indeed sometimes you need to create space; that is only created when you do so decide to listen. Not just to the writer or the professor or the scientist or so-called expert but to all; as if you can learn so much from everyone you meet, for this is true. (S.3.Q15)

This is a good example/analogy to show how our social labels, including snobbery, so strongly define how we view events in life and how we navigate our experiences and encounters. We close ourselves down by our definitions and categories even before we've had a chance to allow for such encounters. Abe asks us to 'listen with an open heart' for we may 'find inspiration within some of the most darkest of places, and in this bring light.' This is the light of our consciousness – a light that can reveal truths to us. We should not pre-define to ourselves where or where not we may find our truths, for then we are already creating our limitations and confinements. Life often has a way of circumnavigating our expectations and presenting us with incredible, spontaneous opportunities.

We may respond to the above by asking, how can we so easily move away from our hierarchies – after all, they are embedded into our social systems? Perhaps it is a case of feeding into those very same systems that constrict us. We rely on them, says Abe, because we 'feel there is but no other option.' We have allowed this 'pyramid of status and acceptance' to be built into our societies, and then we continued to feed into these structures – we nourished them with our own acceptance and agreement. We haven't given ourselves the space yet to feel any different: 'And so long as you are feeding into it, and being fed by it, you see no indifference for you haven't had the space to truly feel this.' (S.3.Q16) Further, there can be almost no effort to move in another direction if there is not first felt any dissatisfaction. Why should we change things if we are comfortable? It is hard to sense, to perceive, that some of our 'comforts' are actually attachments of dissonance that we have become used to. We become invested in certain ways and patterns, and we continue to feed into them, which only strengthens them further. And we may then feel that there is no alternative. However: 'There are always other options - you are an infinite being and just because something worked previously does not mean it does so now.

Give yourselves a break, a breath, a little inch of space, to see this now and to realign, readjust.' (S.3.Q16)

Sometimes it is necessary to reach a breaking point before anything will change. And yet, it is also a strange pattern that people often dig their heels in deeper to hold onto those same conditions that are at breaking point. The deeper we resist, the more rooting out will be required – and this creates the dissonance, the disturbance. It is often the case that the new flows are greater where the resistance grows stronger: 'it is but all dependent on how much humanity goes with or against this new direction. It is of dissonance, and then realignment and allowance. The new flow becomes greater and greater, but sometimes also so does the resistance to it.' (S.3.Q17) Humans are too easily coerced, or persuaded, into perpetuating the separation in our social lives as well as our thinking. We've had hierarchical structures that have been very male dominated, and we play these male-female polarities out through most social systems. When there is a split in our thinking, in conscious experience, then there is also a split in society. Many commentaries talk about the male-female qualities as being 'this' and 'that,' which then separates them out from the wholeness in which they exist. The human being incorporates all qualities, otherwise we would simply not exist. The human being is not one or the other:

> It is true that your conditioning is one of separateness - of Male and Female - like within the brain. Whichever side has been more prominently nurtured and dismissed whilst growing up, this is but influenced by parental society, experience, culture. But you see, what unity is, is merging these two equally. (S.3.Q18)

Just as we have our social hierarchies, we also have our separations operating through many other areas: left brain/right brain; male/female, etc. Whilst it can be useful to perceive such polarities, for they can help us to navigate through the life experience, we also need to recognize the need for their mergence. Sometimes we will use our head/intellect more; other times we shall rely upon our heart/emotions – yet all should be in coherence and balance. Their usage may be more prominent at one time or another, yet they need to exist in harmony rather than one being suppressed at the expense of the other. And this is where we need *allowance*: 'Allowance is key to this natural flow - to rewire, reconnect, and create new pathways within to enable it without.' (S.3.Q18)

There are many ways, practices, and traditions, that can help in this balance of resonance. Some use meditation, visualization, music, etc., to establish this rebalance. We can also take 'time out' to re-align with our 'home resonance' and to root this. It is important that we each find the space 'to refocus, to readjust, to realign.' As Abe repeatedly tells us, 'the resonation is already there' – we just need to find the space and focus to reconfigure it. We don't need to over-complexify these ideas. To find our balance, our resonation, is not rocket-science, as they say. If a person wishes to use certain practices/tools to re-sync back up then this is fine, so long as they realize that these are tools and not the *thing itself*. Of course, it can be said that humans have always used tools throughout their history; tools have helped us navigate through the material world and to mediate our experiences. The danger here, though, is when we start to over-identify with them: 'sometimes you get dragged into the comparison of such things that – "my practice or meditation is but more spiritual, more aligned than your tool is."' (S.3.Q20) There is a tendency to over-try our practices, to push too hard without allowing for space. Readjustment is not a forced process; it is a natural re-alignment and, as such, should be as normal as possible and not strained. Our tools and practices should not end up getting in the way by becoming our crutches. Once the 'work is done' we can put them down again and stop carrying them with us. After all, 'you wouldn't continue to use the hammer if it is not needed for it will only damage the wood.' (S.3.Q20)

The Abe messages speak a great deal about human relations with the world around; yet of paramount is firstly the 'relation to oneself.' If a person rejects a part of themselves, even if they consider this to be a small part, then they are likely to find this aspect externally, as if projected outwards. As Abe says: 'if you reject a part of yourselves, you are in hindsight only going to find it outside of yourselves in that of other people. You project, you try to fix outside of yourselves, helping others when really you need to be more accepting of all your parts.' (S.3.Q21) A person will never be whole, never feel integrated, if there is not this unity within the self. And if a person is not whole, not synched up within themselves, then the world they experience will reflect this. This experience will be unique for each individual, according to their state. Some people may feel a little apprehensive over the repetition of this word 'unity' as if it smells of consensus, collectivity, or even a Borg-like connotation. Far from it. As Abe puts it: 'That is the beauty of humanity and but very few can see this so much now, for within unity there is but much room for uniqueness, for diversity.' (S.3.Q21)

Our uniqueness is also expressed through our distinctive vibration (our 'vibratory signature'), and this emitted frequency is always in communication with the external world. Humans are, therefore, 'always speaking without words.' Humans are embedded within a world of 'silent communication,' yet we seldom realize or acknowledge this. We sense this through our feelings – our gut instinct – and we can learn to be aware of this frequency resonance with the world around us. Often to the contrary, we are taught that we are too sensitive and that we need to acclimatize ourselves to a world of logic and reason. It is important to know, however, that we live 'in a web of vibrational communication' and we 'just need to feel again, to hear.' Likewise, there are vibrational resonances communicating with us, and through us, all the time – communication is not one-way. People often facilitate and nurture vibrational resonance between particular people and places without being consciously aware that they are doing so. In such cases, there may simply be a "good connection" or "good vibe" that a person naturally feels and thus wishes to cultivate. In all likelihood, we've each had this experience of vibrational resonance that felt right. In many instances, people tend to reject these inner sensations or "gut feelings" as not having any external proofs. In this, we often adopt a position of not trusting our own internal nudges. We may feel vulnerable when we are 'without a middleman' or broker to verify or interpret an experience for us. This, again, is a sign of the human conditioning to outsource our inner resources – to project our dependencies onto an external authority. We don't need these artificial brokers in the middle: 'You need to detach, to realign, so that all can receive in this way without the manmade structures…It does not need to be filtered through anything but rather allowed to reroute.' (S.3.Q24)

The vibrational alignment resonates through the human body – this is the primary 'mechanism.' This ability to align with vibrational frequencies has 'never been amiss,' only that 'the connection may have been more harmonious in past times.' In the past, however, the use of the human intellect was less dominant, and the human being operated more on an instinctual level. At times, this also meant more of a survival level. Now, humanity has arrived at a new era: 'you are but in a new era and the intellect has been much too prominent and not allowed this communication and therefore has misaligned all in that you are and in all that you can be.' (S.3.Q25) Some of our vibrational communicative alignment has been distorted due to the over-dominance of the rational intellect. The intellect is important, yet it does try to dictate and lead the way – and it is this that leads to a disequilibrium in the 'wholeness of being.' For this reason, amongst others, some people find like-resonance between them, and with other people there is a vibrational misalignment that results in what we often label as a "strange vibe." We simply do not get on with certain people, and instinctively feel that we are not aligned with them. Then, on those rare occasions, we may feel a strong attachment to a person (beyond the physical) where we may say that we have found a 'soul mate.' This, says Abe, is most likely that two people have recognized the 'HOME resonance' within the other: 'resonation can occur when you see that HOME resonance. And it is but evident in all, and like a little gem it sets off a twinkle in the eye.' (S.3.Q26) It can be that 'twinkle in the eye' that provides one of life's wondrous, energized moments.

It is also the case that modern social conditioning works on the personality and strives to develop dominant personas (vibratory signature). When we come into contact with a dominant personality it is difficult to sync-up with them as their frequency can be artificially distorted. On the other hand, there are people who more humbly allow their home resonance to ripple out, so to say, and we find that it is easier to sync up with such people – often, we are attracted to them and cannot explain this attraction in words. We can say that there is a harmonious frequency in such a case. People are not aware that they are always communicating through resonance. As Abe puts it: 'You are but always talking by resonation.' (S.3.Q27) It is just that humans tend to get themselves caught up in everything else, and they project their reasoning for why things happen as they do onto everything else. Whether we are aware of it or not, we 'try to control these connections as to work harder and faster' for our own needs and end up misaligning the communication between things. That is, we end up creating the very dissonance that affects us. This is part of the 'chasing our own tails' that Abe frequently refers to. As humans, we have not yet fully learned to give ourselves the necessary space 'for things to line themselves up again and re-resonate.' To a large degree we have, as a species, fallen out of our natural flow: 'sometimes you just need to leave things alone to give other things space too - to realign, to recommunicate again.' (S.3.Q27)

This is an important point here, and perhaps one that we do not give enough attention to. As Abe expressed above, we need to 'recommunicate again.' It is easy to dismiss communication as something automatic. Just because we use words, texts, emails – and now far too often emojis – does not mean that we are truly communicating. Words are not necessarily communication: 'words without feelings are just empty words. They have no vibrational resonance as to reach past the material existence. You have to feel that in which you write; you have to feel that in which you speak' (S.3.Q28) Many of us have no doubt had the experience that we are listening to a person who is talking a lot (maybe they are recognized as an educated, intelligent person), yet we remember little of what was said, or what was spoken was tiresome. In such a case, words were spoken – yet little was actually communicated. Communication requires a resonance, not only an exterior echo. It can be that the resonance, the energy frequency, is more important than the content in a communication. Certain objects can serve as instruments – such as books, music, art, etc. – that communicate through vibrational resonance regardless of their content. When we listen to music, for example, what do we find as the most important element: the music or the words? When we feel uplifted by a piece of music, what is it that affects us? Also, how we respond to the form of communication adds to the connection: indeed, do we resonate/respond? Communication also involves how we feed back into it. Communication fails when it is one-way; when it is directed at its target/listener but does not elicit an engagement. Everything comes down to a feeling/vibration: 'You see, speech is vibrational, is it not? It is felt upon the eardrum and converted. It has to be sensed and sense is feeling. You say when something falls upon deaf ears, it is really saying that is does not resonate.' (S.3.Q29) It is the *feeling* that resonates most of the time, not the content.

If humanity has not yet learnt how to be in equilibrium, how to communicate with the world around, then how can we expect to understand the ways of Nature? If we cannot first give ourselves the space we need, how then can we give space to other ecosystems? This comes back to what was discussed in Volume 1 in that humans tend to rush to intervene in situations that they do not fully understand or comprehend. If we act from a splintered mind, as Abe calls it, then we shall develop unbalanced outcomes: a splintered foundation does not produce stability. Realignment 'is but something that happens spontaneously.' If we can allow this space, then things would find their own balance again: 'you do not know what everything should so resonate at, and therefore should let everything else find its own balance, its own hum.' (S.3.Q30) People 'colour' their vibrational signature with their own personal aspects; in other words, we project a resonance that is tinted (and/or tainted) with the vibration of our personality. And if we have been strongly socially conditioned, then our resonance is tinted/tainted stronger or less so, accordingly: 'It is but always in human form going to be tainted in one way or another, for you cannot be void of your own signature' (S.3.Q30) We haven't yet mastered the art of integration, so we leave the head and heart lying separately; but it is the integration that will lead us to *the way back home.* We should feel comfortable with our feelings without having to rationalize them. It seems that people far too often wrap themselves up in protective shells, not feeling safe in coming out. We need to accept others just as much as ourselves: 'This is but so important to allow this space for others to come forth. But hear this, you have to be accepting of self, of true to self - united in all of your being.' (S.3.Q30) This vibrational signature that each person has is their 'base line resonation.' And although we have this baseline, it can still be overridden – a new beat or pulse can be added to it. Our existing baseline resonation can be 'cleaned out' and 'transmuted' – in the words of Abe – and a new vibrational imprint acquired. And it is this vibrational imprint that is passed on genetically: 'This is but contained within your DNA structure and is also dependent upon your own experience and your own resonation. Do you so see this pattern of vibration now and how it is but passed on?' (S.3.Q30) Any expansion of consciousness acquired in our lifetime can be passed on vibrationally 'to be evident in new life.' This is one of the mechanisms for how conscious evolution occurs.

Life experience is the medium where our essential source vibration ('home resonance') is expressed through the mechanism of the human body. The personality is acquired, through social conditioning and other factors, which colours and produces a 'vibrational signature.' Depending on factors, such as a person's upbringing and ego-development, the vibrational signature becomes more attuned, or less aligned, with one's 'home resonance.' This difference is part of the layering that we acquire as we move through the life experience. Abe refers to this as the 'overcoat.' Our personality 'vibrational signature' is the overcoat we wear through life. And it can become more dominant if it is expressed through a more prominent ego. When one aspect is dominant (e.g., the ego-self), then other factors can be suppressed ('home resonance'). It is within this relation of essence/home resonance and personality/vibrational signature that the human being needs to seek balance and harmony – this is the merger. This balance is more difficult to seek in societies that promote the strength of the individual and social individualism. Individualism is not a negative trait, by any means, if it is aligned with a person's natural being. The balance is in the knowing: 'It is never about one or the other but always a knowing - for if you are knowing that you are but oneness then the stickiness of life is not so sticky.' (S.3.Q32) If we can retain an awareness of our connection to Source consciousness, then life does not become so complicated; or, in the words of Abe, life 'is not so sticky.' It comes back to the need to create space for oneself, and to allow our lives to be more 'than this encapsulated being.' We live within the skin, yet the human being is so much more.

Human life has been structured around the stories it tells itself – the mythologies, tales, and identities it has created – and these become the layering that define how we see ourselves. Over time, these layers became more solidified and have crystallized (or rigidified) our perceptions. They then created discord as they formed our separations through social, religious, and political identities and ideologies. Each social environment offered its 'overcoats' for the inhabitants to wear. The earthly existence got turned into a huge shopping mall where we, the shoppers, tried on different overcoats, swapping and changing

74

until we liked a particular fit or fashion. The more we moved away from our natural vibrational essence, the more we name-called those we perceived as 'others:' 'And in some ways causes more discord because of the separation caused - for they will say this is moral and that is not. When you are but back to your natural resonance there is no need for so much naming and blaming.' (S.3.Q33) Allowing the few to have power over the many is not an evolutionary impulse – it is contrary to harmonious growth. The human path of development has become distorted through these structures that are now, as Abe says, 'lording over you.' It is a time for recalibration: 'Time to unify, time to sync back up. As for the mythologies, the stories, they have but served a purpose. But you see, it is now time to not place things outside of yourselves.' (S.3.Q33) An evolved consciousness realizes that all such stories are related to the essential unity and are not separate from it. Yet, as humans, we get so 'wrapped up' in the characters of our own stories that we forget the original meaning of the story itself – we get lost in the myriad of plotlines.

This is not to say that all of a sudden human life on planet Earth falls into harmony and lives happily ever after. This is not going to happen either (not yet anyway). The 'play of unity' does not require that everything exists in a 'unity of being' at any one time. This would signify a more static state of existence. Rather, it suggests that life experiences feed into energies of unity. Ultimately, material and energetic structures that favour separation and resist feeding into alignments of unity will fall, for in the end they are not cosmically sustainable. If the prominent energy upon this planet shifts to one of unity and togetherness, then this will attract others into this alignment. People, structures, and groupings that have previously favoured separation and discord may then be compelled to realign if the prominent energies upon the planet shift. Not only is this scenario possible, it may even be likely, due to cosmic factors which then influence planetary ones. This realignment upon the planet may be chaotic initially, yet such chaos has a function:

> New resonation for you will create new pathways - that in which syncs up. There will always be chaos when change is allowed. But you see, chaos is just the reconstructing; chaos is the realigning - and really, chaos is the space too. (S.3.Q34)

At some point, humanity will have to come back into resonance if it is to continue. For a long time, humanity was focused on its physicalness. And this was all well and good in its time, for humanity needed to learn how to deal with its physical environment in order to grow. And through this growth in physicality, we allowed more and more consciousness. This was part of the 'dance of polarity,' and 'life is change, life is but rhythm.' Yet to continue this flow – this *allowance of consciousness* – we need to come back into alignment with our being, our 'home resonance.' This is what Abe refers to as the regathering of our parts: this is the *way back home.*

This regathering will not gather together everyone. Not everyone is ready for it yet. There are a great many people not yet actively seeking this type of information or understanding. And that is fine. Nothing can be forced: 'We see there is also a divide in people - it is seen, it is evident, so there will not be people who are actively looking for this kind of information and should never be forced upon anyone. It is but an allowance - a resetting, a realigning.' (S.3.Q36) Each person must come to their own place of allowance, and in their own time. This is how things take root and is a personal journey for each individual.

For this reason, the Abe materials do not support or promote any specific tradition or pathway: 'there is many a tradition and the reason we do not bite to any practice or ritual, or sacred place is really our message too - that you are it.' (S.3.Q36) We are told that there is no longer any need to be looking outside of ourselves, trying one practice over another, changing, trying, swapping. As Abe says on more than one occasion: 'You are but us and we are but you.' It is just that in the case of the human life experience, we have a physical 'point of place.'

These body of Abe communications began with the intention to explore the subject of relations: relations to one another, to our world, and to the universe. Although Abe talks in regard to these differing relations, they are also not differing at all – and this is another point that Abe makes. They are all related to the self, for the relation to oneself determines all these other relations. We only have to 'crack open' ourselves to allow more and more relations and connections to open up. As Abe says:

> ... the 'way back home' is home to yourselves; and when we say selves, we do not mean your vibrational signature essence. No, we mean the underlying essence that you are - this beat, if you will, which is in harmony already. You see, it is in the allowing, in the space, that this is allowed to emerge, to strengthen, to be rooted. And we are never one to say that you should but transcend to this state - but ground it, unite it with all of your being. (S.3.Q37)

Our 'way back home' is to the 'underlying essence' that we are. It is a synchronization with the essential core of our existence. By synching up, more of life's vital energies can flow through us and allow us to expand in all ways. Abe asks that we each find something that brings us back into this core alignment when things of the world distract us and pull us into the play of physicality. When we are 'HOME' we feel connected to everything – 'you can feel the world.' When we are 'HOME' we share the space with all and everything. As Abe puts it: 'We would like to say we will meet you there and that is but only when you have finally met yourself.' (S.3.Q37) And when we can meet ourselves, we shall also have met the greater universe.

SECTION FOUR
Contact with the Greater Universe

The next topic of conversation with Abe turned to contact and relations with the greater universe. Of course, this is a large subject in all respects. And yet, as we have come to understand through these Abe communications, it is all in relation to that which resides within us. More and more is being discovered about the universe; and yet, such things are 'always known to the knower.' This again comes back to the phrase of 'what is within is also without.' It is all a pattern of 'inter-looping, interacting, and intertwining.' There is really only one conversation, yet it is being expressed through countless conversations, all throughout existence. And our current conversation is of the loss of connection: 'You but sense and feel the world around you, but you do so feel that you have taken yourself to be out of this system, out of this connection.' (S.4.Q2) Yet, despite what we may feel, it is impossible for us to be 'out of it.' The discord comes from us thinking and believing we are disconnected, which then creates this unnatural separation. Humans experience this disconnection because it has become a part of how they perceive reality, which then reflects back to them: 'what you do outside really does have an effect unto yourselves - it can only ever be this way. It is but madness when looked upon with eyes open.' (S.4.Q2) In a life expression, a person can realize that which they think they are as well as that which they think they are not. Our thinking gets projected and then reflected back to us in so many diverse ways, and this all adds to the cluttering. We have to learn also how to 'reel it in and be still, be quiet,' for at least some moments.

We can only work with what we have, and this determines how we view and learn about the greater universe. If we can expand our understanding on the physical level, then this widens what is accessible to us: 'For in the opening up of the expansiveness in which this universe is, are you not just allowing more pathways to be but built? When more pathways are being created, then are you not then seeing deeper truths, deeper relations?' (S.4.Q3) A deeper understanding allows for more pathways of perception to open up to us; these pathways then allow for greater truths to be known. This is the interconnection, the fractal relation, of how comprehension operates: as we open up a step, we allow more to be known to us that then allows another step to be taken, and so on. Also, everything gets filtered through something, whether it is our consciousness or our instruments (such as the telescopes we build). Of course, the 'more filters the more it does get distorted.' Everything is in relation to the 'mechanism that is receiving' – which in this case means the human being. These relations are not so much 'wrong' or 'right' but instead reflect the state, or receptivity, or where we are at. The external universe is just simply not able to open up to us if we are not ready, or prepared, to receive: 'if you are not internally creating these pathways then you are not so either externally - you are at where you are at.' (S.4.Q3) Each individual defines where they 'are at' in relation to their inner perception. Abe states that they wish to assist us in our reaching into this inner space – in syncing back up – so that we can take new steps forward, un-splintered and in wholeness. All things exist in this dance of relations.

Human science may say that the universe stretches for light-years, beyond our measurable comprehension, yet it is also as close as we wish to make it – for everything is in relation. In many ways, knowledge of the universe has been closed off to us due to our own limitations. We have tried to gain an understanding of the universe/cosmos through an intellectual approach – a rational logic of science developed by human minds. Humanity long ago dropped its intuitive, inner-space probing, such as through meditation and spiritual exercises. Modern humanity became a being of scientific rationalism. As such, the universe responded to this by revealing itself only through the medium of science, which is a limited perspective in our context here. The conversation, as Abe would say, is being made more complex by the layering – the overcoats – that humanity puts over everything. The human layering tends to think in linear, straight lines; in neat packages that have their openings and closings. Our measurements also manage things by 'slice and dice' instead of recognizing how a web of interrelations affects accurate measurement (quantum physics may be an exception here). All such relations, from the human perspective, can never be seen in their entirety: 'But what we see is a highway of communication - no one direction, no one way, but intrinsically intertwined, inter-related, and interpreted wrong.' (S.4.Q5) This immeasurability is not acceptable to modern science – we find such things too disorganized and messy to our intellectual minds. Human minds end up only viewing parts of the pattern and not the bigger picture. And these greater patterns are forever becoming and never static nor completed.

The universe that we perceive is only a snippet of the greater reality. The vastness that lies outside of us can first be connected to from within: 'if you really want to know this vastness in which you see before you - the one that you are but encompassed within - then firstly you must bring it back.' (S.4.Q6) Since there is no perceived, definitive 'starting point of creation' then we have to start from where we are – from within ourselves. We are always where we are now. The expansiveness of creation is always in correlation with our own being. Everything is in a rhythm; perhaps this is why the phrase "the music of the spheres" has been used. Creation is one symphony, and each instrument, each element of the orchestra, needs to get synced up. Otherwise, there are aspects that become entropic: they lose dynamism and vital force, and slide into decline and decay. In the universe, all expressions and choices are allowed; yet such forces can eventually fall into stagnation and wither away from the ongoing vitalism of creative life. When our human body and senses – the 'mechanism' – is out of sync then we are also out of tune: 'For you to resonate these, to tune back up, for when the instrument is finally tuned it can then create a pattern, a rhythm, a beat. This web of consciousness is the beats and can correlate to this greater symphony of being.' (S.4.Q7) The music, the rhythm, starts with us – we are the instrument – and the beat is created when we align and resonate with the interrelations of life and the universe (and everything!). As Abe says, many people 'are not aware of their own rhythm' and will never 'play a part within this great symphony.' What a privilege it is to be a part of the symphony: 'What an advantage, what a blessing, and we would say what a life if but only seen - if only heard, if only allowed.' (S.4.Q7)

A melodious rhythm cannot be created if 'the musical apparatus is but out of tune.' It is the rightful heritage of humanity to be interrelated within this communicative web of consciousness; but human consciousness is splintered. Abe says that humanity is scattered: 'We see it as the ashes of the body left in differing places and this is what we see on a conscious level – scattered, splintered, call it what you will.' (S.4.Q8) We have to bring our pieces back together again. The way forward has to be upon a conscious level. Humanity has largely lived until now through a 'dance of polarities' where one dominates over the other, and then other polarized forces come in vying for dominance. This has been our swinging rhythm; yet it has been more cacophonous than melodic. From the human side, there has been a discord in the universal conversation. And this has been the source of many of our sufferings, for humanity is in 'dis-ease' within its natural environment. Yet how did this come about? How did humanity become de-synced from the universal conversation? In reply to this question, Abe provided a deeply fertile analogy that is worth sharing here in full:

> … a nice flowering plant in which you have never seen starts to naturally grow in your backyard. You see its beauty and maybe you pick a few of the flowers because they smell so sweet. And you pop them into a vase in your kitchen and every time you come in you smell the scent and see the beauty and look out of your window and see them in abundance, naturally flourishing. A friend comes around and sees the flowers, loves the smell, sees the beauty, and sees also they are abundant in your backyard. She asks to see if she could take a clipping and plants in her own backyard and soon has this plant abundant in her backyard. A friend, a scientist, says 'wow, I would like to study this plant' and comes back to the two ladies and says that the plant has so many beneficial components, to not allow any more clippings. For they should be contained and

harvested and therefore taking out of their natural environment where they flourish, and monetize - sell back that in which is but of the nature of things. (S.4.Q9)

As the story shows, something within its natural environment has been taken out and 'contained' – it has been monetized so that it can be sold back. As Abe has said previously (Vol.1), humanity has been splintered into parts and those parts sold back to us. This is the instability, the imbalance, and the cause of the cacophony.

The human imbalance causes a weakness in our inherent capacities, which could be much, much greater than we are currently aware of. Because we have so many external attachments we are 'tugged here, there, and everywhere.' That is why we are being told to 'strip it back to the bare bones' for many of our external attachments are contaminated. Most people do not even suspect there is this rhythm of life that courses through the interrelated web of existence. There are those people, however, who do feel and sense these patterns: 'There have been always ones that never lose this rhythm, this beat - be it a singer, a dancer, a writer, a nurse, or beggar. For they see these patterns, this web, and can but realign.' (S.4.Q10) Such people may act as 'points to reawaken others' like triggers on the spider's web that send out vibrations to attract the spider. Some people are sensitive enough to pick up on these vibrational nudges and to respond to them. To reawaken to our humanity – our true resonance / rhythm – is, says Abe, of 'true beauty.'

There is some element of interference too when it comes to resonance, for vibrational frequencies can be affected by electromagnetic radiation. As many readers are no doubt aware, the world is awash with electro-pollution from the wireless infrastructure of antennas, towers, satellites, and more, all beaming electronic frequencies. In this, there can be interference that causes imbalance in natural earth frequencies as well as within the human electrical body. Abe refers to this, albeit briefly, as vibrational noise: 'it is vibrational noise in which you are but encased and invested in, and that does so contaminate this line. But please do so hear this, it but only takes a nanosecond to look up and catch this rhythm again.' (S.4.Q11) Just as quickly as Abe recognizes the contaminating noise, they also point out that we can 'look up and catch' our rhythm again. What this suggests is that vibrational interference (contamination) can be mitigated through our conscious awareness. And by being aware of something, we can make a choice to disentangle and detach from it – energetically and vibrationally. We are urged to keep the line open and to 'nurture this connection.' Another way that Abe puts it is as this: 'if you are but continuing to look down at your feet then how do you expect to see the beauty in where you are going?' (S.4.Q11) Abe also mentions that our consciousness 'does so leak out in many differing ways;' and from this we lose our centering, our rooting. We have been taught, in modern times especially, to 'concentrate in the head;' and by this we shall gain understanding. Again, this is the dominant intellectual approach, and this lacks cohesion and balance: 'You think if you do so concentrate in the head you will see, you will get something. But the more you strain the less you see, for you are but directing it in one certain place and this is not true.' (S.4.Q12) We also need the bodily feeling to sync back up and rejoin the vital stream. Our languages, social and political systems, our sciences, all speak in parts; and in this, they all display limitations. Yet in respect to the human body/mind, we need to bring this into alignment; through this it will be possible for the human spectrum of perception to be widened and allow greater access to the unified web of consciousness. Everything must be in relation, as Abe never tires of reminding us. Each aspect has its place, and we should not be tempted to get rid of one thing in the hope of a quick fix.

It has been said, such as by various wisdom traditions, that humankind exists in a sort of reality bubble and is limited by this. Also, that the universe we are aware of is part of this bubble reality. Abe's response is that the bubble metaphor is not the most appropriate since this suggests we are encased by something that can be 'popped' and then be exposed to everything outside. Rather, they see it as 'a light of conscious awareness' that is relational according to where the light shines. However, this conscious awareness is not through thoughts alone but also, importantly, involves feeling for 'feeling is the vibrational resonance that you hold of your outside world - and it is but also that in which you hold of your inner too.' (S.4.Q13) And this vibrational resonance of conscious awareness is like 'points of perception' reaching 'further and further,' creating pathways that bring the person to new 'viewing points.' In many wisdom traditions, we are told that it takes a long time, sometimes a lifetime, to gain perceptual clarity to perceive beyond the normal range. In the Abe communications, it is said that firstly we need to allow old patterns of being to fall away. We are not able to gain new perceptions if we are still clinging to old patterns; that is, if we are still under the influence of our major traits of social conditioning. If we remain heavily conditioned, then we may see something without perceiving it: 'you could see something and but still show a blind eye to it and shun it for that is much easier to stay but where you are - is this not true?' (S.4.Q14) Like all things in life, we first have to learn – just like we had to learn to ride a bicycle or drive a car. Once we have learnt a skill, then it becomes easier for us to the point that

86

it becomes natural. It is the same for gaining clarity of perception – effort is still required.

When the subject of effort arises, we may immediately think of physical effort – of action and 'pushing through.' Yet the opposite is equally valid, and sometimes more important: internal work. Abe has said that humanity is entering a resting point: 'It is but time in your human species to go into this dip of this wave pattern. This is seen as the resting point - but really is not so, for much internal work can be done. The master looks as if he is not doing much in a day; but you see, he is but the physical manifestation of this dip.' (S.4.Q15) People are often 'consumed with action' and miss the point for rest and replenishment. And not only human beings but also the whole planet; rest periods are just as necessary as active ones. It is not a question of time but rather of rhythm and fluctuation. Waves are vibrational and vibration is also a wave; and just like in the ocean, waves come to the shore and draw back again. It is a natural rhythm that, when in balance, does not miss a beat. Yet humanity is now not within this natural rhythm, and we are missing the beats. The rhythm for the planet and humanity is now one of rest: not for staying still but for coming back – for regathering, and realignment. Again, it is not a period to be measured by time but through pattern resonance. In such times, much internal work can be done. This is also part of *the way back home* – a place 'of belonging within, of acceptance and nurture.' We have been so focused on the 'outer home,' that we have failed to realize that we had a home already. As Abe puts it: 'But you can but never know what state your own home is in if you are put constantly sleeping on the sofas of others.' (S.4.Q16) Sometimes we are so far away from our home resonance that it feels like we are guests elsewhere. The whole of existence is interrelated through patterns of resonance that attract and align;

these are frequencies that 'pulls the physical existence together.' There is little point in trying to explore the cosmos if we cannot sync-up where we are first. We have to learn how to communicate before dashing off: 'You speak vibrationally and then you get a vibrational response. You just have to listen to that in which is the response and allow yourselves to reset, to create the new pathways.' (S.4.Q16) It is about listening through the whole body, not just with the ears, for the vibrational conversation is silent. There are conversations between dimensions, between points of perception that we have yet to connect with. There is a difference between something that it not yet found and something that is lost. Nothing is lost to us; it only requires our finding it again.

Inter-dimensional travel and related themes are popular tropes now in media programs and movies. It is as if human consciousness is being prepared for these possibilities before their actual realization. By being shown these possibilities, it is likely that relational vibrational resonances will form – 'like a taster, if you will,' as Abe says. We can allow these vibrational resonances of potential to inter-mingle with our own. In this, people are also 'tapping into the field of pure potential' and bringing to light such ideas and inspiration within. Such potentials are within the human being: 'it is all there - you but all have this potential. It's just that you are distracted, and therefore your energy is splintered, and you cannot comprehend it so well for you have conflicting energies of outer influence.' (S.4.Q18) It is often creative people who manifest such 'mind expanding things' because many of them live outside of 'social order mass thinking' and are therefore 'able to keep this expansion, this space, for something other.' What Abe is referring to here is the social conditioning that usually closes down these expansive spaces. It is little wonder then that often it is the mavericks, eccentrics, or cultural creatives that bring forth the more 'way out' or transcendental ideas, for they are less constrained by the influences of mass thinking.

As a collective civilization it seems that we are accelerating away from our point of place – this is the 'flow of the mainstream.' We see this in our advancing technologies and forms of living; we are increasingly within a 24/7 always-on life rhythm. Each individual needs to find their own 'point of place' and to bring one's rhythm back to this: 'to bring it back, reevaluate, and then re-adjust – rest, reset, before moving forwards. That is why life is but this rhythm. But you see, many do so try to flatline it like they will be ahead - will outrun the natural rhythm of the cosmos.' (S.4.Q20) As Abe says, many people end up 'flatlining' their natural rhythm by trying to run ahead of themselves – by trying to outrun the 'rhythm of the cosmos.' And it is this that creates imbalance, dissonance, and distortion. We are repeatedly told that we make things so much harder for ourselves. It is like people running off down short cuts, only to have to navigate their way back because they lost the path. How can we go racing off when we don't even have the full picture? Abe informs us that humanity needs this dip, this space for regathering, just as much as we need the active periods. It is within such 'resting points' that we have the opportunity to see clearer, and perhaps to grasp more of the bigger picture and the 'correlation between all things.' Moving ahead is about coexisting with these natural rhythms, and for each person the path may be different. There is no one ideal location in which to find this rhythm. For some people, it may be sought in the countryside, in rural locations and small communities. For others, they may require more urban settings and more frequent interactions. As Abe puts it: 'We are not to say that everyone should abandon the cities and head for the hills. It is not true, for you can always start from where you are at.' (S.4.Q21) We can be connected to everything from the place we are at – *we* are the connection.

We firstly need to 'bring it back home' to then gain an expanded perception. From this 'higher ground' we shall be able to have a different view; and from here to have 'the strength to reach forth.' And by reaching forth we shall be able to create new pathways externally for us, and this shall also create new patterns of resonance: 'to then come forth with more clarity, more truth, more stability and strength? You can but only evolve, you can but only connect.' (S.4.Q22) Instead of trying too hard to name the unnamable through our external instruments of measurement, we should be forming these connections and understanding from within. Abe insists that we each have the power to bring ourselves back home and back to truth. The question is, would we really want to live by the truth? Would it not be easier to continue within our limited perception bubbles? It seems that this has been the situation for many people. It doesn't help that modern life keeps us 'so over-stimulated and simulated' that we don't know 'which end is up' or 'what is real.' Most people don't even realize that a 'leap of faith' may be required in order to venture beyond these comforting limitations. It is one thing to think about this – to intellectualize the situation and its conditions – and another thing entirely to take action upon it. Truth may not be something euphoric, a big bang: 'you have been but sold a lie for in this you think "Well, I must of missed it all together, for where's the big bang?" But hear this, what you don't so realize is that you are but the big bang and the bang was always silent.' (S.4.Q23) As Abe likes to tell us, those things done in truth are done in silence.

When relations are in resonance, they serve all; it cannot be that one gains over the other. In truthful universal relational resonance, service to others becomes also a service to oneself. And this can be said about the reverse also as nothing is done within a vacuum: 'It is all well and good to be of service to others but if you are but not of service to self too then you are not then serving others well.' (S.4.Q24) To be of service to oneself is not necessarily the same as being selfish. Rather, what Abe suggests is that by allowing oneself we align our relational frequencies with others. This recognizes that all relations are intertwined. If a person acts from purely selfish reasons, then this does not ultimately serve them for it cuts off their resonant alignment with others. These are aspects of imbalanced polarity. When relations are in balance, it is not so easy to distinguish the polarities for there is a unity: 'For if you try as you might to be of service to others, is that really serving anyone well at all? It is but in the act of self-service, of realigning self, then too will it be a natural flow, to be of service.' (S.4.Q24) By realigning ourselves, we then allow the flood of communication and contact to flow. We could say that the universe has been waiting for humanity to awaken so that we can respond. We've never been separated, yet we have been deaf. We have become entrapped within our own maze: 'It has been like a mind maze and you but do not know which way is out now – you're all upside down, confused, as to what is true. You see, it is about clearing the fog, finding a way out of the maze first and foremost.' (S.4.Q25) This fog is the illusion of our reality which has kept humanity within a perceptual slumber. All the connections are there, waiting for us; we just don't yet know in which direction to step.

This maze fog creates an illusory sense of captor and captive when in fact humanity plays both roles. The captive 'doesn't know is that there is no lock and key,' and the captor doesn't know that 'they have but only captured themselves.' This is the bind, says Abe, that humanity currently finds itself within. And freedom comes from a realization of this: 'You realize that you were but always free - you just had to set yourself free.' (S.4.Q26) The realization of the situation can bring freedom, and the confusion can turn into humour once this can be seen clearly. As human beings, we often get side-tracked by the grandeur and the glamour. We become lost within our own fancies. This can also occur through the use of recreational drugs, narcotics, and such consciousness-altering substances. Through such substances we can be 'gifted into a world of what is truly magical' and transcended out of the everyday. When a person lets go of social, mental, and perceptual constraints, they are open to sync and connect with other frequencies. It may give a 'wow' sensation, an explosive experience filled with technicolour. Yet, as Abe says, the truth is not fancy or filled with frills. They give a good analogy to describe this:

> But you see, truth is not fancy - it's not so frilly and explosive and knocks you off of your feet. It is so like you go chasing for love, for the grandeur, and you do so go from one person to another, and you see there was this one whom was there all along - not fancy, not shouting from the rooftops, but an undercurrent of nurture, of natural flow. And you think, why did I miss that splendor, that beauty, that magnificence? (S.4.Q27)

The truth is about finding and connecting with the magnificence in our day-to-day lives; to feel it from the core and resonate deeply with it. We don't need to crack open our minds, as this may also cause a sense of separation when the truth is that we are our own meeting point. Why go out searching for what is already within us? We don't need a fancy holiday away – we need to come back home.

Consciousness expanding substances have been used for millennia by healers, mystics, shamans, and the like. Does this mean they have the same usage today for the modern person? Can they help a person to realize other patterns and relations within the universe and beyond? These are some of the questions we may reasonably ask ourselves. However, Abe suggests that we consider this question from the perspective of evolution. Humanity is now evolving under different energetic conditions: 'here are but vibrational resonances that are not visible and these resonances are rewiring, expanding your consciousness. For you see, you will not need so much the chemical compound to do this...' (S.4.Q28) The human body, its energetic structure, is becoming more sensitive, along with human brains being rewired through the new resonances. Abe suggests that we gather ourselves – become in balance – so as to be better positioned for the 'upgrade.' Although many of these mind-expanding substances can be found in natural settings, we may not have use for them as was the case in the past. We can gain access to expanded consciousness – 'to switch on and switch up' – through alignment with shifting planetary and bodily energies. These substances can show us what is 'but part true,' yet we do not need them now: 'you do not need it now for you can sync back up and be a flow with the cosmic force that is but ingrained in your very being that's magnificent, that is but truly magical, and that is but extraordinarily ordinary.' (S.4.Q28)

The ordinary life is actually extraordinary if we can only view it as such. It is time to experience these wondrous interconnections and interrelated patterns from an attunement within rather than through an induced substance. It is time to turn the tap on from within us. And first, of course, we need to find our *way back home*. As Abe has said from the very beginning, it is time to get back to the bare bones: 'the gift is the gift in itself.'

If we cannot relate to the truth 'in its ordinary everyday attire' then we have even less chance by putting it 'in its fancy robes.' Again, it is about living the truth within the 'extraordinarily ordinary:' 'these vibrational resonances are to be but felt, to connect with, to bring it into your breath - into your day, into your being. It is but all well and good to have an experience, but will it inhabit the day-to-day, the ordinary?' (S.4.Q28) As this way of understanding develops, consciousness-altering substances will seem like antiquated methods, for they too were of their time and place. As the human being evolves, as our internal pathways 'connect, reshuffle, and reconfigure,' we shall find our natural connections and resonances. Such substances will no longer be required. As Abe says, we often get carried away with 'the frill of the ride,' and forget that it is all here already. We only need to reconnect back to it – back to our 'roots as human beings.' By coming back to ourselves, we create the new pathways we need to move ahead: 'You need to but come back home and in this you create pathways within and therefore new viewing posts without.' (S.4.Q29)

As part of our natural development and evolvement as a species, we shall come to make these reconnections with the field of universal consciousness – with the intelligence of the *Continuum*. It need not get made into a 'cosmic show,' says Abe, for we were never apart from it. Within our period of separation, we have been developing other faculties, capabilities, and perceptions – now it is time to bring everything into cohesion and into frequency alignment. From this, our species can then experience a 'new jump in evolutionary terms.' In the beginning, it may start with the few; and these few may appear 'as a little mad, a little different.' Yet there is no need to fall into exhibitionism: 'The big show, the big song and dance about it, really does need to be dropped now for you will then only ever

94

bypass truth, bypass what is here and ordinary.' (S.4.Q30) If the fancy frills continue, then the truth may be overlooked, for it is to be found within the ordinary. The same with enlightenment, says Abe, which is really 'only the light coming back on' as if someone just arrived home – nothing more fanciful. The truth has been 'the even grander show that has been playing out all along right under your nose.' The *way back home* has always been within us, we only had to realize this, resonate with it, and to allow it to be regathered. It is from this regathering that we are able to go forth.

SECTION FIVE
Consciousness, Time & Energy

In the final sessions with Abe that formed Volume 2 of the series, the attention shifted slightly from the theme of relations and relational connections to focusing more upon how to find *The Way Back Home*. Abe stated that they wanted to focus on how 'to deep-seat this' and to 'really bring it back in from a world that constantly pulls you out.' They felt it was important to root and ground this understanding of the 'way back home.' The final two sessions of Volume 2 (and hence these commentaries) explore these issues and topics. However, it was considered appropriate to place them into two separate sessions (Five and Six) as other themes also got discussed. Specifically, the themes of consciousness, time, and energy. Also, many of these messages came from sessions without specific questions. Rather, they just came forth within a free flow of communication. These messages were dated to reference when they appeared/arrived (see Part Two). Where further clarification was required, some follow-on questions were asked. Although not all these messages arrived as responses to questions, I have still referenced them as questions (e.g., S.5.Q1) for continuity of communication.

These sessions began by Abe noting that humans do so like feedback and physical confirmation on their actions and direction. They stated that: 'You do so like feedback. You like to know that you exist materially - you like to but strengthen this in all your endeavours.' (S.5.Q2) Physical confirmation and synchronicity is an indication of where a person is vibrationally. Those moments of synchronicity that sometimes surprise, and bemuse, us are useful hints and nudges to confirm we are on the right path both vibrationally and physically. Often, we humans need these signs since much of what is happening is beyond the physical, and it is harder for us to trust in unseen circumstances in such a dense physical world. We feel many things deep within, in our core being, yet we still feel that we need an overt confirmation. Yet we need to go forward now in trusting the human connection to Source: 'We do so hope that now we can root this within yourselves, within this connection, and we hope that it is to continue and grow and in trust for one another. And also, of that that can guide you - it is of importance to strengthen that now.' (S.5.Q2) The human connection to Source is also that which guides us, if we only learn to listen – this is the rooting resonance. The more a person *allows*, the more they also allow healing vibrations to manifest through their being and person (vibrational signature). Yet most people are still not allowing this flow of vital force (Source energy) to flow through them and into their environments, across the planet. This blockage is, says Abe, like the limescale that builds up in the kettle: 'Like the scale build up in kettle, the flow has but been contaminated and then in this the mechanism is not so effective.' (S.5.Q3) The human being – the 'mechanism' – has become less effective because the Source is not flowing through as it should. Humans are also healers, and this is accomplished by the sharing of energy through our connections. Yet this too has become 'contaminated.' To this, Abe says: 'So now it does so make sense to heal yourselves. But hear this, it is not but a long drawn-out process but like the vinegar that is left to do its magic within the kettle this is too this flow, for in this it will make it sparkling, as good as new.' (S.5.Q3) The Abe communications often emphasize how things can be much simpler than we make them out to be. Humans tend to always make matters more complex, more complicated. It is not about the 'show,' or the 'frills' as we have already been told. We just have to 'allow the flow to work its magic,' and in this there will also be 'prompts and nudges' to provide 'confirmation' to assist us along the way.

It is our duty now, as conscious beings, to take heed of the situation and to rebalance it. Just like a heart that beats too fast or too slow, there is disharmony caused within the body. This applies also to the grander body of life of which humanity is a part, and we are causing this disharmony by being out of resonance with the natural vibrational frequencies. In this, each person can play a part: 'And it starts with one person at a time to truly see this simple coherence of being and the role in which you play to change the winds of time - it is but time now to readjust the sails.' (S.5.Q4) Each person can align with Source resonance; it is not a question of 'channelling' or being a part of a 'special few.' As Abe has stated repeatedly, these communications do not belong to channelling but are a form of *allowance*. This allowance is a part of our natural heritage, only that it has been numbed down. As the human species evolves, this natural capability will develop again: 'this is evolution knowing that in which you are and that in which you can truly receive. And this fountain of knowledge that you can so step into at any time, like your whole body has an order, a natural order, an intelligence.' (S.5.Q4) We can each 'receive' this 'fountain of knowledge' if only we can remove our blockages. These blockages form the old patterns of conditioning and beliefs that have indoctrinated the human race for so long. It may be the case that many of these older patterns will first need to come to the fore – to 'be seen clearly' – before they can be purged. And this may cause some degree of discomfort. Yet, for anything to be truly changed it first needs to be seen for what it is; and this often means bringing it into the light. Of course, we all know that there are people and groups who seek power and use manipulation to achieve this. At the same time, there are so many, many more people who truly wish for peace, harmony, and to seek for advancing human potential. And the secret here is that there is no secret:

> the secret is there is no secret of life, for it is all there in front of you. You just need to clear the view, clear the way, re-sync, then re-adjust. If you are thinking there is but a secret to life that is but only available to a few, is kept in the dark, then you see to it that you are not human. (S.5.Q4)

The very domain of darkness and secrecy is where we lose our humanity. To be human is to keep things in the open, transparent, and flowing. And each human being has these capabilities, the power and the insight, to realign and root the home resonance – our connection with Source. As we do this, realign these connections, we shall be healing ourselves; and in healing ourselves we are also healing others. It is time now for us to be piecing things back together, of finding our wholeness that has become lost, scattered, thrown or sold away. The idea of unity and/or integration may put some people off – maybe it sounds too New Agey? – yet no individual is truly an 'island for one.' In this regard: 'It's like the sun lying to itself that it only shines for itself – it's a myth, an old pattern that need to be rid of now.' (S.5.Q4)

100

Another aspect that Abe brings up (and this again relates to the 'New Age' issue) is that these communications and materials are not self-help: 'self-help can so get you caught up in a bind as to see that you need to fix something. There is nothing needed to be fixed, just rather let go of.' (S.5.Q4) Within the 'self-help' paradigm there is often too much baggage placed upon what is the 'self,' along with too much energy focused (or lost) upon trying to fix or repair something. This then takes away from not seeing 'the underlying truth of your magnificent, extraordinarily ordinary existence.' The magic lives within the ordinary, for life is already extraordinary.

Another theme that has become over-used and popularised is the notion of the ever present NOW. This also gets confusing as 'time is very much a human concept,' and therefore we end up treating it in a 'slice and dice' way. In this, the very notion of 'now' becomes just another concept that we categorize and aim to define. We may end up chasing shadows, says Abe: 'For when you try to catch the present you are but chasing a ghost, a shadow, and it will always be in future tense. It could even be classed as past too, for when caught it is but gone.' (S.5.Q5) The NOW is thus never a time but an internal space where a person can gather themselves. The NOW is a place/space to 'stop, gather, come back and feel.' And in this there is no concept of or need for time: 'Do not try to pull back to past; do not race ahead to future; do not try to stand still to capture the NOW - you can't.' (S.5.Q5) What we can do is to 'just BE home,' and then we are free from the constraints and restrictions of time.

Time plays strongly upon human life – we measure so much by it. We create our timelines, and they stretch deep into our past as well as far into imagined futures. A timeline becomes a tangible canvas for us to paint upon, yet instead of allowing a flow, a process, an arising, as might an artist upon a blank canvas; instead, the human is taught to force or push for an event to manifest. This is an imposition, and it often causes us a disadvantage for we are not correctly listening. If we were in alignment, in resonance, to the whole then we would sense the slight changes, and we would intuitively know how to readjust and realign to shifting vibrational frequencies. This is where we need to be: 'You can feel the Earth externally, you can feel your body internally, you can then feel the cosmos; you can converse easily between these seemingly differing levels - it is an advancement. This is so achieved when synced up, when realigned.' (S.5.Q5) Most people know when they are out-of-sync; they can feel it. It is just that we more often than not reject or decide not to listen to these intuitions and feelings, or we relate them to something else such as an off day. In other words, we don't give us the space to re-gather ourselves – we deny ourselves. And the continuance of this denial only furthers the dissonance and disharmony within us. What ends up being 'real' is that which is real for us. Each person experiences life through the physical body, yet the 'real' is not an isolated phenomenon for it has to operate through us. Abe gives an analogy of the mechanism and the life force:

> ... in your physical existence you can only ever work to the mechanism, for you could ask - is the toaster a toaster or the electricity that runs through it? What would be your answer? For without the current it cannot toast - this is true. So, truth is not something you see but rather something you become. You gather, you accept that your truth is but a collection, a bundle - not you but a system within a system within a system. (S.5.Q5)

102

Our 'reality' is a collaboration, something we are immersed in and not just something we 'do.' It is a participatory arising, an emergence, a becoming, as the vital life force (Source) runs through the mechanism (the human being).

In the reality of separation there is a lot of 'oh, little me' thinking, as if we have subconsciously accepted that we live life as if within some kind of prison. In this, we unknowingly close down our receptivity to the finer flow of consciousness. Without realizing it, we create our own stubbornness, like the mule who refuses to budge. In this mode, people often run around trying to make things happen, trying to force things, and this can further the disconnection. People often shift themselves away from their centre: 'it is in the realisation that you are but a gathering, that you are not a little "me" caught up inside a mechanism - you are but a point of attraction of the whole show.' (S.5.Q6) And yet, caught up within the mechanism we often are. This is the entanglement of life; and from here we make reality seem more complicated. We are our own space, and we can take this with us wherever wo go. Similarly, we take our restrictions and limitations with us also: 'Do not constrict with notions of this and that; it is but a falsity and will too end up keeping you trapped.' (S.5.Q6) External mobility is relational to inner mobility; and here, we need to free ourselves. All the things we end up telling ourselves are like Chinese whispers, and by the time they've gone around the circle they have no resemblance to the original. It seems as if humanity has created its own rabbit holes to go down; we get distracted by our own fascinations and then wonder where we are. And the darker down we go, the less clarity there is. Life only flows according to the space that is allowed. It is up to each person to allow those spaces for themselves.

Consciousness is not a recipe, despite many people trying to grasp it as if it were. God doesn't play dice, Einstein famously said, but if we had some recipe sheet then maybe we could get a handle on it – or so the thinking goes. Within the human realm there has always been a desire to capture what is considered as the 'life force.' Now it is happening in regard to intelligent machines or so-called artificial intelligence; yet unified, pure consciousness is not something to be captured. All life is in coherent relation: 'it has been questioned but many a time upon your planet of what consciousness is - and we would like to say that it is but an interrelated intelligence, a communication, if you will, of the whole thing. One thing, but always of many.' (S.5.Q8) The personal ego recognizes the personality because it has a 'point of place,' and this often extends into a perception that the person exists separately from its environment. This is erroneous thinking and reflects the state of development of the individual – or, the 'evolution of the mechanism,' as Abe calls it. The individual (the 'mechanism') is the filter for the flow of pure consciousness: 'It really is so of but how it is going to be but filtered. If you can allow no filter; in a sense, if you are in this space, you create room for this to come in. And although not differing it is in allowing space - if you do not create so much room it is but filtered.' (S.5.Q8) The more space a person can allow within them – i.e., the less conditioning or internal cluttering – then the less filtering there is, and the more the unified consciousness can flow and be expressed through the individual. The filtering a person puts onto this vital life force is the 'over-speak' of their own vibrational essence. Mostly, what we experience in communication is other people's over-speak, the dominance of their own vibrational signature (their personality). This is not to be dropped, however; rather, a space is to be allowed.

104

As I have explored previously, in Volume 1 of the commentaries, consciousness is not a by-product or something that results from material existence. Consciousness is that which brings about material existence. And those patterns, or pathways, within materiality that are aligned vibrationally with the consciousness field will be more receptive to it. The experience or perception of consciousness expands in relation to the configuration, or receptivity, of the receiver. As Abe often repeats, pathways within create pathways without. That is, as a person opens up to more expansive consciousness, so does this create more internal resonance (re-wiring) that then manifests in greater perceptions of external patterns and relations (pathways). Each element within material existence is evolving and developing its own vantage point, or perception: 'and like the Earth that has its own system, and the body has its own system, and the cosmos but all interrelating, all listening to one another – evolving, incorporating their own vantage, working with but one intelligence.' (S.5.Q8) Abe asks us, would it not be better to be all aligning and working with this one intelligence from which we all manifest, rather than fighting against it like the student 'but always over-talking the teacher?' How can we ever learn anything if first we do not listen? Everyone is speaking, yet so few are listening it seems. Life is vibrational; evolution is vibrational; vibration is the web of communication, the 'continued conversation between all things.' We need to retain this connection, like the child that continues to ring home: 'That connection is not gone no matter where you are - unless you are not willing to listen. Listen to yourselves to connect back up.' (S.5.Q8) There is no hierarchy in this either as each person is 'the birther and the born, the teacher and the taught.'

This life force of consciousness is there for all of us. For some, they see it as a race to harness it for their own creations. Yet such scientists do not recognize consciousness as a harmonious, integrative system of vibrational resonance. This vibrational resonance can be the formation – the 'building blocks' – behind all living systems. If we cannot understand or grasp this, then we miss the point:

> … if you do so sync up again, if you vibrationally allow yourselves to fall back into this integrative system, this life force, this intelligence, you know that it is but in and around everything. Life is but orchestrated and when back in rhythm, back in sync, you can allow yourselves to be both the enjoyer of it and also the conductor. (S.5.Q8)

All life is seeking to fall into rhythm, and when out of sync it pushes to seek for re-integration. Even with complex systems that start to vibrate in dissonance, there is a drive to seek for integration before things go too far. We can sense this same drive within human systems too. They appear to wobble and fluctuate, yet some inner urge seeks for realignment. Abe likens this to the child being pushed out to the deep end that seeks to swim back. There is this continual urge within humanity to find home – the home resonance that is Source frequency. Even from the first breaths of a baby, there is continual becoming, reconfiguration, and recalibration. There is never a start point nor an end point but 'just constant reconfiguration of being, of networking.'

The more a person is under layers of conditioning (which Abe relates to the analogy of the Russian Matryoshka dolls) then the less space they have for allowing the resonance of unity consciousness: 'It is again like the analogy of the dolls - the tighter and tighter the filter, the constrict of your identity, the less you allow to flow.' (S.5.Q9) Yet Abe says that we need to crack these dolls open, otherwise we remain stuck within 'predictable patterns.' We may enjoy the security of such predictability, yet we end up stifling ourselves. We spend our lives just shifting a small amount back and forth within our layered encasing. We may take a peek outside, yet we often contract again: 'You say you want more, and you decide to venture; but you see that it is not known, so you do so clamber back in and shut the doll up again.' (S.5.Q9) We need at some point in our lives to allow for the unknown, for this unknown is the unity of all – and it is also us. We have made ourselves small 'when you are but much more.' Some amount of emptying may be necessary so that a new space can unfold. This emptying can involve all the old, outdated beliefs that we cling to; also, our false fears and insecurities. Where space is, consciousness can flow – and this is all existence. There is never a space of genuine emptiness for once there is room, it is suddenly filled again. The question is what we allow to fill this space: consciousness or external stimuli? We so often get lost in our distractions of pick and choosing, which Abe says is like sorting out our sweets: 'like sorting through a box of smarties stating, "I only like the orange ones." They may have but a differing colour, a slightly differing taste, but in the end all just smarties.' (S.5.Q9)

Whilst many people continue to pick and choose between the different coloured sweets, there are others who have always been listening. Stepping aside from their social-personality filters and listening. They listen to the flow of unity consciousness as it is expressed through them. Some of these people were known as mystics, sages, and great teachers; others were invisible to the world as they continued to share unity consciousness in their everyday lives. It is not about hierarchy – about being a mystic or a teacher – for we are all of the same unity vibration consciousness. What it is about is connecting to the 'WAY BACK HOME.' The resonance of disconnection must break up and fall away as a core unity resonance comes to the fore. We are here to evolve as a species: 'as you evolve you will see more and more evidence to support this oneness, this unity - the pathways are being created.' (S.5.Q10) Recognition of this oneness is an attractor, almost a magnetism, that draws people like 'a moth to a flame.' We may not know quite what it is, yet those people who express or radiate more the 'home resonance' have a quality about them. And such people, like each one of us, also acts as mirrors for others. Every person is a mirror if, as Abe says, we are willing to see clearly: 'And we say not even every person but everything, for you are but in conversation with oneself - it just depends on whether you are but willing to see life as such?' (S.5.Q11) From the unity, everything manifests – this is an essential understanding. It is within the human where polarities become so dominant when in fact there are a myriad – an infinity! – of variations and differing states within the unification.

When we shift from the energy of forcing, we can make space for the energy of allowance – differing energies come in and integrate as within a dance. It does not need to be this 'masculine energy' here or that 'feminine energy' there, but a natural arising in relation to resonance. There are many energies present upon the Earth at this time for this is 'a time of great healing;' as such, we should not try to categorize such energies in black and white for they are within an integrated play, albeit some energies may become more focal at one time than another. However, all energies have their balance; otherwise, 'there is no dance at all.' In our current times, there is much energetic shifting that can be felt. In one sense, these are the healing energies of rebalance and recalibration. Some energies have become too dominant and 'too over-bearing;' and others will come to 'rise again to balance it out.' As Abe puts it: 'We do so say rise in the sense that one allows the other - a constant flow, a constant becoming, not ever in a way as to overlord or push the other out of the picture but always to rebalance.' (S.5.Q14) It is suggested that instead of trying to capture or grasp at an energy and to 'start to run with it,' we should allow ourselves to be the meeting point of these energies. And within and through us we can ground and root these energies – to balance them. It is human conditioning to want to name, categorize, and then box everything as if neatly. Yet this approach does so take away from the natural resonance of the human being – it closes down the heart-space. There is a time for listening and a time for speaking; so too with the energies that shall be fluctuating across the planet, and through humanity, in these times. The merger is about meeting ourselves: 'as humans you fight this whisper; you do so drag it through the mud far too much. It is about meeting yourselves with an open heart, with an open mind - for then you see all can flow.' (S.5.Q15) If we move forward with a 'fearful heart' then we are closed off: 'closed off from self, from what you are.' As Abe asks us, how can we meet anyone in such a place/space if we have not first met ourselves? It is time to drop our proclivity for labelling in order to facilitate the flow of *allowance*.

The human being does not need to fit into any kind of fixed concept – that is just our erroneous belief. It is well beyond time now for a new rhythm: 'now let it rise, let it come forth within your very being. Connect with it, allow it, and let it flow free – flow, for it will merge you with all. It will gently usher you back on path, on track, on rhythm - for in this it is but truth.' (S.5.Q16) The resonance patterns are to arise and emerge from within us. When we are in sync with ourselves, we are also in sync with the whole – all paths are meeting to create one. And from this meeting place we can allow new growth: this is the resonance of evolvement.

SECTION SIX
Clarifying the Way Back Home

In the final session of the Volume Two communications, Abe suggested that it would be 'fitting to clarify THE WAY BACK HOME now' for this term, or understanding, still needs to be explored and unpacked. People are still very much disconnected from a sense of beingness, and many have the feeling that modern life is not allowing them to fully flourish. In this, people seek alternatives to 'hook onto' that often pull them further away from themselves. Yet it does not need to be about 'another religion, another guru, another fad.' The path to the way back home is both simple and yet incredibly elusive for many people. It is indeed hard to find such a subtle pathway 'in a world that does so want you to be out, involved, and always entertained.' (S.6.Q1) The phrase 'the way back home' means more than the letters or words portray. It is easy to think that a 'home' means a place, for humans are conditioned to think and perceive through the lens of the physical. However, Abe says that 'home is but a space, never a place, for in your human existence if there is a space then its purpose is but to be filled.' (S.6.Q2) Space is never empty but always full of vital life, for in the *Continuum* of pure consciousness there is no such thing as an empty space. As such, we should not be afraid of this space in which we, and all things, exist: 'Suspend yourselves there if only for a moment and feel this sense of fullness - not because you are filled but because you have opened to allow. This is but being back home; home from where you can see all paths meet and all things flow.' (S.6.Q2)

Unlike the physical home where we store objects and keep our things, the space of our inner home is where everything can visit without needing to be placed into a spot or given a location. It is the space for the vital flow to continually be expressed. This is the Home within us where we are always sustained and do not need to feed it through external gratifications. If we feel the need to be reaching outwards, then we are being drawn from our Home and enticed with the idea that we need something to fill an 'emptiness.' Yet this is never so, and such actions and beliefs only further splinter us. There is no empty space, and any such place that exists would have to be created by us. As human life became more complex, structured, and developed, more things emerged to take people away from themselves. At first, these were distractions associated with the requirements of everyday living. Yet, as human societies developed further, so did their means of organized distractions and events that drew peoples' attention and focus onto the external. Ideas of fulfilment and gratification became increasingly associated with external objects and experiences. However, humanity is an evolving species, and what was applicable or suitable at one stage of the journey does not necessarily apply for the next. A participation and engagement with the external physical world were a strong necessity for humanity's development. Some forms of engagement soon became entanglements that pulled the human being to and fro, weakening its inner resolve and grounding. Yet life is transactional, and new relations and patterns need to be formed. Humanity has certainly evolved consciously, and some of this new energy was utilized in external seeking and gazing.

112

The human mind and intellect began to explore further its surroundings, ever reaching outwards in curiosity and wonder:

> And the more you look outside yourselves the more things grow to want you to look outside yourselves. This is in many a human connection - from relationships between yourselves, to the food that you consume, the things that you do, the jobs that you work. It is abundant in your modern lifestyles. (S.6.Q3)

The spiral of external attachments expanded further and further, and then began to draw the human being away from its connection to the natural earth. More and more societies began to step outside of the planet's natural systems, and people began to feel as if it was normal, even correct, to separate themselves from environmental systems and relationships. A sense of natural belonging was severed, and then people began to search for substitutes – further and further away from themselves. Humanity has now arrived at a place where it needs to regather and find its belonging: 'finding this way back home - this space in the chaos, a calm, a place of being, of belonging and bringing back. The recognition of the complete picture rather than frantically running around with just a part.' (S.6.Q3)

In seeking meaning, humanity ventured outside of itself and has not looked back. It sought purpose from external gratifications, and from this extended its reach and entanglement ever further away from the inner self. This external gaze and sense of satisfaction had no alternative than to 'splinter' humankind from its recognition of Source connection, and thus to skew the balance. And when out of balance for so long, there is a mounting need for this to be restored. As Abe puts it, humanity has 'hooked' parts of itself to material existence, and this over-dominance of physical entanglement has been detrimental to our flourishing and evolvement as a species. Because of our inherent split, there is a lingering sense of unfulfillment within: 'the more you resonate with the outer gratifications the more you are but splintered; and the more you are but splintered, the more you feel unfulfilled...' (S.6.Q4) This lingering sense is, as Abe says, like an itch that we 'just can't quite scratch.' And due to this splintering within humanity, it is now ever more pressing that collectively and individually we find *our way back home*. Going forward is not necessarily about erasing the past. Whatever vehicle or medium – myths, beliefs, cognitive patterns – were utilized in the past, they served to bring humanity to its current position. We should not discredit past methodologies or ways; at the same time, however, we need to acknowledge when they no longer function to our betterment. All such elements form a part of our growth; and as in all aspects of growth, there are times when we need to drop out of one stage to continue upon another. This is similar to when the young adult 'flees the nest,' and leaves the parental protection to pursue a continuation of personal growth. Yet in this leaving the nest, we often become so engrossed in outer consumables. Whether it is chasing the gods, seeking 'spirituality' under every nook and niche, or enjoying the pleasures that a physical life offers; all in all, they each, in their own way, distract us from the essential. It now makes sense to me what the Persian mystic Jalāl al-Dīn Rumi meant when he stated:

> There is one thing in this world which must never be forgotten. If you were to forget everything else, but did not forget that, then there would be no cause to worry; whereas if you performed and remembered and did not forget every single thing, but forget that one thing, then you would have done nothing whatsoever. It is just as if a king had sent you to the country to carry out a

specified task. You go and perform a hundred other tasks; but if you have not performed that particular task on account of which you had gone to the country, it is as though you have performed nothing at all. So man has come in this world for a particular task, and that is his purpose; if he does not perform it, then he will have done nothing.

It is easy to be put off-track and taken away from ourselves. We easily become stifled by stimulation and then fall into a forgetfulness of our home resonance. Life is a mirror that we hold up to ourselves, only that we started to chase after our reflections.

These reflections soon turned into the vibrational trap of our own making. It is as if we lulled ourselves to sleep and then filled our dreams through the human creative imagination. Sometimes we 'peep out of the top and then decide to put the lid back on again.' Humans have opted more for the comfort, the security, than trust in the unknown self: 'you would but much prefer the comfy slippers of certainty. Albeit it being that in this you also cage yourselves in - you cut yourselves off from the human potential you were born to enhance, to nurture, to evolve to.' (S.6.Q6) It is also important to recognize that our human potential is for us to 'enhance, to nurture, to evolve,' and not for some outside force to come in and 'save' us. The human psyche has been riddled with the notion that 'divine intervention' – or a similar kind of intervention – will be there to reach out and protect or save us at the last moment. This, in my perspective, is a dangerous fallacy. It plays into the victim mode: 'And all the time you play the "poor little me card" and state that something above and beyond yourselves will but save you, the more you push yourselves further from the inherent truth in that you are but the saviours that you have been waiting for.' (S.6.Q7) Abe is correct to state that humanity is its own saviour – not some imagined external force. After all, the truth is that there is no 'outside' as all life, physical and non-physical, is integral to itself within the same unitary expression of Source consciousness. We should not sell ourselves short. When a person, or collective, plays this illusory game of victim and saviour, they 'are but playing both parts.'

The loop of vibrational entrapment is sustained and reinforced through a refusal or denial to see and feel the dissonance in our world/reality. We have to 'feel this dissonance' to truly accept its presence; yet we mostly distract ourselves from recognizing it. It seems we do not truly want to find a permanent solution, but rather a quick fix: 'you want a band aid fix for this deep disconnection in which you feel - it keeps you locked in and disenfranchised from that in which you truly are. Do you see this loop of vibrational communication in which you do so trap yourselves?' (S.6.Q8) This vibrational loop is causing many people to feel a sense of alienation and estrangement within the world, although not quite being able to put their finger on it. And there are those who respond to this internal dissonance (alienation) through certain indulgences that act to numb the senses as a way of a quick 'band aid fix.' This dissonance/alienation is not one thing, however, for all life is relational and 'so tightly intertwined.' The macro and the micro are aspects of this tight intertwining – the 'as above, so below' mantra – that is expressed also across the planet: 'the knowledge of this entire interconnected system upon this planet is but of great importance - of great evolutionary stance.' (S.6.Q9) If we continue to block and resist these inter-relational flows of life then, just like the blocking of a river, the pressure will ultimately burst through: 'If not allowed – if stunted and stopped – will at some point break through and flood your material lives and will overwhelm it.' (S.6.Q9) It is as if humanity has become lost within the shadows of its own collective mind – as if we are all unknowingly living through projections of our unconscious. And until an awakening occurs, where the conscious and unconscious merges, we shall continue existing apart from ourselves. It is time, says Abe, to delve deep within our being and to appreciate that which we are and not what we are told we are: 'And it will not serve this part of your evolutionary movement to keep a space between what you think you are and that in which you know you are within.' (S.6.Q10)

Humanity seems to have forgotten that it has a function upon the planet, just as all aspects of life contribute to the intricate and interrelated web of vibrational communication. Similar to the heart within the physical human body, it can be said that humanity is 'the beating heart of the living organism of the planet.' As a sentient species, human beings emit and transmit a resonance that forms part of the planet's energetics: 'You are but the resonators - you are the receivers, the expressers of this. You are but the heart that does so pump within the Earth.' (S.6.Q11) Yet it appears that humanity got its hands full with running around attempting to run the whole show; trying to intervene and, quite often, mess with the systems already in place. And in this running around, we lost sight of who we are and what we should be doing – and *being*. As Abe says, we are the 'resonators' and the 'receivers;' we are what allows the flows of energy to circulate. Yet humanity has become stagnant within this flow, and the allowance of energy has weakened. This is the fractal relation between the human being and its environment – these are the relations that we need to reharmonize and place into resonance. It is often argued that human beings have free will to choose if, or how, they wish to participate and contribute to the universal schema. If a person chooses not to, then that free will choice has to be honoured. It seems a straightforward argument, on an intellectual level. However, the question it raises is: from where is the so-called free will choice being made? It is from an essential place of being, or from a place of automation, a reflection of self? Humanity is, at present, intertwined in a 'conundrum of being.' In most cases, people are not aware of themselves to a deeply conscious degree. The actions they take are from superficial reflections, such as socially conditioned opinions, engrained beliefs, surface thinking, etc. Very rarely do people take action from a place of deep conscious awareness. If people were able to perceive conscious action, then they would also recognize the profound interconnectedness in all relations – physical as well as non-physical (energetic). And from this heightened perception, free will choice is recognized as something else entirely: 'Hear this, free will is not about choice - and never has been. True free will is in the conscious relation to that in which you truly are; for all the other surface dances and choices are just that - a dance of polarity, a dance of games.' (S.6.Q12)

Do we really have an individual free will in the sense that we are acting alone, apart from the greater tapestry of life – isn't this an egotistical and selfish way to think? The notion of an individual free will is again a result of the human belief in its existence as a separate being, individuated and an island in the cosmos. In truth, there is no separation – only the false persona, the superficially constructed sense of self, sees itself as isolated from the rest of creation. Again, this is the cause of the splintering – the fragmentation and stagnation – within humanity's evolvement. Each person is a physical expression of Source consciousness. When we comprehend and align ourselves with this, then our actions too are aligned and in resonance with the greater whole – we do not act apart from. It may appear paradoxical to our mode of rational thinking, yet true freedom is having no choice. It is only when we put ourselves beyond this unification are we truly not free:

> Only when you put yourselves above it and beyond it are you not free, for in this you are but deluding yourselves. If you can but see - if you can but come back and truly see, truly align - to that in which you are, then that is free will for you are aligning to all that you are. You are not captured by the dancing shadows of your disillusioned minds but are free to see the grander picture of life in which you are a part of. (S.6.Q12)

Genuine freedom then is in aligning and being true to all that we are. This is the stripping it down and getting back to basics that Abe often refers to. It doesn't need jazzing up or putting frills on; it is coming back to ourselves and into alignment with home resonance.

The further away or out of sync we are with home resonance, the more likely we are to make errors. This can be said to be where the concept of 'evil' comes from. We can get lost in the choices we make in error that drive us further out of alignment, and also in the actions that further the splintering from Source connection. Deviation from Source resonance gets heightened and sustained through continual errors of choice that are made without conscious awareness of the truth of the situation. As the phrase goes, "to err is human" – yet must it always be so?[1] Ways can, and should be, changed when they no longer contribute to our betterment. Humans continue to be distracted, and often seek such distractions even when we sense it may be taking us

---

[1] "To err is human, to forgive divine" a quote from Alexander Pope, a 17th century English writer.

in circles. This is the dog chasing its tail analogy that Abe has sometimes referred to: 'It is but a distraction from that in which you are; and like the dog chasing its tail, trying to but capture it, it is so with yourselves. You do not realise that it is there, and there is but nothing to capture for it is already a part of you.' (S.6.Q15) There is no longer any need 'to chase the shadows.' Why keep chasing our own tails in the hope of capturing something that is already within our capacity? It is time to get back to the bare bones; and this means stripping back our misconceptions of spirituality.

As in all subjects, there are facts and fictions, misinterpretations, and misconceptions; and the topic of spirituality is no exception. This is an area that Abe was keen to bring up and discuss and did so without any prompting from our side. Like any story passed through time, Abe said, there are things added on. Humanity is an evolving species and, along the way, has accumulated much; yet now is the time to strip some things away to make for a lighter journey. In our development, humanity has amassed many complexities; some of these complex additions refer to our understandings and beliefs. In this, says Abe, we have lost the 'simplicity of being,' which is the 'nugget of truth' that lies at the heart of all of our religious and spiritual practices. Humanity has created its own hierarchy and divisions: 'it is but never beyond you - and we would not state anything in hierarchical form - for there is no differing in all of life. It is but just the order is different, the pattern is differing - the mechanism. It is just that for too long you have put yourselves apart from this.' (S.6.Q16) What we have come to see as the 'spiritual' or the 'divine' is not apart from us, as if the Godhead is an intelligence somewhere over there in the distance and humanity is here far away. All life is an expression within

Source: it is an emergence from within itself. All existence is 'but one thing expressing in but many a form.' This is the unity. This is 'the true beauty of life – this is the true meaning of oneness.' Yet this understanding of unity, of oneness, was lost when humanity began to put a governing force over and above its place in the world.

Whilst there is some form of an overarching force that transcends our reality, it is not apart from us. As Abe put it: 'it is also a great misunderstanding - for what is governing your world is but also you. You are an interconnected governing system - a system within a system within a system.' (S.6.Q16) We have grown and developed as a species, yet as we did so we continued to place more and more things outside of ourselves; and this has finally splintered us as we fell out of unity. It is not that we now live in a broken world, or that matters are irreparable, for this is not the case. Rather, it is a call for recognition to bring the parts back together – to realign so that humanity can re-emerge whole. In the early prehistoric caves of our ancestors, archaeologists have discovered handprints upon the walls. Our ancestors stained their hands with pigment colours and as well as drawing animal scenes upon the cave walls, some of them also left their handprints stained into the rock for posterity. Why would they do this? One interpretation of this is that our early ancestors were quite literally making their mark to say, "I am here; I exist." It was a way of marking and acknowledging their presence in the world. This gesture was an externalization – a projection to a life outside of the human being. We could say that our ancestors did not want to remain unseen; they wanted to be known outside of themselves. And this urge has continued ever since, through ever increasing forms of external manifestation:

And this through time has been constructed, and many a time also misconstrued, for in this wanting to of exist you had but placed the unseen, the felt, out into the physical world - out on show, pinned it onto something other. But you see, in this you did so lose yourselves. (S.6.Q16)

Humanity entered an ongoing process of pinning itself externally – 'onto something other' – and this drew us out and away from our inner world. We gave authority to an external body and in doing so we also inadvertently shrank back from ourselves. This is what Abe refers to as our 'conundrum of being.'

These early stages were not 'wrong or disillusioned,' for they served their purpose. In their place and time, they were necessary stages. However, this is no longer a way that serves humanity. As we move through stages, we have to allow things to fall away so that we can move forward more efficiently. Some things – beliefs, patterns, perspectives – need to be dropped. There are times when it is necessary to draw back the curtains, to see beyond the veil, to 'see what is beyond the fancy packaging and bright lights – and see the characters without the masks.' (S.6.Q16) We have to accept to see the 'bare bones' without all the layers and packaging (the conditioning) that have been placed over the essential. The old patterns of thinking have created a container that now has reached its capacity and only serves to restrain and limit human advancement, consciously and otherwise. If we continue to ignore the nudges that are attempting to awaken humanity to this situation, we may receive a 'universal kick' instead. Abe urges us to 'stop dilly-dallying on the side lines' – to get off the merry-go-round of chasing our own tails – and allow the vitality of life to flow and find its own space. We are now producing our echoes and listening to them instead

122

of their source within us. By placing authority onto concepts, systems, and ideologies external to us, we have allowed these very systems to govern and lord it over us. The consequence of this is that, in the words of Abe: 'you are but not flourishing as a species.' We are not collectively healthy, and this is apparent now in many aspects of our lives.

There is no need for humanity to suffer in the way it does. So much of this suffering is self-inflicted for it is self-conceived. We suffer because we cling to ideals that we then fight over: 'to suffer is to cling to one thing over another - you do not need to suffer. There will be times that if you cling to a certain construct that you inevitably suffer, for you are wanting something to be sure, to be stagnant, to be still - and this is so not life.' (S.6.Q18) Again, we cause our suffering by attempting to contain life into our imaginary constructs and boxes. This behaviour binds us, and our struggles then tighten these binds further, like the person who attempts to wriggle out of the straitjacket and ends up becoming more bound. Rather than placing ourselves outside of the 'interconnected ecosystem' of life, trying to control things from 'outside,' we should recognize our inherent part of this same unified system. Our most debilitating fiction, says Abe, is that we have set ourselves apart from this creation: 'If there is a God that you wish to praise, realise that you too are it. It is not an ideal that you need to reach to, but a realisation that you were never apart from it - you are it.' (S.6.Q19) If humanity now wishes to evolve further, we really do need to find *our way back home*. And this means to drop the fiction that there is something, some godhead, governing over us, as if we are like 'poor little humans.' We *are* human, and yet we are also so much more. We have the capabilities to grow, evolve, and to become so much that is yet shielded from us by our own blindness. It is not about becoming more 'godly' but to become more thoroughly human.

At the moment, we are in danger of stumping our growth, of arriving to stagnation, if we continue 'by allowing others to lead on what is their truth, their path.' Humanity, the planet, the cosmos, and everything else is like a connected heart with arteries of vital life energy flowing through – all is interrelated.

To comprehend what is meant by Creation we also need to understand emergence. Pathways emerge from unity and resonate with other pathways and forms. Natural resonance allows for new pathways to emerge from Source and to form new connections. Expressions of vital life emerge, grow, and find alignments and resonant couplings – all the time as an expression of the original unity. What humanity needs right now is a clarity of perception: 'you do not need the middleman anymore. You have, and are evolving to have, this direct experience, this direct connection. If you so allow, you do not need the filter as such.' (S.6.Q21) Again, the emphasis here is placed upon the notion of *allowance*. Abe also explains that the vital force in existence is what we would term as love – although not our regular definition of love. Rather, what is love is flow, it is allowance: 'for love really is movement, is unconditional.' This is an important point that will come up in later Abe communications when the notion of allowance is explored in greater depth. For now, it is worth making note that Abe sees no distinction between universal, unconditional love and the phenomenon of allowance. Abe remarks:

> ... what does love truly *feel* like for you? It is expansive, un-constricted, it opens you up - is this not so? For you see, the word 'love' has been over-complicated, over-compensated, for the void you do so feel within - that you feel you must continuously fill. But you see, this very thing is love - is allowance, is space - and should not be susceptible to your human conditions. (S.6.Q22)

124

The phenomenon of love and the human word of love are two very distinct things. The 'love' that Abe recognizes is the unconditional, unconstrained vital flow of life force that allows all expressions to emerge from unification. Such a 'love' is not given by anything 'outside' of ourselves as it is part of our essential being: 'It is truly just an allowance - an allowance of being. It is just so that as humans you call it "love." With much *Allowance* and Light – Abe.' (S.6.Q22) This is the first place in the communications where Abe signs off the message by replacing the phrase 'Love and Light' with '*Allowance* and Light.' Later on, this becomes a permanent replacement. By understanding love as allowance, this also helps us to grasp vibrational resonance as an alignment with allowance.

Just as what we understand as human 'love' is part of an attraction, a vibrational match, so too are the dynamics of evolution. Human sciences have long focused on the physical side of evolution, on material change over time; but this has been at the expense of neglecting the inner – what may be called the 'spiritual' – aspect of evolution. This aspect is one of vibrational matching and resonance; it is the 'meeting back up, the inside out and upside down.' This vibrational resonance of 'meeting up' is itself part of the vital 'love' energy that animates all existence, both material and non-material. The two aspects cannot be pulled apart or separated as they are the intrinsic patterns that make the whole. Materiality cannot exist without its energetic, immaterial component: 'For someone purely focused on materiality is but half the picture; and someone focused purely on spirituality is too. You see, it is always, always, about the dance - that is what makes your very being so treasurable, so diverse, so splendid.' (S.6.Q23) When we are focused on the materiality aspect, we are more liable to get entangled in our shifting attachments. This is part of the human tendency to 'purpose seek' outside of ourselves, and this causes us to shift and change allegiances to external attachments in this desperate search. Yet it is the human being that is the centre and site of meaning creation and purpose. Still, the ingrained habit to go outwards remains strong: 'But sometimes in the space, in the nothing, in this place where you can but not grab onto anything whatsoever, you cannot attach yourselves to anything, any belief system - any THING or ANYONE - as if you are but in the great void.' (S.6.Q24) A person may find themselves in the places they're not looking. The universe, as they say, has a strange way of delivering realizations and epiphanies. Or rather, the truth was never amiss in the first place; we were just shining our torches in the wrong place, like the drunk looking for his keys under the streetlamp although he had dropped them elsewhere. As Abe puts it: 'What if it finally finds you and you but realise it was never amiss, just drowned out by all the noise, by all the activity of your being, of your trying to find something?' (S.6.Q24)

Human beings are often the last ones to give themselves a break. Let's face it, we're often hard on ourselves when we needn't be. Again, this may be part of our conditioning. We don't like not knowing; we feel uncomfortable with the uncertainty of life. We seek structures to prop us up and create an environment of order in our lives. And in this, we forfeit an innate part of our freedoms. By fretting, we reach out for more entanglements to comfort us, not knowing we are also subduing ourselves at the same time. We cannot go forward truthfully if we continue to avoid meeting ourselves; otherwise, we are only walking in shadows. At this point there is a distinction to be made between 'meeting' and 'finding' oneself. By 'meeting' oneself there is a coming together, a mutual involvement, like two friends or lovers meeting in a field. As the Persian poet Jalāl al-Dīn Rumi wrote: 'Out beyond ideas of wrongdoing and rightdoing, there is a field. I will meet you there. When the soul lies down in that grass, the world is too full to talk about language, ideas, even the phrase "each other" doesn't make any sense.' There is no 'each other' for the meeting is a (re)union. Whereas 'finding' oneself implies a search, a journeying – a movement away. Abe puts it as: 'We would like to say that there is but no need to find yourselves. If you are but looking, you are constantly losing yourself to others, to outer structures. For what you do so get entangled in is this conundrum that something is outer - to be sought out. And this is but the illusion.' (S.6.Q24) The spirit is not a seeking, something to be sought, but rather a re(union) with the unity of self. There is no need to put names here, to conceptualize it or try to take ownership of it: *feel* into it. Align with the frequency of home resonance: 'Allow it all to meet there, undefined and unconditioned, and you will but see not a word that will fit it - just feel.' (S.6.Q24)

Humans often become more blocked than liberated through ideals and notions of love, self, spirituality. We have so much baggage created through our mental associations with such concepts – enough to fill a mental national library! Further, our emotional responses often get tied into our mental associations to complete the package. Things lose their neutrality once we 'name it, claim it, grasp it,' and then we add our interpretations on top of it. Not everything requires us to create a language box or mental file for it; some things can be left as an experience unnamed. We can connect with the knowing; we don't always need to define a thing, for this then externalizes it and adds projections onto it. We tend to get mixed up with our meanings: 'Do not get so mixed up in the meaning of things for it is but an interpretation - feel into it and allow it to convey something to you.' (S.6.Q25) We should step back from the urge to claim everything that comes along our path. It is worth remembering here that the wisdom traditions state that truth has no form, yet the means through which people perceive truth have forms. Tools and instruments that help us to get to truth have form, but they are only vehicles. They are not the thing itself and should not be mistaken for it. Everything that surrounds us is also a connection to truth: 'The wind in your hair can tell you as much as you need to know by feeling it. The Earth under your feet can feed you, can breathe into you. For you need to realise that it is but all here - you are a part of it.' (S.6.Q26) It is not so much about being spiritual but rather about being *spirit-full*. This is the allowance – this is the love and the life. Each one of us is a part of it all, just as it All is a part of each one of us. This truth is so very simple and at the same time so overlooked. We miss what is right in front of us.

Another phrase that Abe has used is, 'it was never about being enlightened but to light-up what was previously unseen.' Too much focus on what we think or believe to be 'spiritual' can have the reverse effect of taking us further away from the very thing we are longing for. In many modern cultures, spirituality has become too fanciful and decorated. We often think that 'spirituality' should be so spectacular when it is quite ordinary – and so very extraordinary at the same time. It is our own spectacle seeking that deludes us:

> ... spirituality is not a thing to be chased, but to be seen, to be synced-up with. And you see, it has never been amiss - it has just been overlooked because you were so wanting to find something spectacular, with fireworks and such a display. But you see, it was never lost, it was just not brought light to. (S.6.Q27)

We often get distracted by the fireworks and lose sense of the true light within. We overlook what is there because we had conceived of it differently. It is like the tale of the old lady who upon finding a hummingbird upon her window ledge grabs it and takes to clipping its wings and beak because of believing it to be an ugly sparrow that needs a makeover. The conceptions we have in our heads rule and dictate how we interpret our experiences and expectations. In this, the truth can often be a hard thing to face: 'TRUTH is sometimes hard to face because it is bare and naked and always there but seemingly overlooked in favour of the opposite.' (S.6.Q27) Truth does not need to be 'extravagant' or 'ground shaking' – it is what it is and requires no makeover. Yet we have to 'grow, to see, and to evolve' so that we can meet the truth in that field of lovers – the (re)union.

There is too many 'picking sides' in the domain of what is regarded as 'spirituality.' It seems that this reflects more our human conditioning than it does any essential truths. The realm of spirituality is the unification – the Source, the Continuum – and there are no sides, only interpretations. And it can be these interpretations that cause people to pick and choose sides, which then increases entanglement: 'To see that they are but one in the same, and because your minds have to pick a side, pick and choose and decipher your existence, it is but hard now for you to let go. But you see, it is an entanglement...' (S.6.Q28) The more that we are picking our sides, the more we become entangled in this game – and the more we are then vulnerable to the manipulations and manoeuvring that are attached to such spiritual positions. When we are choosing, we are not allowing life to flow. It is like placing rocks in the stream. The water will eventually find a way around it, yet why have these unnecessary obstacles? It is all too easy to get caught up in the polarities that mark the reality game of life. If we are not careful, not mindful, then this can get us caught up in our own tug-of-war. This is all a form of attachment, like a struggle for entanglement in one thing over another. What Abe suggests we do is to allow it all to flow:

> Get involved, love with all your heart; cry at the loss of a loved one; marvel at the sunset or the birth of a child; love family; love life - but see that underlying current that is never amiss. Flow - allow that to but guide you. You do not need to lose who you are but allow more. You do not need to deny your parts but accept yourself wholly. (S.6.Q29)

Why lose ourselves in the struggle to try to be 'holy' when the real need is simply to be 'wholly'? The human experience involves us in transmuting and transmitting this flow of life – and ultimately transforming it. This is how the ordinary life becomes extraordinary, and this is our gift of being human.

As human beings, we should take care not to get caught up in the words, or the tools, that are the secondary aspects, and neglect the primary. It is so very easy to miss out on what is real for us by chasing these secondary phenomena. The simple truth can become the hardest thing to see as it is continually overlooked. We don't see the heart beating, but we *feel* it. We allow it to continue beating without trying to define it with a liturgy of words. It is time we allow life rather than naming it: 'Don't name it, don't chase it, but nurture, appreciate, and allow what is natural - what is you, what is there. Allow yourselves to be.' (S.6.Q32) This is the prime axiom – to allow ourselves *to be*. For so long we have been caught up in the rhythms, the choices, of others. Without fully realizing it, we get caught in the energy of others, and sync up or entrain with their rhythm even when it is not our own and may be slightly uncomfortable for us.

130

Ultimately, this takes us away from our own rhythm, our home resonance. It is time for each person to root themselves and to ground their home resonance. It has been the human tendency to rush ahead, to charge forth, as if racing to get ahead of ourselves. And the result of this is that so often humanity has taken a destructive path. Both collectively and individually it would be of great benefit to 'stop, listen, and then move forward.' As Abe has said repeatedly, there is an ebb and flow rhythm to life on this planet. We need to take the rest periods as an opportunity to get in sync, to 'rhythm up.' This is all part of the unity of existence: 'It is realising that you have not been allowing it; you've been but too busy, too active. Ebb is allowing your true nature rest and merge with your temporary nature and knowing that they are but one in the same in this form.' (S.6.Q35) Action requires listening; they are complementary aspects of one and the same. And yet, we all too often get contaminated with 'other peoples' do's and don'ts.' Being in sync is about feeling into the flow, the rhythm, that is in harmony and coherence with a 'home resonance.'

A major component in the Abe communications is the message that humans are often the ones that are limiting themselves. Yes, there are constraints placed upon us from our societal structures; still, it is often our own imaginary fears and false boundaries that we place upon us. In one place, Abe states: 'there are no such boundaries - only the line of fear in which you dare not cross.' (S.6.Q36) This is why the 'way back home' refers both to Source as well as to our essential selves. Humans have moved away from their essence, from the natural flow of life, and into an artificial stream of false imaginings, attachments, boundaries, fears, and more. This cluttering has messed with our vibrational frequencies, our harmonic resonance. The result is that often we get stuck within certain 'set frequencies' that fix and limit us. By attaching to certain frequency patterns, we can stagnate ourselves:

> It is in the attachment to them that keeps you stagnant; and as you grow you gather more - you sift and sort and box, and contain varying vibrational resonances, almost as if you are building a house, a home. But you see, you are merely building an outer structure over a home that you already had - you are encasing yourselves in, further and further, like the dolls, like the overcoats. (S.6.Q37)

This is why it is necessary that people clear themselves out so that there can be flow – the 'original flow that enables you to be but connected to all.' We need to clear away the brushwood, so to speak. For far too long humanity has been attached to a non-advantageous frequency range, which is being sustained by distraction. It is imperative that collectively and individually we break out of this debilitating consciousness frequency. Until now, we have been continuously feeding into this frequency range, supported by the media and entertainment industry, socio-political institutions, and various other cultural factors. We have ended up wrestling with ourselves without realizing it: 'You see, it is almost like a tug of war with yourselves; for yourselves it is quite delusional, in a way, to be as such.' (S.6.Q38) This 'tug of war' has distracted us not only from ourselves but also from the flow of life. Life requires our participation, yet harmoniously and consciously. Life is not a one-way street.

Synchronicity is a sign, an indication, that a person is within the natural flow of life. The psychologist C.G. Jung brought this concept to our attention when he correctly identified the role of synchronous events. Synchronicity is a 'dropping back,' as Abe says; and a person knows when they have 'dropped back into the flow:' 'For what is synchronicity other than the natural flow - it is but you meeting life and life meeting you, is it not?' (S.6.Q39) This is the mutual arising – the merger. This merger is a joint endeavour and allows a person to also return to a form of direct connection both with themselves and between themselves and Source. Allowing is meeting, and change comes through motion, not stagnation: 'The reason you do not flow is because you do so prefer the stagnant, stale waters. Allow, and see what does come. For in this, life will meet you - and you will meet it.' (S.6.Q41) We can each 'cut out the middleman' through establishing direct contact in this meeting – this mutual arising – through ourselves. Each person has this direct contact, only that it has been placed in darkness and we are looking elsewhere. We need to focus our light into the right places; not to be swayed away from ourselves in distraction by design. As Abe repeatedly states, we need to unite ourselves by gathering our parts – bringing all into flow instead of fragmentation. If we can unite these aspects within us, then this will also manifest outwardly in our physical lives:

> It is now bringing this together, united in yourselves - vibrational signature, sensory body, and us, Abe - all combined. To see this wholeness, to bring it into physical, to have physical representation of this, your humanness - your true capability - has to be seen now, and you will be but representation of it, of unity. (S.6.Q42)

The human story is changing – it *has* to change now. The stories, myths, and narratives of the past belong to a previous stage of growth. Patterns of human consciousness have changed. It is now about direct contact. For too long we have been putting what is within us outside of us; then we wrestle over definitions, interpretations, and labelling: 'how very exhausting is this,' says Abe. To go forward now, to evolve as a species, means finding our inner clarity and wholeness. Humanity has a new conscious map for future development.

Past sages and wisdom teachings have spoken about the function of the human condition as part of a holy triad: heaven, earth, humankind. In other words, humanity acts as the conduit between Source (heaven - the sacred divine) and material physicality (the earth). Humanity is the vessel that can unify the immaterial with the material – or the spiritualization of matter. This is the merger. This is the *allowance* where a unified consciousness can manifest through physicality. In truth, humanity was never apart from this: 'And what you do so need to realise is that you are never apart from it - you never have been.' (S.6.Q44) The stories we have been telling ourselves have been stories to awaken ourselves gradually. Our very humanness is to allow all that we are and all that we have ever been. All this time, humanity has been growing, evolving, towards knowing our true nature. It is now time to stop getting in our own way and 'have this direct contact.' This is but the journey to take us to wholeness: and from wholeness we shall find THE WAY BACK HOME.

PART TWO

THE ABE COMMUNICATIONS

SECTION ONE
Relations with Ourselves

W̶e are glad to communicate and but to have this relaxed way of communication, and we say it for this time and this stage. For that is all about relation - never forced and a mutual arising. You see, with this writing, and the way in that you are but trusting yourselves and each other, this is but causing and demonstrating this relational value. And you see, this interconnectivity then runs through but all that you do, even the smallest of things.

With continued communication and with much Love and Light – Abe.

1. We would like to begin by asking Abe - is there anything you wish to communicate with us at this moment?

Good morning. It has been but a short while that this connection has been seen to be worked upon. We do see that the energy of the writing is being absorbed and is indeed shifting, making way for new, and that you both have been feeling it, albeit one more than the other for there has been patterns that have so now been broken, been disconnected, rewired if you will. This will take time to take root, but it is creating new

137

pathways. You will see the reflection of this in your outer existence, in your own realities, and indeed it will also be reflected in others, including each of you back to each other - is this of understanding now? We would like to come forth for we feel this time is but a time of rooting things, for we see this energy will be passed but back and forth between you both and it will then balance. Maybe one clearing more than the other, but always in relation to one another - do you see this? We would like to say that we also think it is but time to start out making moves creating this foundation, but this is to be worked in a way that you both feel comfortable. The net has been cast but it would be an idea to seek your own balance as to see where both of your energies are so being pulled. This will give you the correct groundings for as we see it, it is about correlation and not direction. With Love and Light – Abe.

2. Thank you, Abe. We are working in the possible presentation and dissemination of the first collection of communications. Our question now is - is there a specific direction you would wish to take any new communications? Is it now time to begin the second 'harvest', so to speak?

We think it would be time to but collaborate with the resources that you have gathered over the years, and also the people whom you think would be of collaborating force to build upon this foundation, these groundings. We would also see it time to continue with communication - if so both are wanting to continue, and feel at a stage to do so. If you are but asking in which direction, we would see fit for the communication to be going, then we see for it to be of relation - that being to each other, to your world, to the universe. These are but the states that

138

need to be addressed, that need to be aligned, and do indeed need to be looked at in depth - is this of understanding? And as we say, and continue to put forth, it needs to be of relation to that at which you both are at too - is this but seen now?

3. Thank you. The notion of collaboration is well-received and good advice. We note that the essence of this message is 'relations' and 'relationships' - how these are vital to our alignment. Between ourselves, our world, and the larger cosmos. Are we right in feeling that the next communications seek to address the understanding of relations?

It is but so, for if this is not seen, and you do not get the footings right now, you will build something – everything - on un-solid ground. We see it that people do indeed feel that there is a connection. They feel it when they watch a sunrise or in the eyes of a lover; they feel this on a deeper level, but they do so put it outside of themselves. It is good to turn this feeling into new physical pathways - to earth it, to ground it. For people are very dismissive of feelings alone but, as we say, if these two are but in correlation it will be seen in your physical existence and there will be much quicker shifts. It will be short but sharp, and you will not only feel these new pathways internally forming but also see them being built in your reality. This is the path of unity - is this of understanding now?

You see, for anything and everything it has to be of resonance, and if you are but not synced up you will not be allowing to bring forth this unity into physical reality. It will be but always a bit of a daydream, a bit of a 'that is nice' but not a realistic view. Do you see this? For it will continue to have dissonance within and will continue to be shown without. With Love and Light – Abe.

4. Whilst the majority of people remain in 'splintered mind', feeling as separate individuals from life, then it will be difficult for these resonant relations to form. Is there already some change occurring that is shifting people in this regard?

Take it like this, you are but always as separated as you think you are, for you entrap yourselves into such limited perceptions; and in some way, you cannot be totally free of this. What you can be in this form is synced up, unified, for if you do so continue to be splintered, for if your mind still carries this notion, it will not be of resonation to then attract these new pathways, these new neural pathways, and they will continue with these limiting patterns. It is such a shame for you can, and always have, the option to be much more, to let in so much more, if you allow yourselves to be but cracked open. When you ask if there are shifts that are creating this change within people then we would say - but of course. But even those that you do so feel that are so-called 'enlightened ones' still hold onto the notion of this nugget of enlightenment. We see it to be 'of this,' 'of now,' and always 'of here.' If we would like to put this entirely bluntly, it would be this - create a space, create a void, and then allow for things to come together, to build themselves up, for it will be in this void that emergence will happen. Is this of understanding now?

You see, for people to change you need *people* to change. It is but always relational. What is seen without has to be firstly seen within, and when seen within then shines without. Like we said, a multiplying and unity - a wave, a pattern. And it is only

140

seen when things are paused, when there is but a void. With much Love and Light – Abe.

5. Thank you, Abe. We would wish in our further communications to explore these issues of relations - as you have suggested. If you allow it, we would like to establish another round of communications. We look forward to these conversations.

We would like this communication to continue, as long as you are both allowing it to come forth, and as long as need be. You see, it is in the relation, and we would only ever see it to be a mutual arising. With much Love and Light and continued communication – Abe.

You do so see that in the relation between this very connection you are indeed creating unity, and with this it will be relational to others. The multiplying stage is peaked - you are now in the dip; the rest is unity. This is all we would like to say for it will all become evident. In this next communication we would but like you to see this now and allow it in. With much Love and Light – Abe.

We would like to but come forth this morning and explain a little on consciousness and your own conscious experience. You see, there are levels of consciousness but only one flow of consciousness. Let us explain. Consciousness is not an interaction with things, it is not separate - it is an arising. There is just this one flow which is us and which is you, and everything else that you can think of, even something that looks like it cannot be conscious, is at some level. Now, hear this, many other things are operating and flowing with pure conscious experience. More so than what you are, for it does not slice and dice it up; it does not get wrapped up in other vibratory patterns that are so constricting. Humans: one could say you have evolved but you have evolved to separate things. Now it is time to piece it back together but also allow for the separateness too, for unification is but unifying that of a separating system - is it not? Now you see, there are but five differing levels of your conscious experience at present and one could go back to the analogy of the Russian dolls that pure consciousness is restricted and even this is not true for you can never stop the flow. One could liken it more so to being captured. Now see this, you have at the fundamental level uninterrupted consciousness. We would like to say and liken it to that of us, of your natural state of being you. Then you have on the next level your vibratory essence of self, what it is to be a qualitative you - how you experience life. This is gathered by the other four states of consciousness and this is where some people do indeed get trapped in when following a path of enlightenment - going around and around, never truly breaking free. The next level is that of the unconscious; this is the vibratory essence of unconscious behaviour of programming, if you will. This is dropped into when you are not consciously aware and one could say, as you like to put it, on autopilot. The next level is that of sensory vibratory essence; this is your interaction with your world - the feedback, the sensing 'out there, in here,' and also the sensing 'in here, out there.' It is very interactional. And the final level is that of conscious experience; and some people get this confused with mind, and this is not the word we would call upon for this at all. For the word 'mind' is too clogged up with the notion that it is a singular state of conscious experience that can be so neatly packaged. And as you can see, it really is not - it is

142

of differing comings together. Now hear this, we do so speak of there being differing levels; but you see, there is only one river and it flows but within this vibratory pattern. There are many patterns. Remember the word WITHIN for there is nothing that is outside of this stream. You see, the knowing of this allows you to crack these dolls open and loosen these vibratory patterns that do so cling like an overcoat wrapped tightly around a cold body as to give it comfort. This is so how you keep your own true conscious experience trapped and you do it yourselves - is this of understanding now? But do so hear this, and it is very important, on the knowing of these levels and the true understanding of what is really at the essence. What really is you and that is of everything you can see, that you can have these differing conscious experiences for that is the beauty of being human. But completely understand that it is just a play of the one thing - it is but a game. With much Love and Light - Abe.

We would like to state that why we said four that create the vibratory self we did not intend it to be four below, for that would mean our calculation would be wrong; and even if you are not aware of it, you are still within the flow of pure consciousness. This is never discarded albeit a few may try to put it outside of themselves in order to create a problem for even the fifth element needs to be counted. For in this you will be able to see that all of these parts were never parts but one whole expressing, never apart from it, never anywhere to get to - just an opening up and a letting go. For the heat is roaring now, is time to take off the overcoat and feel life truly against your bare skin, your raw nerve. Many will slip back on this overcoat of being as they will feel a whirl of life whip around them and not like the freshness of it. But hear this, that's okay - for at some point the heat will get so intense that you will have no other choice but to remove the overcoat. In this, the heat will turn down for you will feel life and you can so but place it back on again. It is never to be left off entirely because in your world, in your experience, sometimes it is nice to feel cosy so long as you remember the lightness you felt when you removed it - for this has been long lost. We do so hope you are free to see the connection in which we are heading towards with this analogy for we want you to see the easiness of this likened to that of taking on and off a heavy overcoat. It is that simple - it is YOU that makes it oh so much more difficult. We mean this in a way with much Love and Light – Abe.

There is but one more aspect that we would like to bring forth and this is one of resonance in conscious experience. You see, for you to enable pure consciousness to flow consciously, meaning to flow in your conscious world, you have to resonate at it. But hear this, although this is constantly flowing and never amiss, you can so taint it so much as to say wrap it up in such an overcoat that the flow underneath is not recognisable at all. You have to drop it or, as we say, take off the overcoat. This is really done by the realisation that there is indeed an overcoat to be taken off – on, off, on, off. No need to get specific for in the realisation of it you can take it on and off whenever you do so please. Is this of understanding now?

We would like to point you both in the direction to sit with this, to understand it before we move on with conversations again. To so get this symbol deeply aligned in you both for this itself is the pattern, is the dance; is the turning inside out and down and back around on all levels. For this is fractal relation: you have gotten so caught up in the dividing, the fractured splintered part taking it to smaller and smaller bits, it is but time

144

to step back and see the bigger picture, the wholeness of your own being and to that of everything else. You have but long forgotten the relation, the correlation, the unity of such parts. For you see, the true meaning of symbols are that they always point to wholeness of relation. For what cannot so be explained in language can indeed be shown by symbolism and, in this, things are but pieced back together again. Is this of understanding now?

We would also like to state what it means. We but discussed the five states that being of individuals, your conscious experience, do you so remember this? We are now stating the three other states too that are seen. One could liken it to us and you both - this is then the unity represented by that of the circle. The dots of the eight points are all aligned, all synced up neural pathways - do you see this? The lines create these pathways but here you see it all as one. These points are to be of resonance: you, NM, us - the three. But also, the resonation of yourselves - the five. Do you see it is this pattern: the inside out, the multiplication, the unity, the fractal relation - the down the rabbit hole of your awareness? We would like to state that we are but not trying to riddle you or make things complicated, but for you to experience it also consciously. For if you don't, how will you do so ground it for it will all just continue to be pie in the sky. With much Love and Light – Abe.

6. Hello Abe. As indicated, we would like to understand more about the diagram/symbolism of the different states of consciousness. You have stated the five states previously. We would like you to clarify about the three states. You have said that we 'could liken it to us and you both' - can you clarify this? And speak more on this eight-fold unity? Thank you.

You see, it is very difficult in your language to but explain something that is not in parts; for that is what language is designed to do - to but pick out things. What we say in the symbol is that there are five states of your own individual consciousness. And see this, this zero-state is but never apart from it, it is underlying - do you see this? The five states are your own individual conscious experience. But you see, in the smaller Russian doll you then have that again - the three states - and these are but seen as differing things: us, you, NM - individual streams of conscious, each having a seemingly separate experience. And what we say, again, that there is zero-state underlying - always. This is the thread and no matter what level you are at there is always, but always, zero-state - for how can it be any other way? Now then, we have just pure zero-state representing that of the circle, of unity. When these seemingly separate paths of conscious experience are but lined up, and the dolls are but cracked open, it then creates pathways for you. See, you speak of differing dimensions in your human experience; but you see, it is what is aligning, what is allowed. Dimensions are just differing states of conscious experience. When you truly get this, the pathways will be formed, and it will but be that the

146

light of awareness has been but flipped up a notch. Tell me, you will be rewiring humanity, resetting. Is this of understanding now?

We would also like to say that the symbol used is to point out unity in such a way that you see it is not something separating but encompassed and intertwined and very much connected. It is thought that everything is separating; but it is always of resonance that these points do so sync up and make their way back to wholeness, unity, zero-state, home - call it what you will. But hear this, you are never apart from it; you are just overriding it, contaminating the line in which they are out of resonance. Is this understood now? You are but down the rabbit hole. The symbol gives you something that the language cannot - do you so see? Love and Light – Abe.

7. We understand this concept of zero-state underlying all, and the differing states of consciousness are pathways that can be aligned. We wonder if the symbol can be more than an eight-fold unity? The octagon is a known mystical symbol. Is there an alignment here with this diagram? And can these symbols assist our understanding - do they impact our subconscious level? Thank you.

They are used in a sense to cut out the middleman and that is but one of language. You see, everything is but over-examined, over-explained, and therefore over-used. It loses the original meaning and the meaning is but always this Unity. Symbolism has always been used when language fails - do you see? Why do you think that your companies do so have logos? They do not have to speak a word for it to be engrained in you - for how many children do so know the labels of things? You see, it is a way to resonate. Geometry has been used to show these patterns and you see that they are interconnected, always - this is but the same. We are not saying that things cannot and should not be explained. But you see, drawing the pattern of that in which you do so experience will link it up, will resonate. There are but always differing levels; sometimes you do not need words. With Love and Light – Abe.

8. And so, the unified person is when all five states of consciousness are aligned and consciously experienced? A person is aware of their unified-zero state, vibratory essence, the unconscious, sensory vibratory essence, and conscious experience? The fractals are these states operating independent of our conscious awareness, and yet they form a unity, a whole?

This is correct. Firstly, resonate - join up your individual, for this will then link it up to the three in this synchronization. It is but like a light. Your conscious experience is much more - you are simply just taking off the overcoat which was so weighing you down. For when this resonates, when these five states resonate, you see the unity in everything; and in this, you see the ludicrousness of past ways, of past separation. You see that for what you have always been chasing or rejecting is just part of you. Is this of understanding now? But do hear this, when this is realized you will have a surge of energy and for some it will be uncomfortable; that is why it is but always a journey. With much Love and Light – Abe.

We would also like to add this - it is but always a choice of being. It is but never to be put upon others for you will always, but always, loose the meaning. You will be feeding into a system of control. You are only ever right when it is right for you; everything else is but to be left alone - do you so see this? For it is never about a following of other but a knowing of self that what is truth. With Love and Light – Abe.

9. How can the average person attempt to join up their individual parts? Many of us long for unity and belonging. Separation is not always a choice. What can you say to assist people in this journey toward unity?

You see, this is the overall purpose to THE WAY BACK HOME. It is but always about you - you have for so long tried to manage, tried to control. But you see, it is but always a reflection of you. The fractal relation is seeing that you are but unified. But hear this, people need to resonate with this material, this truth. They but have to feel this dissonance in self. You see, your world just distracts you. It creates noise so that you cannot feel it links you up to something else. You are wired up to the system, constantly gaming, playing - you are but a reflection of a system. That is why a person who does so stop and who has had enough of the distraction, the noise, will see them going off sometimes, searching outside themselves for peace, for quiet. This is well and good, but you need to walk in the noise again and show people that silence is here too, in your very own being. Is this of understanding now?

You see, it was never about the material as such; but it is more so your understanding, your light. For when you shine out you are resonating, you are grounding this energy here and now. You show others that here is the light, the quiet in the noise. They have but a choice to see it, for they will resonate deeply to it. It is never about shouting from the rooftops but aligning yourselves first and foremost. When you have but walked this path of realization yourselves, you are a beacon of truth and it is but always your truth, and those who so feel it will be drawn to you. But do so hear this, you have but the choice too. With much Love and Light – Abe.

10. You have mentioned several times that we are 'down the rabbit hole' and that we need to realize our unity in our relations with others and the world around us. Our religious texts also mention the 'Fall'. Are these terms related? And did something happen to us, this planet, to cause this state of separation?

You see, it is never about an event as such; albeit a few that do indeed seem to further this divide. But you see, sometimes a fall is but good; it just all depends upon that in which you are so falling from. For a fall from grace may seem to stable you again, for then you will begin to learn yourselves. You wake up and shake off this hierarchical dew and begin to see the interconnectedness of your own being, this unity, slowly piecing yourself back together. This power shift that is happening at present, which in generations before has always been sought in outer systems, now people are claiming back their own power - gathering themselves back up. You see, the rabbit hole, in the context of which we speak, are these layers of conditioning; of the falsities that have limited your conscious experiences, have kept you trapped and splintered. But hear this, this has indeed been a process of generations, never just a specific person. But see, for you to indeed be down the rabbit hole you have but had to of taken that journey too. And also see that you are the only one whom can then resurface. Is this of understanding now?

11. Can it be said that many people are now, slowly, coming out of the rabbit hole and regaining back their personal power? Sometimes it feels like the contrary as young people are hypnotized by their phones, their online lifestyles, and superficial distractions. It seems as if we are in a turbulent interim period where awareness is struggling against inertia and conditioning.

It is so this way - but it is a journey and you but have to root this. Liken it to coming out of a dark tunnel and suddenly you are blinded by the light and the sounds and smells. It will but take time to adjust, and the best thing to do is to keep grounded. In this world of polarity, it always seems fitting to place things outside of yourselves; and in this you seem to tire yourselves out on the placement of things. And in this, including people, you are but so deeply conditioned. You are far down the rabbit hole and only when you see this will you begin to rise again from the depths. For you see, it is not about stripping everything away either. It is about listening and trusting, and we do so say it is but a journey. The thing is, will you stop at every given chance – will you question or shake in fear? Or you may even run back in this cave once you feel the bright light of perception. For some, it may seem too exposed, too raw, and they do so like the comfort of the darkened cave. Or will you love yourselves enough to give yourself time - to adjust time, to feel time to be? With much Love and Light – Abe.

We would also like to say that people only change when you change. It is not about saying 'oh well, if I do all this hard work and no one else ever changes, then what will so be the point of it all?' That is not your concern. See, life is always becoming, always seeking balance within and without. And we would say, do not make this all you have and do; and also, do not make what you don't do, all you think about. Is this of understanding now? The whole point of grounding this energy right now is that you do so bring it into the noise of your own life. It is not to be separated or kept sacred like it has so been in the past - something that you slip on and off like a pair of shoes. It is but something that shines through your life and is but all you do, even in the times you do not so think it is - you have to LIGHTEN up for others to see. With much Love and Light – Abe.

12. Could you say more about the relations between people and what we need to learn (or remember) regarding our inherent interconnectivity? Thank you.

We see that relations are just that – interconnections; and you see that your experience puts conditions on these so-called relations. And you see, you then knock them off - you un-sync them. You see, if you are unconditional love then you give unconditional love. It is never about what they do so do or don't do. They only mirror the parts of yourselves that you don't like or have suppressed - allow it to come up. If it has been suppressed, it is clearly something that you do not wish to experience or do not like about yourselves. Face it, make peace with it, and allow it to ride away some parts. People will show you who you want to be - allow that too. Make the changes; be true to you, to this beautiful expression of one. But hear this, it

152

does not need to be sifted through and sorted. It is trusting that life will show you where you are so stuck or blocking, or stagnant, contaminating the line. And then once seen, poof - it disappears. It isn't a long process. It is what you make it to be. Do not put yourselves under lock and key for the conditions to be but right so that you can get yourselves out of this constricted conditioned box that tells you who you are and comes with a set of instructions that you yourselves did not write. Allow life to show you who you are, who you all are, and see the unity in your being. There are no steps, for no two people are the same. For that is the beauty of life. That is the beauty of one - that you can have but so many variations of one thing. It is realizing that you are uniquely interconnected to all there is and all there ever will be. But you yourself is just colouring - it is flavouring it. And also, the real gem is that there is not but you either. It is all an intermingling of just one - a syncing up, a play of UNITY. You just need to allow life to show you, for it to be able to meet you. You see, what do you feel when you do so flip the channel to Abe? It is again not about flipping the channel as much but to allow this through. You let it colour your whole being. You always have what you need. You always have all that you are to be, now - if that isn't love, if that isn't beauty, then what is? With much Love and Light – Abe.

We would but lastly like to add that people will only meet you at the place in which you are coming from, are vibrating from. That is why it is always good to take time to listen. With much Love and Light – Abe.

13. Thank you. If life is showing you in others where you are stuck, then how do you know if it is that you are no longer

resonating with someone or that you are stuck in a pattern and they are just showing you that part in which you are not accepting of yourself?

You see, it again is relational for you show them, and they also show you. It is interconnected. It all depends if one is open; and if one is then not for you. See, it is about resonation too. For someone who cannot see this truth will not resonate with someone who does. And you see, you can love people, all people, unconditionally; but you can resonate with people and that is key. Is this of understanding now? We would also like to add that if but two people can see and know this truth then they will only ever but dance. It will be effortless - an effortless connection, unconditioned and liberating; unrestricted and free; true and authentic. And is this not what all humans do so want? With much Love and Light – Abe.

14. Thank you, Abe. It is important then that each person work on themselves. It is not about changing the world or fighting the system head on. It is about us being the new way ahead. By allowing each of us to connect with unity consciousness, and allow it to be grounded, we are creating the journey out of the rabbit hole. Would you agree?

This is exactly so. It is but always about this home state, this syncing back up to what you truly are. Only, but only, when you do so piece yourself back together to unify and pick up all those pieces will you be able to step forward. This stage is about your individual conscious experience - about humanity's evolvement on a conscious level. So it makes sense to cut the cords to a world that is so very divided and start to piece it all back together again

- so that you can take this new step forward. With much Love and Light – Abe.

15. Thank you. You say 'cut the cords' to this divided world of ours. Are you referring here to our conditioning and social programs? Could you say more on this?

The meaning of so 'cutting the cords' are these very many parts of consciousness, like little tentacles, that do so place themselves upon people, situations, establishments, religion - all being outside of yourselves. Drop them, for now they may very well sync back up again. But while you are connected to all this - and let us say it is a two-way vibrational communication - you are but locked in. You have but no other place to go - allow the pathways to all drop, and in this you drop yourself, and what it means to be you. Is this of understanding now?

16. Our sense of this is that we are to work on dropping our 'personalities' which are conditioned layers, and to strip ourselves back, bit by bit, back to the essence. We are locked-in to our false sense of 'self,' with our opinions, reasonings, beliefs, etc. Cutting the cords means throwing off these externally acquired 'belongings.' Could you comment on this?

Yes, this is so. The way like an unwrapping, a travel through and back up the rabbit hole. Yes, your 'self' is really now nothing but a condition at present; for it is all dependent on outer. It is not relational, is not synced up - it is illusory. But hear this, self is also whole and unconditioned at essence, and you can allow them to meet with a sense of yourself again, as a mutual arising. See it again like this, a collection of five states - there is but not

155

one thing at all for 'self' really is the colour of zero-state, and so everyone has a different pen, a different colour. For it is coloured by these states, this collection. Allow it to happen spontaneously in mutual arising. This is but to be said creativity - creative creatures are but what you all are. See this, in cutting cords you do not have to painstakingly go around saying 'no, not that, not this.' Just drop it all as easy as that - like in meditation, you lose your sense of a stagnant 'I' - this is but so for cutting cords. Is this of understanding now?

17. In terms of our relations with others, and the world around us, we would like to ask about the nature of belonging. Many people are feeling a need to belong, to belong to something, as if this is an innate feeling. Yet this need to belong often gets transferred into other areas, often material. Could you comment on this?

Yes. For you see, for you to belong in something other - in people, in groups, religion, anything - that so does take your fancy; but in this fanciful belonging you are really just longing to be - do you see this? You are but searching outside of yourselves to find someone or something that accepts you for who you are, who does so reassure you that you are ok. It is quite a neurotic way that you humans have begun to flow, essentially with this innate need to belong. But you see, you could flit from group to group, from person to person - what you really need to see is that you are but okay. You are better than that; you are but great, for you were always belonging. You were but tricked, deceived; what is true really is that you just long to 'be.' With much Love and Light – Abe.

18. Is therefore most of our human belonging a delusion, created by our cultural programs? Is there not an essential, innate sense of belonging that represents our core connection to Unity?

You see, a need to belong is a conditional state; not all but the way in which you think of the word 'belong.' For you are but seeking representation outside of yourselves. Notice the word 'representation,' for this is key. You are wanting this gathering to reassure you, to back you up - that this way is of truth. That is why there are so, so many groups; we would not to be able to decide to whom we belong - can you? You see, like we say, you long to be, to rest, in this space. Tell us, what does it so feel like when you are but not caring whether you belong to this group or that one? It is never about that; it is belonging to 'you' first and foremost. For if you are never belonging here, now, you are but never HOME - is this of understanding now? We wouldn't say that all of your human belonging is that of a delusion. What we would like to say is that, really, you are just longing to BE. With Love and Light – Abe.

There is but a sense of belonging that lies unseen, underlying, and therefore always searching outside. You never need to belong for you already belong; you are but in a dog-chasing-tail scenario - is this seen? This is why we say you really do long to 'be' for there is no need to belong, for you always do and always have - and to something far more expansive than you can imagine. Can you see how you do as humans go around and around? You separate and then you have to but search from what you think you are separated from - like the times you lose your glasses and then you realize they were but on your head, and you laugh for you had been searching for something in which you already have. It is not lost for when you sync back up you are no longer splintered and therefore you belong, deeply connected to so much more – unified. You see, people only need to belong externally because they are longing to 'be' that in which you already belong to; and until this is seen you will but be chasing your tails. It may be fun for a while, but it does soon become tiresome. With much Love and Light – Abe

19. We would like to discuss more with you about internal and external connectivity and relations. Our external connectivity, networking, and global linking are patterns that will force people to realize their inherent unity. That is, perhaps our external 'coming together' will function like a mirror to show us our internal connectivity within a collective consciousness. Could you comment upon this?

You see, it is but forever mirrored; but you must see first and foremost that connectivity is relational. For you to see it in your outer world you but have to feel it within; it has to resonate - this is but so. So, you see, there has to be that initial spark to start that fire - one of action. For you see, if you are disconnected from what you are it is seen in your world. But hear this, it is but transactional and the discourse you feel outside of yourselves, you feel inward. There is never a specific event as such, although some do so grab a hold of one end of the rope, pulling it more towards discourse and disconnection. But see this, there are just as many people wanting connection and community pulling so on the other side. It is about this fine balance of being, first and foremost - is this of understanding now? You see, we do so see that you get caught up with the notion of 'is it the chicken or the egg that came first?' but we would like to say a mutual arising. With Love and Light – Abe

20. Classic brain studies have shown the difference between the functioning of the left and right brain hemispheres. In most cases, each side is not communicating with the other and usually one side is dominant. Could the re-wiring of our human brains that you have spoken of also refer in some way to the linking up and communication of these two brain hemispheres to create an integral consciousness?

This is but so. This rewiring is of essence - to receive more, to work more so in coherence. Now, it is like an upgrading if you will; a resonance is sparked to create new pathways within, and you see it creates this without - and then you see it without. It is but confirmation of your inner. This is the relation we so speak of. Is this of understanding now?

21. Is has been said by many great philosophers and mystics that 'Everything is Mind.' That is, our known reality is both that which is thought itself as well as the thing that is thought about - thinker and thought together. Thinker and thought are two aspects of the same unified reality - is this so?

This is also fractal relation. For you see, you can think yourself into such a dark place, even if it is so but beautiful and sunny outside. See how many times you have but changed your mind about a person or situation and seen with your own eyes it's change. You see, it is this inter-relation that is happening; of one flow, one unity. Everything is in communication, for your body tells you it needs food. You think 'I am hungry' then you act and fetch food and eat. The food is eaten, the body is happy - or sometimes not, depending on the intake - and you have a harmonized communication system. But you see, as human beings you have but splintered yourselves from this vast network, and in this you have but segregated yourselves. These pathways in which we speak are pathways within piecing this network back together, mending the line. Then when this is but unified, your vibrational communicative web will become more and more vast; more and more getting online with this cosmic consciousness - linking back up. This is evolution; this is unity. You have but been splintered far too long - it does not work this way anymore. It will be too stagnant; it has been too stagnant - is this of understanding now? Tell us, are you the thinker and the thought? Or is thought a vibrational message coherent to the vibrational essence of you? It is but not differing things. With Love and Light – Abe

22. Our known reality is a consensus reality in that it exists because we all believe in it. That is, it can change according to our level of perception. If we shift our perceptions we can 'call forth' a different, hopefully better, reality. Is this not the situation at this moment - hence, our perceptions are critical?

It is but so. For whatever you do so shine the light of perception upon, is highlighted. You have to but make sure now that you are but unified, are wired up correctly in a sense, to make any moves forward; especially if you do so want to give them good foundations, good groundings. Is this of understanding now?

23. Other realities exist, according to levels of perception. Perhaps it occurs that other realities slip into ours, causing a disturbance? Or maybe other realities intervene - accidentally or deliberately - that create a shift in our known reality? Could you comment upon this?

It is really but so. But we would like to say only vibrationally. For if you are not wired up correctly, you cannot see clearly. Vibration is transmuted only ever by the organism, or a device that does so. There is but a distortion, not only in your reality but in others. You see, life is like this - forever becoming, this forever dividing of but one thing. And in essence, to but see and know it all, you have to at some point make your way back to unity - your WAY BACK HOME. Is this of understanding now?

24. We have been thinking about what some people consider masculine and feminine energies. People often say that we need one or the other, or that we move through successive masculine-type and feminine-type energetic eras. Yet is this not also a cause of division? Is it not necessary to integrate both these aspects to create a unity, a whole, that incorporates everything? Are we not creating our own divisions about speaking in terms of 'this' and 'that' type of energy?

But of course, and it is so very evident for your stereotypes of masculine and feminine. For you see, you but all have these within - it can be but no other way. It is about the fine balance. It is but likened to that of what you call brain states. You have but separated this too into a masculine side and a feminine side, and really there is no such thing. It is of division, and these are but qualities that you have but given an identity. That is all, nothing

161

more, and all a part of unity. It is time to wake up to this knowing if you do so want to go forward. We see that there are but many New Age philosophies now that speak of this divine masculine and divine feminine, and the purpose of this life is to unite. This is but so, but it is of an inner state - it is always this. It is but bringing yourself back to this. It is also said that there are levels, dimensions. This is but raising not necessarily your vibration but your whole being, bringing it all back into alignment. We understand that the fifth dimension is one of great attention. But you see, we would rather put it as gathering these five states in that you are connecting up, are rewiring, and ready to but receive more. Is this of understanding now?

25. Without Question

We would but like to come forth to add something today, and we are not quite sure at all where you would like to place it - but feel it is an addition that need to be added at this time. You see, intuition is a gut feeling in your science. Now you are but realising that the gut is now classed as a second brain. But you see, brains are but receivers of vibration; therefore, the whole body could be classed as one giant brain. For what part can you really say that in which is a true receiver - is it not the whole? It is but your human capacity that does so allow you to work in parts. The physical brain creates pathways, neural pathways - is this not true? And you can see that the gut may not have this capacity to create pathways, but you will see that indeed it does, by way of communicating with the brain. But you see, the difference is in the brain - these pathways resonate so are therefore stuck, in a sense, until you allow new resonance. For you see, you are a whole system - as within, so without - and

162

vibratory communication is key. Allowing is key. What we would like to say is this - the feeling in the gut is vibratory knowing. It then gets transferred through the brain and also filtered through it, and is then projected by your heart. You see, all these things are but interlocking, relational to one another. You know this of your bodily parts - they are only effective as a whole system, only resonation as a whole system. You see, when these things are synced up, are in unison, you will see that in which you feel. Then thinking and then projecting will all be in accordance to this initial nudge. Is this of understanding now? For you see, you are but pure potentiality until you do so create the pathways within - and then so without. With much Love and Light – Abe.

26. Without Question

We would like to but come forth in a way to share that we are not ever discounting your human-ness by discrediting all that you have but built - the stories, the language, all help in this connection. It would go against that in which we want to convey now. What we really want you to see is beyond this. For you see, you have been enchanted by the word and language, and logic explanation for things; and therefore, lost meaning for meaning only comes when seen wholly. You see, in this you do not really have the full story. We never discredit one part over another but more so want you to see all in its entirety. Is this of understanding now?

SECTION TWO
The Reality Game

1. We talked about how this is an unprecedented time for connectivity, and for nurturing relations between people. Yet there is an epidemic of loneliness in the world. People are seemingly feeling lonelier now than ever. Why this contradiction, and how can we address it?

You see, loneliness is only ever felt when you are splintered, when you see yourselves as a lonely island of me. This is but then projected, for you are stressed and annoyed at others pushing people away, using them for your own gains. You really are communal creatures; you just need to but lighten up a little. To lighten the load of this constant bashing of doing life and allow it to do you for a while. You see, loneliness is an epidemic for you have shut off your heart space - you are cold. In a sense, you are in fear of others, of life, of love; and therefore, will be cold and stranded upon this island of me. Is this of understanding now? To address, you have to come back to self; and we say this with great love - that you have gave yourself away. You have but allowed to sell your parts to the devil and bought them back from the snakes. In part, you are but fearful and when you divorced from fear you automatically resonate with love. You see, when you are in but a bad mood you cut yourself off from others; you cut yourselves off from your heart - you close it down. We are not saying don't feel, for that is what you are. We are just saying, don't close the heart and do not buy into fear. With much Love and Light – Abe.

2. It seems that people - individually and collectively - are being blamed for their disconnection from the greater Reality. Has the loss of connection with the greater Unity been our responsibility alone? And is it only an individual responsibility to try to regain it?

You have lost yourselves to so many things, it is sad to say; and see it in such this way. You have to but take responsibility, to come back, for even some of the people whom have so tried to do good in the world forgotten to come back to this first - to resonate. First, they but have this knowing; they wake up and see the injustice in the world. But you see, true strength will come from gathering your parts first, for you will have good groundings to stand your ground and but help others. If so, this foundation is strong - is in resonation. You see, it is not about connecting back up out there as such, for you are unity that will automatically align to that in which you resonate at. You have to flow within to have balance and strength within - to then carry this through the world. Find your own light before lighting others. With much Love and Light – Abe.

3. Can we then say that we are being 'tricked' by this reality we are experiencing? That it is like a fabricated bubble that keeps us in splintered minds and disconnected from unity? The

166

falsity of our reality has been mentioned by many ancient wisdom traditions. Could you comment on this?

In a sense, you are but tricking yourselves. For you see, if it is based 'out there' you are in search for the gamester, the pied piper, that does so lead you along. But we say that you always have the power to wake up; to see that YOUR reality is but an illusion and you have been plugged into it for far too long. You are but feeding into this system that keeps you trapped. For you see, it is but always relational. Is this of understanding now?

We would also like to add that if you do so see that there are but others who control this game, this illusion, you will see to it that you are but always trapped. With much Love and Light – Abe.

4. Yet is it not the case that by seeing that 'others' control this game - this illusion - it empowers us to find ways to 'break out' by awakening? For if we don't see that it's a game, why would we want to wake-up?

Yes, but they are the ones that are but not willing to break this chain. They benefit from it and you do not. Once this is seen, would you not want to shake off that dew, that connection? There will always be ones that do not want to get out of their seats of comfort, and you can never force that. They have to see it to believe it and then to believe it they will act. You can be a resonance to which they have long forgotten. But hear this, you only have control over that in which you are wakeful to. With much Love and Light – Abe.

5. From your perspective - the perspective of Abe - how do you view this 'false reality' that we are trapped into? And how do you view those 'others' who are controlling this game? Has Abe been trying to awaken humanity to this 'game' throughout the ages?

You see, this is but the thing about relation, and what does so keep you locked into a system that does not serve you. It is this mutual arising - you have to meet it there like everything else. If you are asking what it does so look like from our perspective then we would say like you are but forever chasing your tails. You see, reality is only reality if you do so meet it. You have to meet it; you have to but keep playing and participating for anything to be upheld as a reality - your reality. The thing is, the system knows how to play into this by fear, by keeping you trapped. But what they do not realize is that love is so much more powerful than fear. You see this, it builds new worlds, new realities. We are here to act as an alarm going off; to say - 'this is not what life is;' 'this is not what I have to be;' 'this is not MY reality.' It is about aligning within. It is about your own resonation of being. We have but much to talk on this. But you see, the key is always this - where and what are you meeting? With Love and Light – Abe.

6. And so, if enough people shifted how they saw or 'wished to see' reality, then this would change the 'consensus game,' so to speak? We are like in a tug-of-war between a given, controlled reality, and with a truer reality that is in unity? To put it crudely, are we in a battle for our minds?

It is but always so, that you are in a tug-of-war, and you are in a tug-of-war to reclaim yourselves. For like we say, you are but splintered and an outdated system sells you back your parts and never in full - never to feel whole. You see, you have so much power, more than you do so think, and you have been but taught that power is money and status and it is not. Power is knowledge; power is truth; power is working in cohesion - this is but true power for it is true of whom you so are. With much Love and Light – Abe.

We would also like to say it is the time for but a break in the clouds. With much Love and Light – Abe.

Maybe it is so that we should state the relation to which people do awake. For you see, it is always vibrational to break this spell of an illusory reality in which you have so been taught - that keeps you spellbound and caught into it, feeding and taking, taking and feeding. You but so have to break that chain. How it is done so is with a space, a break in the line of connection. Is this of understanding now?

7. You have mentioned how our false reality is being manipulated and controlled by fear, and that we need 'triggers' to act as alarms to wake us up. Have not cultural events, sometimes disasters, acted as these 'alarms'? If so, how do such cultural triggers operate, and have they been deliberately caused?

It is so this way. But realize this - you do not need such a wake up. It has all been well and good in the past; but you see, your culture was anaesthetized and was but kept in this

169

unconscious cycle. And although the effects are still being shook off, they are not over, one could say. But hear this, it is not the EVENTS that are so much of importance here but the energy that it does so entail; and the vibrational resonance that comes from it. Do you but understand this? For you see, you are but feeling this shift - most are. It is so whether you learn to jump with it or not. Many things can awaken you; it does not have to be catastrophic for it could be a tiny whisper that does so catch you. And in this, you feel your heart swell and begin to open again, to let the light in. Sometimes what looks like catastrophe at ground level is really rooting below the surface something really quite extraordinary. With much Love and Light – Abe.

8. As you say, it is time for a break in the clouds. Does this mean that humanity is winning this struggle against a false reality? And/Or that it is now time to break through this illusion?

We would like to say a bit of both. There is a break in the clouds in which you can see that people are waking up, but they also could slip into falsity of the illusion of the illusion. Is this of understanding now?

9. We would like to discuss more about breaking the spell of an illusory reality. You have said that humanity needs to break the chain, and this is done by creating a space or break in the line of connection. Could you clarify what you mean by this and explain more?

The break is just that; a break from yourself - a break from reality, your conscious reality whilst still wide awake. You see, it

170

is very hard to write a letter if you do not have the space in-between. It is the space that really shows the meaning. Words are filled-in all your day, every waking moment. Sometimes it is the break that does so speak louder. You see, when you break, you let go; you do not have to fill the space - you allow it to be there. The break is really the connection of things - but you do not see it as so for you have to but fill the space, fill the gaps. Is this of understanding now? You see, this connection is broken to the continuance of doing, of filling the space. This space then allows you to see that you are but connected - you are but unity - you just don't need to talk about it; you don't need to fill it. And in this you are but breathing; you are meeting it there. With much Love and Light – Abe.

10. It is interesting that you say our cultures were anaesthetized and kept in a cycle of unconsciousness. Could you clarify and explain more about this? And why did this occur?

You see, this wasn't an administered anesthetic. There was not one so doing this; it has been a growth of vibrational resonance. If we were to say there was but any administer, we would say it was but individually taken, willingly, for you have been long mesmerized by power, by gain, when true power is resonance, is less - is coming back HOME. You see, the culture has been anaesthetized, and when you do so come around there is but another administered; and you have but unconsciously taken this shot - vibrationally hooking up and plugging in, resonating, lining up, and therefore participating. What we say, and this is with great love, is it is but time to stop; to have a break, to see, to feel, to stop numbing and dumbing yourselves down. It is but a shame to live like this. It is but even a greater shame to die like this. But hear this, to really know what is true reality - what is but not a mirage - you have to feel it; and when you are numb you cannot feel anything. You are unconscious of your own being – feel, feel, feel again; and you will but have your reality, your truth. With much Love and Light – Abe.

11. Could it be that what appear to be catastrophic or unpleasant cultural events, are really shielding some important vibrational shift or catalyst?

We would like to say not shielding, for it does not need this. It rather brings back up this feeling again - to feel even if that is but grief of despair. And when this is felt, you look to others; you relate to others. You see, most of the time your culture has you going along in autopilot and you see these vagabonds, and people whom are not in the race, and they see these patterns. Many even numb these patterns out for it is like a lonely graveyard for them. They distract themselves as to go back sleep; not all, but some. For you see, it is hard for you to be awake when many are asleep, are 'under' in a sense. For you are but talking to a brick wall and, we may be straying, but at essence what we are trying to say is that it is not to shield it - but rather, to resonate with you again. Sometimes these catastrophes create space to see that things aren't working in the way they should. You feel again. You get out of your seats and go see what all the commotion is. Is this of understanding now?

12. It is also possible during these transition times that - as you say - people could slip further into falsity of the illusion of the

illusion. Could you say more about this? Also, what you mean by the 'illusion of the illusion'?

You see, your culture is but great at getting you to willingly participate; and we say it like we do, so just blame your culture. But you see, you are but participating. This always has to be vibrational relation - the illusion of the illusion is but this. You see, humans find a back door, an exit, and some do so go out that door. Some may never do so for they have all they need but here. But some do, and then they come back and do so tell the others about this exit backstage; and it gets around, word gets out, and more people go out and see 'wow - the sunshine upon our faces.' And they go back in and it just isn't the same. But you see, your culture can put up another exit door that does so mimic the original exit door. And in this you are but caught in a sort of loop - a pattern, a cycle, if you will. Is this of understanding now?

13. Can it be said that by 'breaking the spell' we need to break a vibrational pattern that is dominant in our cultures and our reality? Are we trapped in this vibrational pattern? And if so, how can we begin to break out of this pattern?

Yes, it is so. And it is but not as difficult as you do so see. You see, you have to feel again; for a person who is 'under' is not going to sustain - they are but guided here, there, and everywhere. You need to feel - feel to the core of your very essence. It's like a spark but can grow to a great glow and will guide others. There is not anything you have to do as such. But see it like the antennas, the connections of all that you do so hold onto are connected up to. Just drop it - drop them all. We are not saying to do nothing; but you see, at some point you need to breathe and come back home, rather than all these vibrational wires linked up to so many things now - this is entanglement. With much Love and Light – Abe.

14. The big question here is WHY? Why does human culture wish for people to be caught up within the spell – the trap – of the endless loops, the anesthetized numbness? What is the objective and intention here for that?

It is but to keep you apart, to keep this division; for if you knew your power, they would completely crumble, would they not? We say - what would be the point of an illusion if it were not upheld and fed into? And you see, this isn't just your culture or something outside of yourselves either - this is a definite divide within your psyche. Is this of understanding now? For you see, they are just upholding that in which you think you are, and that is one of great division of being - and you are in a loop, in a rabbit hole. Is this of understanding now?

15. Thank you, Abe. It would seem that those people who hold power in our cultures are also divided and splintered in their psyches. Is it a case of the blind leading the blind, just for the sake of maintaining some illusory idea of power and social control?

This is but correct. But whilst there are people of power - and you but allow that illusion to stick - you are but upholding this illusion too. There has to be a shift from within, from within yourselves, for they are sitting pretty and have no intention of doing so. For the ones who are so winning the game do not feel as if they want to quit, whether it be an illusion or not. Is this of understanding now?

16. Would you say that there are those in power who are aware of the nature of the splintered human psyche and are maintaining and continuing this illusory distraction for as long as possible because they wish to block the development of human consciousness?

We would like to say that there are but some that hold the key to this knowing, but not in its entirety, for they too are but coming from a splintered mind. As you see, it is interwoven into their structures, into their lives. For something to be splintered, you have to be yourselves splintered - do you see this? It has to be of resonation of your being, and as humans you can go around blaming people at the top as you have done for so long. But you see, it is not moving anything and therefore just causing more and more division. Is this of understanding now? You see, your human stance is one of love, and conditioning and generational entanglement does so fog this line, this vibratory essence. With much Love and Light – Abe.

17. It seems that between our current state of 'splintered consciousness' and unification, there are many degrees. It's not just a question of going from one to the other. There are many states of consciousness between here and unification - is this not so? We also feel that those people in the 'lower' resonance of consciousness have no idea of what's going on at the 'next level', so to speak. Although there is a fine line between these

states, there is a huge gap in perception. Could Abe comment on this?

It is so this. And you see, with this symbol you have that what is unification. But you also have these eight dots that is of almost a joining, a stage - a pathway. You can but only keep stepping forth on a pathway in which you do not know - it is *of* faith and not *in* faith. For something to save you, or direct you, of something other but faith in yourselves, in what you truly are - when you know this you know unification. For you can see it as clear as day that you yourself are guiding yourselves and everyone else. Is this of understanding now? You see, perception is not differing stages as such but more like a growth, a linking up. Be slow with yourselves - allow it to link up itself to allow these new neural pathways to form, to resonate, to connect, and in this it can be solidified. With much Love and Light – Abe.

18. You have said before that Abe would like to talk more about relations in terms of humans relating to the world around them. Does this involve our relations with our pseudo-reality? What aspects does Abe consider are important to discuss in this regard?

Yes, it is so. For you see, you are entangled in this reality. You are but completely invested. What we want to come forth as - and we say it again - it is a break in the clouds, a break in the connection, a rock on the path. Not abruptly, but gently to feel the sun upon your faces again. As the light cracks through the clouds, it shines but light upon your reality that you have so been invested in for so long, trying to but make it work. Be gentle with yourselves, to allow that space to see again. You see, you can pull

176

your heavy carriages over the rock in the path and risk your carriage being broken, breaking a wheel - giving you time to repair it, to rest. And you can but also stop and take time to remove the rock. But you do so see both of these things give space. With much Love and Light – Abe.

19. Thank you, Abe. We understand this need to take a step back from our entanglement in our reality. As you say, many people are invested in these entanglements – this reality is so real for them. These people will think that what Abe is saying is the 'false reality.' Can we reach out to such people, or must everyone come to such realizations through their own willingness?

You can but always shine this unity, and this must always be so when people do such want to come forward. They will do so for only then will they truly absorb that in which you are both bringing forth. For you see, for it to solidify in your physical reality it has to be of resonation, of relation - to meet up. It is but pointless to talk flower language to a seed for there is still much growth. But hear this, you always have the power to step yourselves back, to join anyone as to where they are at if so wanted. Is this of understanding now?

20. We also get a sense that 'something' is breaking through into this illusion. As if the cracks are beginning to appear. Perhaps the current sense of uncertainty/confusion with many people today is a result of this 'wobble' in the illusion-reality? Could you comment on this?

It is such this way, yes. It does so feel that things are as you put it - in 'wobble' - of the illusion as to which you are so tightly constricted to. And this may seem like utter devastation to some, like their whole world that they have but become so reliant on is crashing to the ground, for you have become accustomed to this illusion. But you see, like when you look behind the curtain or under the bed and realize there are no monsters of life, just empty space, and you relax and wonder why you did not so realize this before that. Your angst and depression and anxiety are a sign that you are clinging to but a monster in which you have to battle - allow the space in which you are but so frightened to have, and in this there will be much growth. With much Love and Light – Abe.

21. Modern life is now creating many questions – and even attacks – upon the notion of reality: from 'fake news,' to artificial life, to 'alternative facts' – phrases that have suddenly become popular. Are these contributing to a shift in our construction of reality?

You see, what does so happen when you see that some are but losing control, they do so become flustered. They become a dither to things so they are to throw out all that can set confusion or send you deeper down the rabbit hole. But hear this, this is of not one person losing control at the top but of others whom do so feel attacked. To say that this reality that you have invested but all your life unto this point is a sham, you will have people that will lash out and try to uphold this falsity. So long as you can decipher through this mess you can sail to the shore. Is this of understanding now?

178

22. Is this 'false reality' only being maintained by forces upon and within this planet - or are there forces external to the planet (cosmic elements) that are contributing to our illusory reality?

No. It is but a collective achievement - and we say achievement very loosely. For you see, if all is unity then it but has a knock-on effect, if you will. To think that there are darker forces but beyond your capabilities as a human being is very outdated. For it may have worked previously to shift perception so that these new pathways can be created, but now it does have to be dropped. We come forth and say this with much love and light for your species. But you see, you are but your own worst enemies and also your only saviours. Is this of understanding now?

23. Thank you. Have these entrapments in reality-illusion occurred with previous species or civilizations upon this planet? If so, what were the consequences? Or has this been an ongoing accumulation of misdirected perception within our species?

See it like so - you have a seed; you are but a beginner - you do not know what these seeds will give. You learn that you have to plant the seeds for them to grow; you then realize you have to water these seeds if no rainfall. You tend to this, you learn as you go - you see, you are but the beginners of unity. Like we say, a constant becoming. You are not so much to say evolving, in a sense as evolving so that you are becoming a finished product as such. No, you are making your way back home consciously - to ground this, to so solidify this. Now you are but a plant that is growing; but you are also the soil that nourishes and the gardener that tends and nurtures. Is this of understanding now? If you are but asking straight out as to whether YOUR species has ever had true perception, we would say that - no. It has but always been tainted, for you are but in a physical reality with much to fire the senses. And we do so see that you look at the ancient civilizations that seem to of lived more harmoniously with their planet, with each other, and the cosmos. But hear this, it is but time to go forward consciously with that in which you are at now - do you see this? For what was once their physical reality, although not so overloaded as of like it may be so today, was still tainted. With much Love and Light – Abe.

We would like to also add that you can but learn much about these ancient civilizations and how they connected. But hear this, do not get so caught up in it or else you will be but taking steps back. It needs also to be adapted and worked in a way as so it is relational now. With much Love and Light – Abe.

24. You have noted how our modern life today is 'overloaded' as you say. Does this refer to overload of our senses? And/Or overload with physical gadgets, technologies, and our possessions? And with this 'modern overload' will it not be more difficult to break from this illusory spell toward true perception?

See it like this, that your ancient civilization has but gone shopping - vibrational shopping - and we say in such a way as we really want you to see the light-heartedness of it. They are collecting this and that, putting it in the trolley, adding it to the cart - round and round they go, seeing more that they seemingly need when in truth a few fine ingredients would suffice. But you see, they had but come with an empty vibration and everything seems so enticing, so they keep adding. This is but the point at which you are at - the cart is full, you are overloaded, and there is but no slight chance that you can but consume it all or use it all. Do you see? The overload is of a vibrational essence and is but easily dropped, easily minimized if you so want to. But hear this, you have to want to. Is this of understanding now? You see, we say as this is all vibrational for it is really this way now. You cannot let go of your outer clutter, your outer connections whilst you are but still vibrationally attached - it is but the other way around. Use what you have brought forth up to now to enhance life, not to compensate for a life not lived. With much Love and Light – Abe.

But do so hear this too, this has been over time in your physical existence that this accumulation has happened, and it will not be an overnight process, an instant gratification. You do so see this?

25. Thank you, Abe - yes, this is a good analogy with the shopping cart. To de-clutter our vibrational overload, would this suggest a physical de-clutter of our lives - such as stepping into a simpler lifestyle? Does it also suggest stepping back from our reliance on technologies - or do you refer principally to a mental-emotional de-cluttering?

We would relate more so to a mental decluttering. For you see, you are attached to things physically, where the attachments to the physical items are the emotions in which you hold mentally. Is this of understanding now? You see, there will be people more willing to leave behind the mental clutter due to tiredness of upholding these vibrational loads more so than they would initially the physical clutter. And this is a good thing for then it will set in motion. But hear this, you can rid or be rid of something physical and not at all rid yourselves of the vibrational essence of it. Therefore, we see it fit to concentrate on the vibrational essence first and foremost - you see this now? Your reliance on technology should be brought back, not thrown away; but brought back so that you can redefine that in which you could be using it for - and going forth un-splintered, unattached or overloaded, to have mental clarity. With much Love and Light – Abe.

26. Thank you. There seems to be a great influx of what are termed 'channeled' messages at this time which mostly speak towards this need for our species to 'clean itself up' and raise our consciousness. Is this the case that a lot of assistance is emerging now from different places/vibrational realms because the situation has become so bad/difficult for humanity on this planet?

We would like to not say it to be of assistance but rather a knowing, a waking up as so. You see, you will only receive for what stage you are at, vibrational wise. It is relational, and this is what we speak of when we speak of fractal relation. For what looks like fragmented, differing realities, perceptions, realms, is really one - is unity. Do you so see this now? Your species is splintered because of the vibrational resonance of which they are at individually. There are few who are resonating higher and we do so see this; and there are ones that are of lower. But hear this, this does not mean a hierarchy at all - it just means that vibrationally they are younger, they are still growing. And you cannot be a seed one day and a flower two seconds later - it is but a process. Is this of understanding now?

There are but ones whom have had a higher resonance enabling them to be alarm clocks, if you will. But you see, some of those do not because they run out of battery; they get tired or too heavy with these vibrations. With much Love and Light – Abe.

You see that you have had so many apocalyptic theories of the world ending, of disaster striking. But you see, the real disaster in the physical will be not enabling these vibrations to take route now - or rather, arise. You see, apocalyptic is really the breaking down of an old way of being because the vibrational resonance that you have brought into your being, or rather allowed. By bringing back your connections, your feelers, to your physical world that you do so feel something is amiss, is unreal, you have but brought them back in. In this, you are clearing societal residue from your vibratory essence. It is no longer continuing to feed into it by being hooked up and invested in it. You take a step back from being consumed within it and just watch for a brief moment. You see, you give space for this essence that has been but so long overridden to come forth - to now allow to make new pathways. The thing is, when great change occurs there is but destruction - for it lends way for a new beginning, a fresh start. You have to keep your head about it, but also an open heart too. With much Love and Light – Abe.

27. Thank you, Abe. You say it is essential that we unify our vibrational resonance amid the distractions of modern life. Is the human vibrational resonance affected by digital

environments? We ask because there is an increasing development of augmented reality projects. Also, the coming emergence of higher bandwidth 5G mobile phone networks. How are these new environments affecting human resonance?

It but does so interfere, for every resonance is susceptible to change, to distortion. But do so hear this, when your own resonance is of unity - of grounded true unity within - then you see there are not so many things that can so distort it; that can contaminate it in a way as to redirect it to get caught up in other resonances. If you are so saying that resonance of this kind affects your own true resonance, then see it like this - you are only affected by that in which you allow to affect you. For you see, it is not at what these differing vibrational resonances do but more so in your own grounded resonance - your truth. Not in such a way to stand stiff in a storm, no, for you could easily break - but like the bamboo that is so flexible to enable it to be touched but not broken. Is this of understanding now? You see, every vibration is felt to someone whether you know it or not - and manmade digital vibrations are no different. The thing you have to understand is that these things can evolve your species when used in the correct way. But you also see that they can also control and manipulate. It is about grounding this unity using what is needed and realizing your own need for connection and relation to that of all of your world. For when you have but one part, you leave other things out of balance. Unity is whole and not dismissing one thing over another - so long as there is unity there is balance. With Love and Light – Abe.

28. You have spoken much about taking a 'step back' and 'taking a pause' to assess our vibrational states. Can human

resonance be assisted, realigned – and possibly even healed? – by being close to Nature, and spending time in natural, non-urban, environments? Is Nature closer to a genuine reality and has less of an 'illusory' factor?

You see, in your built-up areas there is but much vibrational influence – over-stimulation, if you will - so many differing vibrations. And you see that anyone who is highly susceptible or even those whom are not to all, these differing energies, these vibrations, it is like an overload of exterior stimulation when in essence it is vibrational. You see, when you are but knowing of vibrational resonance you know this; and so, when you are out in nature you have space again - you have resonance flowing and not distorted and disrupted. So much like light bouncing off of a surface, shooting off in many directions; and to some this feels like hectic madness, and for others not so much for it is their reality. But you see, when you do so have a break from this hysteria you can too see that it is but madness, is void of connection or any sense of true self - that you have but become a machine. Not even the machine but a part becoming void of your inherent human nature - and for what? It is not that we think people are stupid but rather have been limited, have been told that your reality is real and to get on with it - when you see that there is but a break, an exit, the thing is you just need to look up, stop, and see. With much Love and Light – Abe.

If we are to be direct in saying as to whether nature can heal, we would say - but of course, it is your home. It is part of your essence whilst in human form. You have but a deep vibrational relation to it, so to cut out this is to cut out part of who you are, and in this it is not unity. Is this of understanding now?

29. Our current reality has much to overload the human senses. This is contributing to a vibrational dissonance and is distracting people 'from themselves' so to say. And yet this is a direction in which we see modern life (or 'reality') is developing further, not lessening. Maybe we need to rethink our lives? Could Abe comment on this?

You see, Unity is wholeness of being - meaning that new ways of being is not put out of that equation. You see, it is in your genes, in your essence, to but advance as a species. We are not to stunt that at all - it is good to go forward. But hear this, if it is used in a way as to manipulate, to control, to divide, to box up each individual inside your own conscious experience - then it has but missed the point completely and will not be to your own advancement but rather to your own demise. Do you so see this? For unity – well, unification - is the essence of putting things back together as to see the whole picture again. To widen your own consciousness so that it isn't so tightly constricted inside such definitive boxes; and again, cracking open these Russian dolls. You see, anything that you do so lose yourselves to, and see that this is putting yourself into something else - be it a person, a religion, work, or even a coffee machine - that you do so want, and as stupid as this does so sound, it is but truth. These vibrational antennas are out and connected up, and it is not such a bad thing as such, so long as you know how and when to shut these back down - to bring them back in. Is this of understanding now?

We would like to but come forth this morning and just touch upon vibrational resonance, and that of differing vibration so that it is clear and not one of confusion. For we see that many people now are working upon their vibrational resonance and

186

trying to rise it. What we would like to say is that this is but counter-productive, and in this can make your resonation dip considerably. You see, if you but try to raise your vibration by way of positive thoughts you are in essence saying that you are not already of high resonance - and this would not be of truth. You are sugar coating that in which you need to clear; it's like a band-aid problem - a medication problem. You are masking the pain but not actually rooting out that which is embedded in your own vibration. And in this your default setting is but the same. You see, in the recognition of these patterns within, you allow them to fall. For when you see the root cause of your pain, you realize the medication was but masking it. It was a block in the neural pathway, but it did not make a new one, and was but still of resonation to these old patterns - it was just a delay. Is this of understanding now? You see, we are not but saying that a positive thought is bad. No, not at all; it is but good to be optimistic. But it is also good to be realistic sometimes too and see that you are already of high vibration. You just are a little but dusty - you need a vibrational clean out. With much Love and Light – Abe.

30. You say that some people are trying to raise their vibrational resonance – what are some of the practices that people are using here that you feel are not appropriate, or necessary?

Yes, we do. And we say this with great love that the very fact that you are but trying to raise something is the hiccup here. For you see, you are that high vibration - it is just that you but cling to all the baggage, the contamination. Unwilling - maybe some unwittingly - unable to release, to let go. You see, this energy that so does come in is already allowing anyway - it is but a clearing out, if you will, to connect you back up to your natural resonation. It is a wakeup to the spirit. It is not that these higher energies are not of you, but just like when catastrophes happen in your physical existence, and what these energies are that come in, are not above and beyond all that you are. They are just a reminder. With Love and Light – Abe.

31. Would you say that vibrational resonance has a strong connection with our mental states? Such that, people with depression or lack of self-worth, or who just don't trust or believe in themselves, are lowering their vibrational resonance?

This is but so. It is relational always to what you do so feel within. But hear this, it is but also something that is taught in your society and in this you hook up vibrational resonance to these structures, these patterns and pathways. This is why we say drop it, bring it all back, and even for the moment just drop yourselves - give yourselves a rest. Is this of understanding now?

32. What about people with disorders such as schizophrenia, autism, and others – how does this relate to their contact with their vibrational resonance?

We would like to say that with these types of mental connections it is that you are but wired up different; and believe us when we say that this is not wrong. There are pathways that are not yet of normal functioning amongst many. What really is to be taught here is not to medicate and sedate and lock away these conditions but allowing them to re-resonate so that you can

188

but be sensitive to these vibrational resonances, but not overloaded. And you see, that is why this whole thing is a growth and not flooding all at once. For you see, the mechanism also has to resonate with the vibratory essence otherwise the fuse will be blown. Is this of understanding now?

33. Also, are mental disorders somehow related to distortions in vibrational resonance and/or external cultural vibrational distortions?

It can but be this way too, for many a vibration are but influential to that of your own. At all times it is whether you have rooted these new neural connections, these pathways; for if not, you will be swayed back and forth and eventually snapped in two. You see, your strength is not just dependent upon how strong the body is, it is also dependent upon how strong is your resonation, and how easily influenced and manipulated it is. For when you give but yourself away to something, when you link up, it takes a little away. And the more and more things you but link your energy up to, the more you can be but influenced. We are not saying to not link up but do so make sure that the things that you are linking up to are but feeding back in equal quantities, of equal resonation. If not, they will not serve you. Is this of understanding now?

We would but like to add, this is why it is but good to keep a check - for you are always growing. You are but clearing things out and more often than not you forget to spring clean your vibration. You forget to draw back the links, the vibrational resonance to things - draw them back, take a break and reevaluate as often as necessary. It is never too late to start over

and over again, clearing as you go. With much Love and Light –
Abe.

34. In terms of creating harmonious (or even healing) vibrational environments in our homes, are there things we can actively do? Such as the arrangement of our homes/furniture, practices, etc? Or can we 'clean' our home environments by irradiating our own internal vibratory state?

The best thing you can do is but open a window - allow things to flow. It is but this simple. You need air to breath - is this not true?

You see, life becomes so much more complicated than need be. You can but arrange your house in a certain way, but if you do not so like it that way it will not have the desired effect. Is this of understanding now? It is but always of resonation. With Love and Light – Abe.

35. How does vibratory resonance function with animals? For example, many people keep pets in their lives which they form close ties with. Can we say people become 'vibrationally aligned' with their pets? And do pets – and animals in general – serve to form harmonious vibrational connections with humans?

You see this, the animal brain does not have such complexity as does the human brain. But hear this, they're not so contaminated. This is not to say that humans are over-complicated. They can but do very much with the ways in which the human brain has evolved, but it does so need a vibrational

190

clear-out. Have you known or ever had an experience in which a certain animal just does not like you or has been stand off from you? For you see, all mechanisms are differing in size, proportion, and that in which is essential for their own survival. Pets have been rewired to be reliant on humans, and this does so date right back to when the first wild dog was fed by a villager. You see, there has to be one of resonation - someone who does so not like dogs, for example, will have reason not to. They will pick up on this; animals are susceptible to these energies and are also part of this unity - they just are rewired. Humans, on the other hand, do indeed have the upper hand at present as they are more self-aware - to enable relations, to initiate them, and change the neural connections. But hear this, so are animals. With much Love and Light – Abe.

36. You have mentioned how pets have been rewired to be reliant upon humans. How does this relate to other animals in general? Is there a vibrational bond, or relationship, between humanity and the animal kingdom? If so, has humanity been honouring this bond or breaking with it?

But of course, there is this bond, this resonation, for you are really not apart from the animal kingdom yourselves. You see, you have but far too many groupings of things. For you see, a dog will be loved and pampered but on the other hand a spider would be squished without second thought. And you see, this kind of mentality is abound in your societies. Is this of understanding now? You cannot keep separating things down and down; well, you can but realize this - it all comes back to unity. There is but no other way: break it apart, see how things work if need be, but do so remember to piece it all back together again. There has been, and will always be, a bond for it is evident when you see the simple truth of unity. Your survival is dependent upon these connections. With much Love and Light – Abe.

37. And so, part of our crises at this present time upon this planet is that we have broken, or rather stopped honouring, these relations of unification with the natural world, as well as the animal kingdom. Would you say that eco-system thinking is fundamental to how physical relations operate on all material planets?

It is, yes. But of course, relations do not just need fixing back up with each other but with all - how you resonate to your planet, to the animals that do so help to sustain your lives. You see, you have but gone down this rabbit hole - you are but alone. Make your way back out firstly to self, then more outer and outer. For when you do realize the intricate web of existence that you are so encased in, you are but a part of, you will realize that one part taken out intentionally - not coming from unity - will but upset this balance. But hear this, as one thing raises from unification, other things will too. And in this you can see that which is rebalancing and that in which is being destroyed - in this you are but destroying yourselves. Is this of understanding now?

38. Thank you, Abe. If humanity is introducing technology into this intricate ecosystem without unity consciousness, then will this disturb and upset the balance? Is it better to say humanity needs to return to unity consciousness before

introducing advanced technology into the planetary ecosystem?

We would like to but say this: to Unify is but key to your species survival now. We do not want to be so dire, but it is of essence to bring it all back in - bring it all back. Unify self - that is but vital in going forward. Your vibrational resonance must be one of unity, of connection, of the known oneness. Not of just saying we are all one but of you resonating at it - of shining this. Therefore, when this is truly rooted, truly grounded of strength and certainty in your very being, other vibrations will not be able to penetrate it. Only then can you step forth from this place of great strength and build a new world. Let the structures fall, cut your ties, and see them plummet. But wait for unity to grow and ground from within before taking steps forward from this place of calm and ease. With much Love and Light – Abe.

We would like to come forth this morning and, on this note, say that it is never about the practise, but what it does so move in you. It is never about the place but what you resonate at yourselves. For you see, your home has a vibrational resonance - everything does. You are not to be rid of it, any of it, but sync back up. There is but an intricate grid, and although you see life as timelines, it is never as so - this suggests a stretch forward in time. And what we would like to say is, a web of communication between all things - intricately intertwined. Is this of understanding now? When you unify, when you truly allow unification of consciousness, you will feel this grid all around you; and the patterns will but become evident. For in this you will see the patterns - the connection, the relation, and the beauty. With much Love and Light – Abe.

SECTION THREE
Relations with the World Around Us

Thank you, Abe. To return to issues of our relations with the world around us, we would like to consider how we deal with our social and cultural systems. Specifically, how these may now be broken systems that are being perpetuated. In this regard, we wish to consider some themes of power, domination, alienation, entrapment, authority, vulnerability, attachment, identity, and more.

1. It seems that modern life is creating greater alienation amongst people. Some of this is being caused by work practices even though we are experiencing a time of greater freedoms and access to information and higher standards of living. Why this contradiction?

You see, the contradiction is but within yourselves. For you see, many younger ones and infant - many older too - are great with technological advancement. But they do not know how to conduct themselves in the fine art of conversation. They have lost their confidence because they do so have a 'go between,' and we see that this is not across the board but a significant amount. You see, whenever there is something placed between yourselves, be it a gadget or even the mental wall that you create to guard yourselves, it is always a second-hand exchange. And by true default this is not what you honestly want as a species - you want connection. It is part of your very fabric. You see, it is time to drop any sort of middleman if you truly want to connect. For you see, alienation is a defense mechanism that you have built up for yourselves. Like we say, it is a divide, a split, mainly within yourselves. You are then allowing for this divide to be widened and fed into. Is this of understanding now?

2. We feel the difficulties today are that people increasingly give their power away to external forces. At the same time, dominant social power is becoming more invisible as it gets placed within our automated institutions and bureaucracies. Is the answer to change our systems first - or change ourselves?

It is always for you to take it back to yourselves first and foremost – otherwise, what would be the point? You need to bring it all back in - to then re-reach, reassess, and recalibrate. Is this of understanding now? You cannot rewire your world. It does not work that way, albeit a few do so try, sometimes successfully. But it is never sustainable, it never sticks. You are the foundation in which a new world needs to be built upon - each and every one of you are a part of this foundation. With Love and Light – Abe.

3. Most people will agree that unity and unification are noble and 'true' paths to pursue. Yet few will act upon this. It seems as if social reality operates like a form of amnesia causing

people to forget their true, genuine path. How can people start to take their own power back?

You see, many would think of it to be something that is above and beyond an ideology, if you will. But hear this, it is your human trait - it is who you are. It is a process of becoming, and is a path that goes against, in a way, all that you have been taught. Life is a division of you, and this is your current programming; but it is changing, it is developing, and develop it you must. We talk that it is of an instant seeing, which it is. For you see, when you see unity it cannot be unseen, although many do try. They know it is truth, but they are not wanting to clear out the vibration so that it can be rooted, can be your default - for this is what it needs to be. You need to give it time to be rooted, to create resonation within your brain so that these pathways can then join up, can strengthen. Is this of understanding now? You see, with anything it is reprogramming yourself first. You have to bring back in these wires, these links to everything that you have been so taught; and take time to reassess, to question bit by bit, piece by piece. Like we repeat, it is a becoming and humanity will not change overnight the programming that has been embedded within you. But it is time to start to cut it back - back to the basics for that is where the truth lies. That is where you power lays. With much Love and Light – Abe.

4. Perhaps the truth is also that people - individually and collectively - hypnotize themselves. As part of the socializing process we develop ideologies, religious and 'spiritual' doctrines, and manifestos for living. It seems as if these are

traits of a lower stage of civilization. Is this so, and can we surpass these activities in the near future?

It is but a vicious cycle you do so get yourselves into. For you see, many would think that unity is void of self-expression, and it just is not so. You see, that is the real beauty of unity - that it can but take so many forms and still be of one thing. We would like to say that there is not any forms of stages, although it does seem so. There is not a ranking in which you do so have to work your way through - this is but another ideology. And we say where you do ever break this pattern, you are where you are at – consciously, socially, and spiritually. The thing to know is that you are all a work in progress in which may never be complete. And that is the beauty of life, and to go on and live. Now, this may seem to some as a meaningless existence. It is not, for if you are willing to continue to strip away the layers despite what you are told, you will be truly living, truly participating. Is this of understanding now? You see, many do call this life a game and it is rightly so. But what you miss sometimes is that games are meant to be played - only this game has no winners for you all have this gift of the game of life. With much Love and Light – Abe.

5. Humanity is a collective species. It is also a social species, needing forms of community and togetherness. This social need has also been exploited and has created weakness in people. Is the way home to strengthen our collective spirit or first to develop our sense of individuality-within-unity?

We would say again, it is definitely about your own truth in unity - it but has to be this way. Like we say, this is your strength,

198

your foundation firstly - this is where you truly ground it. It can be no other way. For you see, it is fine to meddle out there in the world, but it will be swung and swayed. You will not have the strength, and indeed the capacity, to create these pathways without firstly doing so within. It is indeed so - as within, so without. It is but always this way; it is just that it has been tarred with the notion of witchery or new age philosophy in which people tend to shy from. This is because it resonates profoundly but is scary, for the barriers and illusion that you have built around you now will have to be dropped - and some are just not ready. As this resonation of being syncs up more and more, as your consciousness evolves in more and more people, they will see what a slog it was to always do it the other way around. But you see, you are taught so that indeed you have to move the pieces around the board when in fact you could sync up with the pieces - and in this, not sort and sift or fruitlessly place at all. With much Love and Light – Abe.

We would like to come forth and really allow you to see that you but always had the power - you were just so frivolous and quick to give it away. You thought it lay in the things that are external to your very being. In this you are tossed to and fro with life's circumstances. Unity doesn't mean everything will be happily ever after – no, but it does so allow you to see the connection in things and the wholeness. It is not about life giving you constant happy gifts and continually being positive - it is really about the beauty of wholeness and that wholeness starts with you. In unity, you are given back your power for you see that things are not good and bad, but just that you withstand because your happiness is not dependent upon things outside of you. You are not resisting one experience over another, but you are strong and can honestly, truthfully, and open-heartedly relate to your world around. Is this of understanding now? For if you place your happiness upon external things you are but merely tossed to and fro, and in this can never find it - can never sustain it. With much Love and Light – Abe.

6. You say that we place gadgets as a go-between in our conversations. Isn't this also the same for how many people live their lives? They place go-betweens to mediate direct connection, both with the world around them and themselves. It is a form of projection. In this, we do not know how to truly be with ourselves. Isn't this also like living within secondary forms - as if living within a veiled reality?

Yes, this is true. For you do so place yourselves, or more so that in which you consider to be yourselves, in-between all interactions. This is why we say vulnerability is key, for you are not upholding this filter, taking things the wrong way, distorting truth. Gadgets are but a physical manifestation of that in which you already hold. Is this of understanding now?

7. As part of our becoming, and to return 'back home,' should we not be shifting to use an updated vocabulary? Many of our words and languages emphasize the division and separateness of life. To access a more unified consciousness, should we not be using a vocabulary that speaks of the holistic, the integral, the whole seeing? Isn't it true to say that the language/vocabulary we use contributes to the programming we have?

Language will always be a divider. But you see, the language does not need to change but merely the conditions, the meanings of it. And that only comes about by firstly unifying self. You see, words are dividers - it conceptualizes that in which cannot be conceptualized. But you see, it does not need to be dropped - it just needs to be seen in a new light. Is this of understanding now? We would hear you say that well, for unification, all we have are words to allow people to understand. And if these are so still stuck in conditions of separateness, of division, then how will it ever come across? And we would say, you could also talk and change the language to be that of unification. But it would still be divided; it would still not allow the person to see this. It has to resonate within - you have to have the space first. Do you see this now?

8. Are we trying 'too hard' to try to 'be' something, to 'get' somewhere, and all these phrases and ideologies of accomplishment? Haven't we already accomplished 'the art of being'? Now we need to see clearly where we are instead of running ahead without a roadmap? Could Abe comment?

You see, there is no road map. It is but likened to taking a step from truth each and every time; and the step appearing in unison with the foot being placed back down. You only ever see clearly when you are back here, and it does seem contradictory in a way that so many speak of a 'no-self.' This is but true, but it does not help you in this process to try to diminish it. You would be but caught up in a never-ending battle. For how can you diminish a 'nothing'? For you see, that is the human contract, the human story. No, it is about bringing it back in - no longer hooks placed in many a thing, an experience, a person. No, it is about really bringing it home. Not to say that you are stuck within this body, a whim to all of its conditions, but free as a bird to soar. Is this of understanding now? It is about being and allowing and doing all in unison. With much Love and Light – Abe.

9. The evolution of consciousness is still a 'New Age' concept to many people. And yet it is necessary to shift from older forms of thinking. After all, consciousness is accessed - it is 'allowed' - rather than created in our vibratory mind. Isn't it imperative that humanity understands that consciousness is allowed rather than created if we are to truly participate with our world and reality?

It is but so an allowance. You see, you as humans, you seem to claim so much and in this do so make life hard for yourselves. For then, you have to make something happen that in which happens spontaneously. With Love and Light – Abe.

10. As you have said, people are swayed by the world around them - 'tossed to and fro with life's circumstances.' Many people are trying hard to change the world - to impact it, to force human action upon it. The world is responding in ways we cannot fully understand. How can we more genuinely relate to the world and should we be forcing ourselves upon it?

You see, when something is forced upon anything you but know that something is not wanting it, is resisting - it is but not resonating. You have to sync up to know what is truly of alignment and you only know this when you are but truly aligned with yourselves. Is this of understanding now?

11. We talk often about not relying on external things. Or by not placing our expectations externally - by 'coming home' to our inner nature. Many people will consider this approach ineffective in that it does not help to deal with current global issues and such social and environmental crisis? What does it really mean to 'be effective'? Is it not also important to act externally and to place our aims, intentions, and some degree of expectations upon the world outside of us?

You see, what would be the point of placing something that is so magnetized to just go back to where it started off again? You see, you would have to move the magnet - that magnet is but you and your own resonation, your own patterns. You do so, and we say this with great love, you do so make a lot of work for yourselves. And you see that, always out there, things need fixing, need aligning. But then they bounce back - they realign to that resonation and that is you. It is but an endless loop. You need to be the one that breaks these patterns first - or else, what would be the point of any action? You are only going to allow things to spring back. Is this of understanding now?

12. One philosopher (G.I. Gurdjieff) said that people should not identify with things external to them. By identifying we forget ourselves. In order to remember internally, we need to stop identifying externally. Could Abe comment on this?

It is so this way. And although this does seem a selfish act, or somewhat lazy way to be, it is not. Tend to this first - it is of essence, for you will not be able to align. You will not make new pathways without for you have not tended to the already established pathways within. It will be but futile work and in this a fight, a struggle. Is this of understanding now?

13. To return to the question of language, and how it is a divider. We can also say that certain forms of language have been utilized - such as by poets and mystics - specifically to trigger new pathways in consciousness - is this not so? For example, certain forms of tales, nonsensical poems/writings, imaginative texts - have not these been used consciously by people to help develop an evolution of consciousness with human culture?

It is. But hear this, it is not so much the words but the way in which it gives to create space. Do you see this commonality within all of these texts? They are not defining things for they are just giving space to but turn back in - to give space to question. Only in space can you arise, can you question - is this not true? Do you see this clearly now? You see, what we are not doing is diminishing great works. It is not so these are but catalysts on the road to evolution, but it does so still define things. It is so this way, for this is your language. It is in the trickiness of creating space - and if you do so create this in language, you create this in others. With much Love and Light – Abe.

14. How would people experience and relate to the world around them if they shifted from a rational-logical state of consciousness into an integral, unified, holistic form of consciousness? What primarily would change?

You see, it would change in a way so that, like yourself, things are seen as unified. It is within your own seeing clearly.

204

But hear this, it is not a one-off and you instantly see unification - you need to clean out all that has been keeping you from seeing it. Is this of understanding now? You see, it has to be rooted - it has to be established. It has to be your own default setting - this is the work of it. With much Love and Light – Abe.

15. Is it correct in saying that in order to evolve as a species we need to evolve through various forms of consciousness? It has been said that humanity began with an archaic mode of consciousness; then passed to magical, to mythical, to mental. And now is shifting into an integral mode of consciousness. As these modes of consciousness shift, so does our perception of the world and the way we interact with it. What would Abe say about this?

We would like to say again about the Russian dolls - a doll within a doll within a doll. The smaller down, the more confined it is. And evolution is but cracking these open so that indeed there are none. It is almost like the air inside the smallest is but the same as all around outside of it - you are constricted in space. But you see, the more and more space is being given, the more you crack open. It is not that it is not present, it's just that you are but expanding the space for more air flow. Is this of understanding now?

These confinements, we would like to add, are that of your signatures, of bodily constrictions, and the vibratory essence that does so go with it. You are but the constrictor and also the space. With much Love and Light – Abe.

We would but like to come forth this morning with an important message; and although it does not sound like it is, it is an important step on this journey. You see, in your societies there is a hierarchical system. It is evident in many a thing, from the clothes that you wear to the food that you eat, to the job that you work. And are all differing labels, differing conditions. You do so put upon people for you think 'ahhh, the professor - I bet he would be an interesting chap.' But you see, it may not be true, and an old drunk at your local pub may indeed have more a true word to say that would 'wow' you. You see, you do so place these hierarchical systems between you and other people. You create barriers when indeed sometimes you need to create space; that is only created when you do so decide to listen. Not just to the writer or the professor or the scientist or so-called expert but to all; as if you can learn so much from everyone you meet, for this is true. But do so hear this, this works but both ways, for snobbery has been put into the higher class when indeed it works both ways - do you see this subtly clever divide? Listen with an open heart - you will find inspiration within some of the most darkest of places, and in this bring light. Light is not something being of a holy presence, as depicted in times gone by, but the light of your consciousness - the light of truth. It is okay to listen to people with the knowledge they hold, that they have picked up and studied. But you see, sometimes it is the one that has nothing to lose in terms of status that really does speak the truth. With much Love and Light - Abe.

16. Thank you, Abe. You are right in pointing out the hierarchical nature of our societies. Humanity has been conditioned by status and hierarchy for as long as our history records - from priests to royalty, from religions to

governments. We feel many of these to be controlling and social management systems. Is it now time to both individually and socially move away from our reliance upon such status systems? Can our societies function without hierarchical systems?

You see, the only reason you do so rely on them is when you feel there is but no other option. For you see, a drug addict or gang member could see life as so constantly feeding into something that does not so either benefit self or society. And you see, with society you have built this pyramid of status and acceptance, and now do not so know how to get away from it. You see, there has to be that dissatisfaction of one's being to move into another direction - that dissonance of being. And so long as you are feeding into it, and being fed by it, you see no indifference for you haven't had the space to truly feel this. But you see, as long as these structures do so upheld this dissonance, this false premise, and you are but vibrationally attached to it, invested in it, you see it is feeding you and you are but feeding it and strengthening it. There are always other options - you are an infinite being and just because something worked previously does not mean it does so now. Give yourselves a break, a breath, a little inch of space, to see this now and to realign, readjust. With much Love and Light - Abe.

17. Even as we advance towards technologically modern societies, there is a widening gap between the 'haves' and 'have-nots' - between the rich and the poor. And this gap continues to widen. This is contrary to a consciousness of unification. Can Abe see this situation changing, or will this

situation deepen until we have a collective shift in our thinking patterns?

You see, for anything to change - and to change significantly - it has to but get to breaking point. And the more and more people that do so hold onto these conditions, that do no longer serve them, the deeper they dig their heels in. To say no, to resist what is trying to reform, the deeper it will have to go to root out. You see, it is but all dependent on how much humanity goes with or against this new direction. It is of dissonance, and then realignment and allowance. The new flow becomes greater and greater, but sometimes also so does the resistance to it. Is this of understanding now?

18. Our modes of living - our hierarchical structures, for example - are the results of a limited consciousness that perceives a 'separateness.' We feel this is due to the dominance of the brain's left hemisphere. Our neuroscience has talked about integrated left-right hemisphere brain functioning. Is it the case that we need to integrate our left-right brain hemispheres to re-wire our brain patterns to access a unity consciousness? Isn't it true that the right-brain hemisphere has greater access to the unified field?

You see, that over times gone hierarchical structures have but been very male orientated and it is but true that your science has depicted the two hemispheres as male and female. But you see, there is but this split in your conscious experience and therefore a split in society. You see this is evident, but you do so also see that it is becoming closed in your thinking towards that of female and male qualities. What is true, and many people don't see, is that you have but both qualities - or you would not be human. But what has been taught, and then pathways created within, are of these seemingly separate hemispheres. It is true that your conditioning is one of separateness - of Male and Female - like within the brain. Whichever side has been more prominently nurtured and dismissed whilst growing up, this is but influenced by parental society, experience, culture. But you see, what unity is, is merging these two equally. For there are but times that you will use your head more, become more focused, more logic and reason. But there will also be times when you will but nurture and care. And this is not dependent on your physical qualities - this is for EVERY person EVERYWHERE. And also, to allow this flow of continuance rather than suppress one over the other due to your own conditioning - let it flow and but balance itself out despite what your society says is right and wrong. Allowance is key to this natural flow - to rewire, reconnect, and create new pathways within to enable it without. Is this of understanding now?

19. Is it also the case that many religious-spiritual-wisdom traditions have used techniques such as music, meditation, visualization, and readings, to assist in this re-wiring toward left-right brain integration?

It can be so with resonance, yes. It can but rebalance. But hear this, in your own rebalance, in your own space, you can take time out. You have the space in-between this constant resonation to make new pathways. We are not saying these do not help, not at all - it can give the space to refocus, to readjust, to realign. But you see, the resonation is already there. You just need space to reconfigure; and if these do help, then be it so. With much Love and Light - Abe.

We would also like to add but one thing - that life is so simple, and humans come up with many complex ideas to help to realign to that of truth. What needs to be seen now is not in others, as for one to teach you these visualizations or to listen to the music or readings. If this so does help, does allow you to sync back up, use these tools and realize they are but tools. They are there to use. But please, please, do so hear this - it is not so much about the thing but more so how you respond to this thing. It is not so much about what that is doing to me but the more so about the space you are allowing for yourself, for something else to emerge - it is never not there. Is this of understanding now?

20. It is true that all the exercises, rituals, or practices we use – whether yoga, meditation, visualizations, etc – are tools. Yet are not tools needed at this stage as a form of guidance to help a person find their genuine space, their way to an awakened consciousness? Has not humanity always used tools in order to mediate between their physical state and Reality? Tools are how we navigate through and experience the material world – is this not so?

Yes, it can be so. But that is indeed if that works for you; and as differing you are, there are but differing tools to create space. What does so give you your space? You do so know that no matter what, when you give space you do so allow all that is but already. There is nothing amiss, there is nothing other - it is in the allowance of it, is it not? And you can but reach this by simply doing nothing. We are not dismissing these tools, these

210

activities. But you see, sometimes you get dragged into the comparison of such things that - 'my practice or meditation is but more spiritual, more aligned than your tool is.' The path, when you see there are but many paths and many tools, what we want to put forth that it does not take years to have to perfect a practice - it is always available, always present. You just need to drop it for a moment to allow something new, something true. You see, you can all easily become aligned - you just need space to readjust and these things are well and good. But hear this, they can also get in the way of real progress for tools are just that - a tool. And once the work is but done you can place them back down again. For you see, you wouldn't continue to use the hammer if it is not needed for it will only damage the wood. Is this of understanding now?

21. Humanity is out-of-balance in its relations with the world around it – this much is obvious. Could Abe describe how should our relations be like with the external world? In an ideal situation, what would our relations be like?

Firstly, you have to see that the relation to oneself is of paramount. Now, it can be so that your own relationship with what you class as yourselves has to be one of acceptance, of allowing all your parts. For if you reject a part of yourselves, you are in hindsight only going to find it outside of yourselves in that of other people. You project, you try to fix outside of yourselves, helping others when really you need to be more accepting of all your parts. For if not, there is never unity, there is never wholeness within your being; and therefore, it can never be in your physical reality. You are but not synced up. Is this of understanding now? If you are but asking a direct question as to what all relations should be like, then I am afraid it is not as simple as that for each one is differing, is unique. That is the beauty of humanity and but very few can see this so much now, for within unity there is but much room for uniqueness, for diversity. With much Love and Light - Abe.

22. It seems like the faculty of human communication is dimmed, or not working at a high capacity. We communicate largely through the form of language. Is it not the case that the natural world is constantly in a form of 'sense communication' with humans, yet we fail to perceive this? Could Abe say more about how the external world is communicating – or trying to communicate – with humans?

You see, you are always in communication with your external world, for you are but always emitting a frequency. And therefore, are always speaking without words; and this is true for everything. When you realize this silent communication that does so come up as feelings, you can but learn again, to be sensitive again, to vibrational resonance. But you see, your culture has taught many whom are sensitive that you are too sensitive. And this can be so if you do not strengthen this, for you can be tossed to and fro from all the vibratory communication that some are not aware of. You see, many try to shut it down for it doesn't benefit them in a world of logic and reason. But you see, this can also be your greatest gift - you just have to become more aware of it, to strengthen your own resonance so not to be so deeply affected. We see that we may have strayed a little, but this is important to know for you are but in a web of vibrational communication - you just need to feel again, to hear. Is this of understanding now?

23. Are there external factors which influence the perception and sensibility of human communication? For example, the phases of the moon. Does the moon affect the human communicative faculties – and how?

There is, like we say, vibratory resonance communicating to and through you, and from you all the time. But if we take the moon, for example, it is seen as a very much feminine energy. The moon does not communicate, but what do you so feel when you look up at it and give the space to perceive it? We ask this for you then sync up - you hear it whisper vibrationally for you have created space, a vacuum, for something to connect. You have created vibrational resonance. In a way, it is all dependent upon that of what you are pointing at. Is this of understanding now? It is but of intentional alignment; the same way that you would hang up on the phone to speak to another. This is but the same, and it is done through your very own resonance - you just need to sync up. With much Love and Light - Abe.

24. Going back to the issue of our vibrational communication with the external environment, you say that we live in a web of vibrations. At this current time, our modern societies are close to unveiling a new wavelength of wireless communications called 5G. Many people are saying this is dangerous as it can affect human health and even create greater dissonance. What would Abe say to this?

You see, you do not need something as so. For you see, the whole point of the fifth dimension or the fifth state, and we liken it to that in which you but call 5G, is not something apart from that in which you are - just a different resonance of being, of consciousness. And you see, that for us to come forth in such a way there is but no tool to do so for the brain is evolving to accept these resonances without a middleman. You need to detach, to realign, so that all can receive in this way without the manmade structures. Is this of understanding now? It does not need to be filtered through anything but rather allowed to reroute. With Love and Light - Abe.

25. We would like to return to the subject of intentional alignment. It seems, as you indicate, that it is possible for humans to have a vibrational communication with the external world, such as with the moon or with Nature. Is this an ability that humanity has forgotten - and was it ever active within humanity in past times? And in our present era, how may we develop this capacity for intentional alignment and communication?

You see, it has but always been a trait of yours as human beings. For you see, this has never been amiss, but it was but always dependent upon the mechanism in which it was filtered through. Yes, the connection may have been more harmonious in past times, but the intellect was very low and did so make it a survival game. Humanity has done good work and not all is dire. For you see, you have but done many things and many a good things, although we do not like to define it as such. But hear this, you are but in a new era and the intellect has been much too prominent and not allowed this communication and therefore has misaligned all in that you are and in all that you can be. For it would be a shame to waste all this acquired intellect upon such travesty, for you are but missing out upon your own development - your own wholeness of being. Is this of understanding now?

26. It is said that many species in Nature exhibit a group-soul - is this true? And what can Abe say about the human group-soul - is the 'way back home' to our unity also about reunifying and consciously expressing the human group-soul?

You see, you are but one soul - if you would like to state it this way. But we do not relate so well with the word 'soul' for it does so have this notion of being something other and really it is an interaction - not even that, but emergence. For you see, it is all but one and for us to say any different it would be untrue. But hear this, there are signatures that do so relate, that resonate - this is when you would say you have found a 'soul mate.' But you see, it could just be that they are resonating the same - you have but similar signatures. Is this of understanding now? There is also the fact that resonation can occur when you see that HOME resonance. And it is but evident in all, and like a little gem it sets off a twinkle in the eye. And you meet that in this way by simply being around someone whose own signature is not so prominent in that they allow this home resonance - this unity. You can but only want to sync up; you are but attracted and you do not know why sometimes. Do you see this?

27. For example, the insects known as bees are generally respected and loved by humanity. We are in awe of their abilities to pollinate flowers and create honey. Bees are said to exist in a group-soul. Is there a possibility for the human group soul to communicate with the group soul of a bee colony?

You are but always communicating, but you are not so aware - you resonate, and they do so pick it up. You are but always talking by resonation. You see, you do so allow some unity. For you see that the bees pollinate the flowers and they collect honey - you have but this natural resonance, this natural order of being. And things can sometimes get too caught up, for when you see this unity you can try to control these connections as to work harder and faster for your own needs. But you see, you misalign this communication between things and therefore create dissonance. We can see that this may seem like it is going against what others say or sometimes that in which we have said. But you see, you do need this space for things to line themselves up again and re-resonate - to sync up by themselves, for it falls back into its natural flow of communication. And this is true that sometimes you just need to leave things alone to give other things space too - to realign, to recommunicate again. With Love and Light - Abe.

28. The philosopher-mystic Rudolf Steiner said that human speech is a spiritual activity as well as an art form, lending itself to real interaction with both higher spiritual worlds and the human world of social conversation. Could Abe comment on this?

It may have been so, and is an articulated way for your species to communicate. We are but not dismissing it in any way, shape or form. But words without feelings are just empty words. They have no vibrational resonance as to reach past the material existence. You have to feel that in which you write; you have to feel that in which you speak - have you not come across a person that is but monotone? For in their very speech they could talk about something that could so interest you deeply, but they have no feeling behind it, and it soon becomes tiresome to listen. And you do so wonder why you liked this subject in the first place at all - is this seen now?

29. In this way, the resonance is often more important that the subject of what is being communicated? So certain books, for example, can have an effect, or function, through a vibrational resonance regardless of their written content? Isn't this the same with these Abe Communications - that is, the vibrational resonance you are transmitting is just as, or maybe more, important that the actual content?

It is but to do with the intention that gives words meaning, that give words resonance. And it is true, it is not always about the topic but how it does so make you feel - how it allows resonation or not. It is so indeed with the resonation, and also with Abe. But you see, what does so allow you to resonate with these words? Is it because it is engaging or is it but a topic you like? We ask because like everything, it is what you feed back into also. For it has to have this feeling, and the feeling is allowing Nicola but to type; if it was not of resonation to her we would not be able to come forth - there would be dissonance. You see, speech is vibrational, is it not? It is felt upon the eardrum and converted. It has to be sensed and sense is feeling. You say when something falls upon deaf ears, it is really saying that is does not resonate. And it is not the actual content that does not resonate but the feeling - this feeling is HOME. Do you see this connection here?

30. To return to the question of allowing the natural flow of communication, such as in Nature - this suggests that our current thinking about intervening with the environment to reduce, or stop, climate change is wrong thinking. Would you say it is best to step back and allow Nature to readjust and find her balance? Will it not make things worse if humanity tries to intervene in these processes with its current split consciousness?

Oh yes, this is so. We do so feel very strongly in this sense; that is why we say firstly give yourselves space, for then it may allow you to then do but the same for everything else. You see, realignment can but happen - it is but something that happens spontaneously. And this is such of all life - it finds but its own balance. For you see, when you stop trawling the oceans and poisoning them, they repopulate. For if you were to allow this space, things would so find its own harmonious balance again - do you see this great paradox? For you see, you do not know what everything should so resonate at, and therefore should let everything else find its own balance, its own hum. With Love and Light - Abe.

You see, feeling is vibration that is not tainted initially. It is this HOME vibration - that is, until the head gets a hold and converts it. But you see, it is not about one or the other. It is but always in human form going to be tainted in one way or another, for you cannot be void of your own signature - and would be an endless pursuit to try to do so. We are saying feel again, give space - for this unity is about allowing both and that is allowing feelings again, whatever that may be. And you see vulnerability as a curse, but it is really a gift for it is a vibration, a truth - and then you can through your own signature express this. You are

218

but uniting head and heart - masculine and feminine, ying and yang. This is but the point of it all - this is THE WAY BACK HOME. With much Love and Light - Abe.

There is but one last thing we would like to state today and that is this - you see, the problem is not so much feeling. You all feel, that is human - albeit a few who close it down significantly. But you see, it is not the problem that you do not feel as much as it is that you rationalize far too much that in which you do feel. Imagine if it was so that you as human beings communicated more so what you feel - if you allowed this vulnerability to another. Would you not be more so true? Wouldn't the other then open more and more up to you because you would feel comfortable to do so? For you would also be true, creating close bonds, resonance, intimate relationships - not just with the ones you love but the same to all of humanity. Almost like a constant edging forward, allowing people to come out of their protective shells, little by little, knowing that it is safe to feel. In fact, it is beautiful, it is freeing, it is true. This is but so important to allow this space for others to come forth. But hear this, you have to be accepting of self, of true to self - united in all of your being. For this is true Unity; and we never state Unity is perfect, but it is beautiful - it is but true. For you see, in all of this to have a ripple effect you have to start at where it all started, and it all starts with you - then your close relations, and then out further, and further. With much Love and Light – Abe.

We do so also see within your existence that resonation is hijacked in a way to get what YOU WANT - but what you want is not always that in which you need. And to have unity in motion you need to allow space, like we say, for first this to move and flow. You see, we have not yet spoken upon this signature;

219

in a way, this soul as you call it. But you see, it does so have a pattern, a beat, for it is within your physical existence now and is susceptible to this base line resonation - one could say of cause and effect. But hear this, this too can be overridden - you are never but doomed because of what has happened before. It all depends thereafter on what you do now, what you send out. But you do so have this baseline - some would call it karma or ancestral karma - but it is just resonance and does not have to stick. It too can be but cleaned out - and is more often than not transmuted. But this is what is passed on genetically - a genetic vibrational imprint of resonation. This is but contained within your DNA structure and is also dependent upon your own experience and your own resonation. Do you so see this pattern of vibration now and how it is but passed on? You see, through time and your own expansion in consciousness you then allow this to be evident in new life. You can nurture this natural progression within your children for conscious evolution. With much Love and Light – Abe.

31. You have said that some people have a resonance signature that is not so prominent, in that they allow this 'home resonance.' Does to have a less prominent personal signature suggest a person with less ego? For us, it seems that the ego strengthens the personal resonance in a way that overrides the 'home resonance' that is unity. What would Abe say to this?

That is but true, and we speak of the overcoat again. And it is but all very well to have this signature so long as you are so aware of it. Is this of understanding now? For you see, for any one thing to be of prominence it does so leave out other factors that in which form unity and are your very essence. With much Love and Light – Abe.

32. It seems that to find the resonance of unity, a person needs to balance the resonance of ego and of the sense of the individual, with the resonance of being more than an individual body. This could be disruptive for some people, especially today when our societies teach the need for individualism. Does 'the way back home' require that people lose their attachments to individualism? What can Abe say to this?

It is not so much in individualism being lost, but more so a coming back home to your natural being. It is never about one or the other but always a knowing - for if you are knowing that you are but oneness then the stickiness of life is not so sticky. You can allow it a little more, it flows. You need to always create a little space for this to be seen, for in this space you see that you are more than this encapsulated being. Is this of understanding now?

33. Human societies and cultures have been built upon the stories we tell ourselves - tales, mythologies, group-identity, for example. These stories (or ideologies) have been necessary for creating social order and structure. Do we still need these same structures of order? Is it now time to leave these mythologies behind? Should we be developing new mythologies/stories to replace them?

You see, and this will sound counter-productive to that in which you have been long taught - but you do not need these social structures. When you are back in unity with your own being you see that these are really just structures layered upon that in which you already are at nature. And in some ways causes more discord because of the separation caused - for they will say this is moral and that is not. When you are but back to your natural resonance there is no need for so much naming and blaming. Life will not fall into chaos because you do not have someone lording over you. Tell us, has this worked so far in this time of evolution - or has it caused much separation, much discord? And we do so say this with much love for life - to change, you but have to change first and you have to at some point, you have to piece it all back together again. You have to see the bigger picture - humanity are a part and not the whole. Time to unify, time to sync back up. As for the mythologies, the stories, they have but served a purpose. But you see, it is now time to not place things outside of yourselves. For you see, in these stories they are taking to be of real, but many were an analogy to that in which you already are. Now that you have evolved, and continue to do so on a consciousness level, you will see that many a story can be linked back to this unity. For you see, as humans you can get wrapped up so much with the character and forget the meaning - the nugget of truth it was really pointing at. With much Love and Light – Abe.

34. Thank you, Abe. You say that we do not need our social structures when we are back in unity with our own being. This may be true, yet we are not in unity with our being - not yet. And so, we need some sort of social structure, do we not? To not have social structure would result in chaos. In general, people need some sort of order. A life without a form of social order would be more disruptive. Could Abe comment on this?

You see, yes, the whole of your planet will not be of unity of being, not at any one time - this is also the play of unity. But you see, your structures will but fall because you are not feeding into them. But this does not mean that others will not reform in your physical existence that does so resonate to the prominent energy at that time on your planet. Is this of understanding now? You see, it is not about the falling, for this is inevitable. New resonation for you will create new pathways - that in which syncs up. There will always be chaos when change is allowed. But you see, chaos is just the reconstructing; chaos is the realigning - and really, chaos is the space too. With much Love and Light – Abe.

35. These Abe communications focus strongly on unity and coming back to our natural resonance. Is this not more an evolutionary goal than a short-term possibility? Is human unification, as Abe sees it, not a potential for far, far into humanity's future?

See this, you but always have to come back. You have for far too long been focused on your physical reality. It is all well and good to know that this is part of your existence for you see it is what you are. One could say the human being is spirit and matter. As your bodies have evolved your physicalness, you have but allowed more and more consciousness. Being zero-state, you are but the dance of polarity - you are also the unity, it just needs to be uncovered. You see, there is but no long or short of it and if you are asking of where this is meant to be and stay put, then we would say of course not - life is change, life is but rhythm. But to allow this flow you but need to come back into your being - to gather the parts that have defined you as separated beings within the world around you. Is this of understanding now?

36. Does Abe consider that these communications will be for everyone? Or will they appeal to people who are resonating in a certain way as to be seeking for answers, seeking for change in their lives? What type of people does Abe feel will respond to these messages? And will it not take time for these messages to be absorbed, take root, and create new pathways in people's minds?

We see that there is a divide in consciousness. We see there is also a divide in people - it is seen, it is evident, so there will not be people whom are actively looking for this kind of information and should never be forced upon anyone. It is but an allowance - a resetting, a realigning. For anything to be forced would go directly against that in which we wish to convey. You do so see, like anything new it is all dependent upon the individual - for how quickly they become to the state of allowing, for in this allowing is where things truly take route, where the true journey can begin. Hear this, there is many a tradition and the reason we do not bite to any practice or ritual or sacred place is really our message too - that you are it. There is no longer a need to look outside yourselves, confusing always, holding off to perfect this practice and that, and in this never really practicing it at all. You are but us and we are but you. It is just that you have the point of place, the physicality - nothing is ever above or beyond but here in the allowing. With Love and Light – Abe.

37. Abe stated at the beginning of these recent communications that you wished to explore in-depth the subject of relations - 'that being to each other, to your world, to the universe.' We have explored relations being to each other. And we have now discussed our relations to the world. Before we consider moving on to discuss relations to the universe, is there any other areas that Abe would wish to cover regarding our relations to the world?

We would like to but say one thing, and that is this: although we talk about differing relations, we really also want you to see the differing levels of which are not ever really differing at all - never really apart from one another. For the relation to oneself determines all these other levels; and again, can be but likened to the Russian doll analogy. You just have to crack open yourselves to allow more and more connection. With much Love and Light and continued communication – Abe.

There is but one thing that we would like to come forth and discuss today before moving on, and in some way is still on relation to self. You see, the 'way back home' is home to yourselves; and when we say selves, we do not mean your vibrational signature essence. No, we mean the underlying essence that you are - this beat, if you will, which is in harmony already. You see, it is in the allowing, in the space, that this is allowed to emerge, to strengthen, to be rooted. And we are never one to say that you should but transcend to this state - but ground it, unite it with all of your being. Or more so, allow it to sync, to rhythm you up. Is this of understanding now? You see, in this syncing-up life can but flow - it is allowed, it is but whole, and it is therefore unification within. We do not denounce such practices that will give space, will allow this arising. But you see, what we say is that it is not necessary. Find something that does so bring you back to this when you feel that you are being pulled out into the world - always try to bring yourselves BACK HOME. In this home place you can feel your body - you can feel the world. You can but feel and be with all of your loved ones, truly and openly. You can connect to the shop keeper, the banker, or the baker, because you are HOME - and you are open in that space. We would like to say we will meet you there and that is but only when you have finally met yourself. With much Love and Light – Abe.

SECTION FOUR
Contact with the Greater Universe

1. Thank you, Abe, for your communications regarding our relations with each other and to the world around us. As suggested, we would now like to move on to discuss our relations to the universe. This is a large subject. Could Abe possibly give some indications of where we might begin, and which topics are to be considered within this subject area?

We would like to say that, yes, it is a large area in terms of undiscovered knowledge. But as we say, is likened to the system that does so reside within. There is but always new knowledge of these systems being discovered but is always known to the knower - the ones who do so have this within - and therefore must reflect outside. We feel it be appropriate to start with this - with this seemingly separateness of being but never apart from the whole system. We would say this would be a good starting point so that what is within is also without. We think this the right place to start now. As for topics, and what we will continue to say for this whole relations conversation, is to go with it and feel - feel what is to be asked for we have no specification of how this should go. But more so, FEEL this connection and allow it to flow effortlessly - this triad of being necessary for these communications to come forth in such a way. With much Love and Light – Abe.

2. Thank you, Abe, for your continued communications and guidance. We shall proceed with questions and dialogue regarding human relations to the universe. To begin, you have said that a good place to start is with our feeling of separateness of being when in reality we are never apart from the whole system. What are some of the features of this whole system? We may recognize some 'sense' of its presence without being consciously aware of it. How do we feel its presence in our physical lives?

Ahh, another new direction. But you see, all the same - all inter-looping, interacting, and intertwining. What looks like differing conversations can always be really seen as just the one conversation. You do so feel that there are things that need to be directed and that is but well and good to get back to the bare bones again. But realize this too will but have to be dropped for if you are to see any truth, to fall back into the system harmoniously. You but sense and feel the world around you, but you do so feel that you have taken yourself to be out of this system, out of this connection. But in essence, you are but really accessing your part. For you see, you cannot ever be above it. You can never be out of it. You can think you are, and that is where this discourse happens. But you see, you are not, and affect it in such a way to what you do outside really does have an effect unto yourselves - it can only ever be this way. It is but madness when looked upon with eyes open. You are but only ever realizing what you are, and sometimes that in which you are not. If you are but wanting to know how you can become more sensitive to these vibrational connections, these pathways, this grid, then we would say bring it back - reel it in and be still, be quiet, and just be - if only just for a moment. With much Love and Light – Abe.

3. Most of the universe exists only in our speculations, or imagination, as we have no direct experience of it. We have only glimpsed it through our devices (telescopes). Perhaps what we are viewing is not the real universe at all but our filtered interpretation of it? Does our view of the universe have a relation to the universe-as-reality?

You see, you can but only work with that in which you have on a physical level to widen this scope, to access more. For in the opening up of the expansiveness in which this universe is, are you not just allowing more pathways to be but built? When more pathways are being created, then are you not then seeing deeper truths, deeper relations? This is but true on all levels, from the microscopic to the infinite. You are but seeing this interconnected relation, their fractal relation, and this is allowing you to be but placed back with it. If you are stating if the relation to which you use your tools for viewing are of un- truth, then you see it is not but black and white. For you see, everything is but filtered through something, and the more filters the more it does get distorted. But hear this, this analogy again of the Russian dolls, it has to be but cracked open; and it also has to be in relation to that of the mechanism that is receiving. It is equal relation to that of which you are at now and is never wrong or right but.....this now. Is this of understanding now? For you see, if you are not internally creating these pathways then you are not so either externally - you are at where you are at. What we are here for is to sync you back up, to reach back to this inner space, this inner knowing, so that you can but take new steps forward - un-splintered, creating unity, realizing you're already wholeness. That softness is not always weak, and hardness is not always strong, but always a dance, always relative. With much Love and Light – Abe.

4. Our human science tells us that the universe stretches for unknowable light-years, beyond our comprehension. For many people, the universe is so far away from us that it is not worth thinking about. Yet are we not intricately connected to the universe? And how?

Yes, we say you are but never apart. And you see, this is the importance; not just for yourselves to keep balance but also on other levels, for they all are affected in one way or another - maybe not the same but of some affect. You see, like the way your body functions - the cells, the organs, the nervous system - when out of sync, when out of the conversation, there is discourse on differing levels - there is but Dis-ease. This is true without. You may not be able to comprehend your power of being, and this is so of all life. You see, as humans you do so like to use things to the benefit of self; and in this, you forget about the whole workings and that in which it will displace. Sometimes it is well and good to but leave things alone to regain their own balance again. It is this so for the bringing back to self - you become aware, you come back to your body, to the senses, and your senses can but feel when all synced up. As within the five states, you are whole body experiencing awake, consciously awake, and are of these patterns for you are not weakened but hold steady this core. Is this of understanding now? For in this core you can feel this pattern, this grid - this is but why we feel the exercise is good, it strengthens this core. But it also has to resonate with you in this - you will sense this grid, you will feel it. We do realize that on this question we may have strayed a little from the original meaning. But again, you see, it is but always relative - always but ONE conversation and we would like you to see in the complexity of conversation, of but language, there really is simplicity. With much Love and Light – Abe.

5. You have said previously that we are connected in a web of relations that are also timelines. Humans have often thought of timelines as linear. Yet you say that our timelines are in a web. Does this refer to our timelines after physical incarnation? Could you say more about this?

You see, you do so think of things as linear, as neat packages starting and finishing, and this is also well and good. But see this, it is not truth. It is by ways of measurement so that you can but slice and dice. But what we see is a highway of communication - no one direction, no one way, but intrinsically intertwined, inter-related, and interpreted wrong. For you see, as human beings you would find this incredibly overwhelming and incredibly disorganized, and in some way destructive for it is not measurable. For anything that is so intertwined can never be measured in whole, only ever in parts - and that is why there is never but a complete picture. It is patterned, there is but a beat. But you see, it is not stretched out but just a forever becoming - do you see this now? With much Love and Light – Abe.

6. Thank you for your answers so far about human relations with the universe. We would like to begin now by going back to the essential. What is the universe? Human scientists have given us a 'picture' of the universe as a collection of galaxies, star clusters, solar systems, etc. Yet this is only a physical image according to our filtered reality. We ask Abe - What is the universe?

Ah, you see, such vastness to be perceived and also such a vast answer would also have to be given. For although just one - as you see your entirety of your bodily system too - you see the universe. But you see only a snippet. The more so you see within, and see this interaction of complexities, the more so you see the direct relation to that of your outer systems spanning further afield, creating more and more. But you see, it is all but in relation from the smallest to what you see as the largest - an interrelation, a fractal relation of what looks like interdependent things, interdependent in space and time. And although your sciences are spanning and scanning and discovering, there is still so much to comprehend. For you see, what is inside you is directly relational to that outside of you; and also, that which is outside of you is directly relational to that within. For you see, if you really want to know this vastness in which you see before you - the one that you are but encompassed within - then firstly you must bring it back. For you see, there is never a definitive starting point of creation, but you can always start from here and know all - and what is here for us is within for you. And you do so see that the great expansiveness is but nothing without the correlation of your own being. Is this of understanding now?

7. Thank you, Abe. In your description, the universe is an interrelated, intertwined web of communication which, as you say, has a beat. If humans were able to develop their internal pathways, they would be able to enter into this web of communication and conversation – is this not so? How would you describe this experience?

There is but always a rhythm, a beat, at all differing levels. But hear this, only one symphony you correlate to the overall in that the rhythm is but synced up - is this of understanding now? This web of communication, this symphony, these vibrational patterns, can be synced back up. And this is but only done so when your conscious experience is then synced up, like the symbol. This can represent this correlation, the five states of being of your own being is where it needs to be firstly brought back to - do you so see this? For you to resonate these, to tune back up, for when the instrument is finally tuned it can then create a pattern, a rhythm, a beat. This web of consciousness is the beats and can correlate to this greater symphony of being. For you see, it is a web, a pattern - many complex patterns creating just one thing. But it always has to start at the instrument - the music is only created then by interconnection, interrelation. It is indeed, in one way, a complex system of particulars finding its way back to one another to unite. Its just that so many are not aware of their own rhythm and therefore will never be allowing to see or hear or play a part within this great symphony. What an advantage, what a blessing, and we would say what a life if but only seen - if only heard, if only allowed. With much Love and Light – Abe.

8. Are we right in saying that the true function of the human being is to be in communication with this 'universal conversational web' whilst at the same time being in physical incarnation? Did humans ever have this capacity, and used it, yet it has now been forgotten? By Abe wishing to get humans 'back in sync' – does this signify also in-sync with this universal web?

It is so. In sync with yourselves first and foremost, for you are but scattered. We see it as the ashes of the body left in differing places and this is what we see on a conscious level – scattered, splintered, call it what you will. But hear this, you have to bring these pieces back. Your consciousness, for every analogy we have described so far, is in the way to show that your strength now is on a conscious level. Is this of understanding now? You see, through your existence up to now it has been but a dance of polarities, one dominating over the other. But you can also see that this is cycles too - it is not of bad or of good but of rebalance - do you but understand this now? It is true that it is to be synced up with this web. But you see, you cannot create a rhythm if the musical apparatus is but out of tune - can you see this, do you not?

9. Abe has stated that when out of the universal conversation, there is discord on differing levels – a form of 'dis-ease.' It seems that the human nervous system is currently out-of-sync with the universal web – is this so? And if so, how did this de-syncing come about? Was it purely environmental factors, or were there other factors involved?

You see, it cannot be blamed upon any one thing, for you yourselves have to resonate at such a level too. It has been but a build-up and take it like so: a nice flowering plant in which you have never seen starts to naturally grow in your backyard. You see its beauty and maybe you pick a few of the flowers because they smell so sweet. And you pop them into a vase in your kitchen and every time you come in you smell the scent and see the beauty and look out of your window and see them in abundance, naturally flourishing. A friend comes around and sees the flowers, loves the smell, sees the beauty, and sees also they are abundant in your backyard. She asks to see if she could take a clipping and plants in her own backyard and soon has this plant abundant in her backyard. A friend, a scientist, says 'wow, I would like to study this plant' and comes back to the two ladies and says that the plant has so many beneficial components, to not allow any more clippings. For they should be contained and harvested and therefore taking out of their natural environment where they flourish, and monetize - sell back that in which is but of the nature of things. You see, with this story it is brought out of balance - an etching further and further, one side creating instability. For stability is but of balance - of the dance, the beat, the rhythm - for these create this symphony of existence on all levels. With much Love and Light – Abe.

10. Abe has said that 'you may not be able to comprehend your power of being' regarding our ability to affect the balance and harmony of universal relations, and therefore sometimes it is good to leave things alone. Does this mean that humanity is currently negatively affecting in some way the universal web? Is humanity mis-aligned in its evolutionary relationship with the universal balance?

It is but so - if you are but not unified in your being; if these but five states are not aligned. For you see, there is weakness in a thing that does so have many attachments for it is but tugged here, there, and everywhere. It is but time to strip it back to the bare bones for so much has been contaminated. You are but so out of rhythm that you do not even know there is but a rhythm of yourselves - never mind that symphony in which the beat, the rhythm, does so belong. If you cannot sync up to this, then you cannot sync up to these patterns. There have been always ones that never lose this rhythm, this beat - be it a singer, a dancer, a writer, a nurse, or beggar. For they see these patterns, this web, and can but realign. These could be said as the points to reawaken others, like spiders in point of place feeling the vibrations then quick to respond. But this web is not for purpose to capture - oh no, not in the slightest. But to flow again, to sync up, and reawaken your humanity, your rhythm - this is of true beauty. With much Love and Light – Abe.

11. We wonder if current very high levels of electromagnetic radiation – what many call electro-pollution – are affecting the human nervous system in a way that decreases the ability to sync or tune-in with the universal communicating web? If so, is this a purely accidental side-effect or is there some degree of human intention involved?

You see, what we would like to steer this question more towards would be of one that is not intentional but again relational. And you see, it's always of balance; and you can but never be balanced if you are splintered. We know you understand this by now, but we see that it is important to get across here. Nothing is ever good or bad but the thinking or resonation to it - the imbalance of oneself you could say. That yes, this can interfere with this rhythm in a way that if you are but in constant flow of this then you are not able to sync up for it is vibrational noise in which you are but encased and invested in, and that does so contaminate this line. But please do so hear this, it but only takes a nanosecond to look up and catch this rhythm again - it just depends if you keep that line open, if you continue to nurture this connection. Do you see this now?

We would but also like to add this: if you are but continuing to look down at your feet then how do you expect to see the beauty in where you are going? With much Love and Light – Abe.

12. Abe, you have said on several occasions that what is external to us is a reflection of what is internal – 'as above, so below.' Does this suggest that the more aligned we become – that is, the more access to consciousness we have – the more relations in the universe open up to us? If so, this would also suggest that not only do our sciences have a limited physical relation to the universe but that the way ahead to develop relations is psycho-spiritual and not scientific. Could you comment on this?

It but must always start from this for you to step forward. And as said previously, in a way of it taking just a nanosecond, we see it as being unscattered - your vibration gathered. You see, your consciousness does so leak out in many differing ways; that is why we do so state these five differing states. For many still see that it be of just the head; but you see, this is not true. You think if you do so concentrate in the head you will see, you will get something. But the more you strain the less you see, for you are but directing it in one certain place and this is not true. It is about all body, all feeling, uniting and syncing it all back up - in this you can only ever be back in this stream. For you see, you are not splintered, you are not fractured. Your sciences speak in parts, and this is again all well and good but for it to be understood at all, must be described in such a way as to see this relation, this pattern. We see this as shifting though, and has been shifting, and eventually will always come back to the one governing system - the one flow. It is but inevitable they do so have limitation. But hear this, they are also widening the spectrum for your human conceptions - this too is relational in its process. We would never say to rid of one for all does so have its place; but rather a look at what you are within before trying to master all the external first. This is a real step to truth, a real evolutionary leap in your conscious awareness. With much Love and Light – Abe.

13. Some of the wisdom traditions have made the analogy that humankind is in some kind of 'reality bubble' and within this bubble consists also our known universe. Is the universe as we can perceive it only that aspect which exists within our limited reality bubble?

You see, it is - and it is also not that way. For you see a bubble as something you are but encased in - a protection if you will - and then if popped you are but exposed to it all. We would rather see it is a light of conscious awareness; in a way, as what you hold within you will but see outside - it is relational and much common sense now. But people see that they can change by just forcing new thoughts - and that is not the way for it is always in the feeling. And we go back over many a thing we have said unto now, that the feeling is the vibrational resonance that you hold of your outside world - and it is but also that in which you hold of your inner too. Is this of understanding now?

We would also like to state that it too could be just seen as differing points reaching further and further - not really of linear points but more so of the points of perception. You create a pathway to then stand at another viewing point. But you see, these viewing points need to be firstly linked up within for you to ever see more without. With much Love and Light – Abe.

14. We have been led to believe that to develop our perceptions, in order to perceive beyond our limited splintered perspective, is a lifetime of initiatory self-development. And yet Abe says that 'it but only takes a nanosecond to look up and catch this rhythm again.' Is it really so easy to re-align ourselves, and how can the average person achieve this?

Ah, we just stated this nanosecond meaning at the start of conversation and yes, it is true, to snap and be able to but see these patterns. But you see, for anything to stick and to be natural to your being, you would firstly have to disconnect; or more so, allow old patterns of being to fall away. This means seeing this pattern and allowing yourself to sync back up with it. For you see, you could see something and but still show a blind eye to it and shun it for that is much easier to stay but where you are - is this not true? We wouldn't like to state that it is a lifetime notion, although it is well to be conscious and here. But you see, when you learn to drive you but have to put in effort - you have to learn. This is the beauty of human nature too; but after a while driving does become natural - it is easy not to have to think of it. What we say is not to slog away at being a driver but keep checking in that you have not but picked up bad habits or habits of others along the way. With Love and Light – Abe.

15. Over history, many religions have tried to develop cosmologies in order to understand how humanity relates to the grander sacred cosmic order. And yet it can be said that these interpretations have been found lacking in relation to the needs of today. Is it not the case that external social-cultural and religious institutions are no longer sufficient to provide for the developmental needs of humanity? Is the way forward - the way back home - now an individual inward path that each person must be responsible for?

This is but a great question and does so tie it all in well and neatly. It is but time in your human species to go into this dip of this wave pattern. This is seen as the resting point - but really is not so, for much internal work can be done. The master looks as if he is not doing much in a day; but you see, he is but the physical manifestation of this dip. You see, and we say with great love, that humans have been long consumed with action and pushing through, trying to but straighten out this wave. But what you didn't see is that you need to replenish and reset - and so, in this, so does the whole planet. It is but a rhythm, a lull - a shhhhhhh. Is this of understanding now? You see, home is a sacred place - the hub, the gathering. It is not but something in your physical space but a place of belonging within, of acceptance and nurture. It's just that you have been more focused on the outer home to realize that you had a home already. With much Love and Light – Abe.

16. It is understood that there is a natural attraction between physical particles - an energetic attraction - that forms the underlying energetics of the material universe. This suggests there are also energetic attractions between human relations and our cosmic environment. Could you say something about these energetic attractions and alignments?

Ahh yes, this is so. And these attractions are but on all levels - attraction to each other, attraction to a place. Attraction is what creates systems for this is but always what your dominant resonance is of; it pulls the physical existence together - it shapes it. But you can but never know what state your own home is in if you are put constantly sleeping on the sofas of others. Is this of understanding now? You see, again, to connect up to the larger cosmos, and ride safely through these dimensions, you but have to sync up where you are. It has to come back - when you are gathered, you are united. When you are united, it is in relation to your world and then out further. It is but like a tiny drop causing a big splash - you always vibrate out. You speak vibrationally and then you get a vibrational response. You just have to listen to that in which is the response and allow yourselves to reset, to create the new pathways. For you see, like you said - as above, so below. This inter-relation, this attraction of vibration, needs to be heard now - not through your ears for it is but silent. Listen to what you do so feel. With much Love and Light – Abe.

17. When we talk about relations with the universe, we usually consider the 'one universe' that we know of. Would it not be more correct now to consider in terms of dimensional universes rather than a singular one? How does human

relations function within dimensional universes, and what are our connections between these dimensions?

Dimensions is again un-connected points of perception - you have but not found the means to connect. You have not yet reached this vibrational resonance, and this is so for too much power would blow the system - would but blow the fuse. Just like within, this is so outside. It is all here, all one, just not yet perceivable. You see, for your human thinking, if something is not found it is lost. But you see, lost is just that it hasn't but been found yet - do you so see that this pattern is internal and is so external? Is this of understanding now?

18. In recent years there have been an increase in media programs and movies that have storylines involving inter-dimensional travel and contact. It seems that human consciousness is being prepared to accept the idea that dimensional relations exist as part of our broader reality. Is it the case that humanity is now being prepared to shift to a broader conscious perspective, and these cultural programs are part of this preparation?

It is but so this way, for if you are shown possibility you are but gathered that tiny vibrational resonance - like a taster, if you will. You allow it in, to inter-mingle with your own vibrational resonance, of something being a possibility. But you see, these people who do so bring these possibilities forth are just tapping into the field of pure potential and therefore bring it to light, bring it to human perception. But hear this, it is all there - you but all have this potential. It's just that you are distracted, and therefore your energy is splintered, and you cannot comprehend

242

it so well for you have conflicting energies of outer influence. You see, many a creative person, or people, that do so bring forth mind expanding things usually fit outside the realm of cultural, or more so, social order mass thinking - and therefore, are able to keep this expansion, this space, for something other. In space there is everything - pure potential in silence. There is also this, but as humans you have become afraid of this void, this space - why is this so?

We would also like to state that these things, these points of perception, are also but linking up on the outer, from one to another, creating new pathways for others to have a new perspective - a new view. And then it is relational - as within, so without - pathways and walkways for others to create new pathways. And in this, walkways for others to come. With much Love and Light – Abe.

19. You have stated on more than one occasion that our species has entered into a dip in the wave pattern - a kind of resting point. You have said that this is a good time to do inner work rather than pushing ourselves into action. We suppose that this 'wave dip' is a cosmic phenomenon that is also impacting our planet right now. Could you speak more about this resting period, and for how long it is expected to last in earth time?

You see, this is but the pattern, the wave, for everything is vibration and therefore is a wave. You have this fluctuation of being - but you see, these waves are distorted, in a sense, as the enclosure like an ocean. In an ocean it is complex yet simple - it is complicated yet simple. For you see, if you are but out this natural rhythm you but miss a beat – you're off-sync, out of tune, missing the underlying truth. For you have built up this vibrational bubble, if you like, one within another within another, like the doll analogue. Is this understood now? You see, this resting period is not intentionally a place of rest but a place of coming back - and like the wave that washes to shore, it takes differing particles (sand, etc.) with it on each wave. We would like to say again, it is but not a length of time as such but more so a rhythm. And we feel this may not answer it properly or for any way for you to grab onto or latch up with. But you see, this is but the very point of it to be so also. It is never about the time, it is always about the pattern - never to measure but to feel, to rest yourselves, for only then can you fall back into rhythm, can sync up. With much Love and Light – Abe.

20. To continue with the subject of this resting period, we would like to know more about how we may synchronize with it through our social-cultural systems. It seems contrary to a resting period to be accelerating with our technologies, into artificial intelligence and digitized environments. Would it be more appropriate at this time to slow down these external advancements and develop our internal faculties?

You see, as a person of never going with the flow of mainstream do you but see that you have kept this rhythm? And you see, this rhythm has guided you in a way that you could not rhythm yourself? It would of course be ideal for this to be so - but you see, it has to start somewhere. It has to slow down - you cannot expect others to do so, but you can keep your point of place. It is always but a good idea to bring it back, reevaluate, and then re-adjust – rest, reset, before moving forwards. That is why life is but this rhythm. But you see, many do so try to flatline

244

it like they will be ahead - will outrun the natural rhythm of the cosmos. But you must see that you just make it so much harder on yourselves in the end - you but have to go back. You run off stating you know a quicker route, but it never appears that way for you have to follow this rhythm. For you see, your life is but linear and your life is polarity - how on Earth could you but know it all and race off for you do not have the full picture? You but need this dip as much as you need the high - it is but this way. With much Love and Light – Abe.

21. Also, Abe has spoken about the importance of community and the benefits of rural living. Would such rural-community sustainable lifestyles be more appropriate to develop and engage in during our species resting period?

You see, it is always about getting back into sync with this beat - this flow, this wave. And we would never dismiss your advancement as a species, but we feel that it is this resting point that allows you to see clearly - to see the larger picture, to see the correlation between all things. And in that sense, it makes sense to advance in a way that coexists with this rhythm. Is this of understanding now? We are not to say that everyone should abandon the cities and head for the hills. It is not true, for you can always start from where you are at. Falling back into the rhythm of the cosmos allows you to feel this rhythm again - feel this beat, feel this deep-seated truth, see your humanity. With much Love and Light – Abe.

22. In recent communications, Abe has spoken about the rise in the pathways of perception and the awareness of

multidimensions. Are these multidimensional pathways set to increase in our species' perception during this resting period? And would this not be an ideal time to gather ourselves and 'bring ourselves home' by focusing on self-developing our internal potentials? As you say, it is a time for stillness and allowance of ourselves rather than pushing for external gains.

It is so, yes. We believe that once you rest, you can bring it all back - all the conscious antennas of attachment. It is but to realign - this is but our purpose, for you to bring it back home to then have a wider perception; a higher ground, if you will, to see differently. Only when you gather can you but have the strength to reach forth. Only when reaching forth can you create these new pathways externally. Do you see, these stepping back to then come forth with more clarity, more truth, more stability and strength? You can but only evolve, you can but only connect, and you but can only see the harmony and totality of your very being within this time-space conundrum you are in right now. It is just pure magic, pure living. We say this with such great love for you, to see and experience whilst in this form. With much Love and Light – Abe.

We would also like to say that sometimes we feel we don't give you the bite, the nugget of truth that you so seek as human beings. But you see, with this you cannot hold onto anything. It is like trying to make something unnamable be named; and for that, it is only ever felt, only ever dropped back into. We do hope you take this vagueness as but a positive, as a stepping-stone to really know that you always have the power to bring yourselves back home, back to truth. And although we speak, it is but always from a place of nurture - not distinction or direction. For you could really latch onto this too, and that would not be our point at all. Do you see this clearly? Do you see this truth?

246

23. To continue this thread, we'd like to say that it seems the subject of relations with the greater universe brings an awkward response from some people. It is as if the subject of a 'greater universe' triggers a fear and/or uncertainty reaction. People are afraid of what they don't know, and this fear keeps them trapped within limited perceptions. Could you comment upon this?

It is so this way, for they want to know the secrets but not to really live by them. For if they do live by them, they do so realize a kind of 'Is that it?' But you see that you have been so over-stimulated and simulated that you do not know which end is up now, what is real, and then you do not take the leap of faith. You would rather think about it and not live it. But you see, it isn't something euphoric. And in this, you have been but sold a lie for in this you think 'Well, I must of missed it all together, for where's the big bang?' But hear this, what you don't so realize is that you are but the big bang and the bang was always silent. For you see, things that are but done in silence are but done in truth. Is this of understanding now?

24. Is it not the case that by realizing and nurturing our relations with a wider universe, humans are shifting from service-to-self to service-to-others? Does it not benefit the grander whole by humans willingly wishing to be of service to more than ourselves? What can you say about this?

You see, we would like to but put this in context in a way that shows that in serving others you do so serve yourselves, for these two are not so defined as you may think so. It is all well and good to be of service to others but if you are but not of service to self too then you are not then serving others well. For it is not about one over the other, but in the realization of knowing that the two are but in relation, are intertwined. That what you do for self-interest only will not serve you; and also, in service to just others will not serve you to move forward now for you are seeing in polarity still. It is about knowing and seeing so clearly that the two are not as definitive as once thought - that is but the key here. Is this seen now?

We would also like to add that in this drawing back you see that service to others becomes a self-service, in a way, because they are no differing - do you so see this now? For you can have but a person who does so serve others, is for service to others, and not like it at all in the end. For if you try as you might to be of service to others, is that really serving anyone well at all? It is but in the act of self-service, of realigning self, then too will it be a natural flow, to be of service. Then it is a spontaneous happening, not a forced action. We do so hope that you can see that in which we are trying to convey here? For they are so tightly interwoven, like very much everything else. With much Love and Light – Abe.

25. It seems to us that the universe has been waiting for humanity to awaken so that it can reach out to the human race and engage with them - to communicate and form relations. Does this sound fanciful? Is there some truth to this?

It would sound fanciful to some - but you see, you have never been separated as such, just distorted, engaged, if you will. Like the man with the treat who does so say 'Here dog, take my treat' and another will say 'No, over here.' It has been like a mind maze and you but do not know which way is out now – you're all upside down, confused, as to what is true. You see, it is about clearing the fog, finding a way out of the maze first and foremost. And in this, you can have rest - you can but gather your parts yourselves and but realign, readjust. Then in this rest you will but see that there is but so much more that you are connected with once the trouble of working out which way to go has been lifted. Is this of understanding now?

26. Abe, you have mentioned before that our human conceptions are both the captive and the captor. Could you say more about this, and how it may affect our relations with a grander reality?

Yes, but of course. For the captive thinks it does have the captor, and what the captive doesn't know is that there is no lock and key. And what the captor doesn't know is that they have but only captured themselves for in the lock not being, and the captive staying, you are but both. Do you see this bind, this trap? If you will, it is so to free yourselves from this pattern you would have to realize that you are but both in this. You realize that you were but always free - you just had to set yourself free. We do hope this is of sense, and although a little confusing can also show the bind within the bind. It is but humorous when it is but seen, albeit being frightening and troublesome at the time. For you see, realization of it is freedom from it. With much Love and Light – Abe.

27. In the last few decades there has emerged the cultural-recreational use of drugs, narcotic, and consciousness-altering

substances. **Various of these substances have been experimented with to gain awareness/insight into transcendental states. Some people have made strong claims for insight into the collective intelligence (zero-field?) as well as into cosmic-universal realities. Could Abe comment upon this?**

You see, it is all about letting go of that in which you hold onto so tightly, day in and day out. You see, whenever this is but let go of you will sync up, it is but true. But you see, you do not need to experiment with these as such for they do to alter your perception. We are well aware that many do so transcend, are gifted into a world of what is truly magical is an experience. And you see, it is but that - an experience, a differing viewpoint. But hear this, although mind altering substances can but open up the mind, can crack it open, it too can also destroy it. For when you are but in this state you can see that 'wow, that was beautiful' - but you see, it can also create a sense of separation, of a differing world, for it is amiss here in its splendid technicolour. But you see, truth is not fancy - it's not so frilly and explosive and knocks you off of your feet. It is so like you go chasing for love, for the grandeur, and you do so go from one person to another, and you see there was this one whom was there all along - not fancy, not shouting from the rooftops, but an undercurrent of nurture, of natural flow. And you think, why did I miss that splendor, that beauty, that magnificence? And you see, you can get caught up so in this trap of grandeur - and please know that we may have strayed a little but you see, it is not now about the explosive for you are but human, you are the meeting point. And once you can see this magnificence in your day-to-day lives, truly feel it from your core - resonate deeply with it - you will see that these things are okay but they are very much not needed now, not to experience this, for in the ordinary everyday there is something quite extraordinary, something quite grandeur. You just don't need to be searching for it, for it is here with you. With much Love and Light – Abe.

28. Mind-expanding substances have been used for millennia for consciousness exploration, such as with shamans and mystics. These days, they have entered more into the social-cultural domain. There may be some risks here. Are such substances necessary for consciousness exploration - or re-wiring - and what do they tell us about our contact with reality?

You see, they are not necessary; and yes, have been used for millennia by shamans and mystics alike. But you see, you are but evolving and although it may seem in many ways that you are evolving the wrong way, it is not so true for these energies are but causing you to do so. There are but vibrational resonances that are not visible and these resonances are rewiring, expanding your consciousness. For you see, you will not need so much the chemical compound to do this; and you also see that these chemicals are abound in nature. They are but potent when taken and do give you another viewpoint of your reality. But please do so hear this - like we said before, it can but crack you open. But it can also give you a sense of too much, for we say it is a becoming - it is about seeing the beauty here, now, in the ordinary. You see, you do not need to see these connections for your bodies are becoming more sensitive; your brains are but being rewired. The thing to do is to bring it back - gather yourselves for this upgrade, if you will, in your conscious awareness. You see, you all have this ability to become healers and you all have the ability to become so-called mystics. For you see, you are but all made of the same stuff; you all have access to it - it's just that you forgot you turned it off. It is but time now to switch on and switch up. Is this of understanding now? We say with great love that these substances do allow you to see what is but part true and can expand the mind. But hear this, it too is not a full representation of what life is. It can show you the patterns, but you do not need it now for you can sync back up and be a flow with the cosmic force that is but ingrained in your very being that's magnificent, that is but truly magical, and that is but extraordinarily ordinary. With much Love and Light – Abe.

We would but like to come forth in such a way as to discuss these vibrational resonances. For you see, what was said with regards as mind altering drugs you can but see that they alter your conscious experience. We understand that many have experienced a light switching on for them in a way that nothing else has; for in the seeing of this beauty you can see the connections, the beauty of it all here - and how much is really not seen in the day-to-day, in the normal conscious experience? And although this is well and good, we think that now is a time to develop this within, and can only be done this way by gathering yourselves - by but finding your way back home. It doesn't need to be drug induced, it can be as simple or as hard as you but wish it to be. For like we said at the beginning, it is but to be one of bare bones - the gift is the gift in itself; it doesn't need the fancy bow and sparkly paper. Do you see that in which we are getting across now? We do so hope, for if it is not seen in its ordinary everyday attire it will never stick in its fancy robes. You see, these vibrational resonances are to be but felt, to connect with, to bring it into your breath - into your day, into your being. It is but all well and good to have an experience, but will it inhabit the day-to-day, the ordinary? Will you still see the wondrous - will you

252

feel the deep connection with it all or will it be but a place that you do so visit? With much Love and Light – Abe.

29. Thank you, Abe, for your answers regarding the use of drugs for consciousness-altering experiences. We understand what you say, that such experiences are temporary and unnecessary. We don't need to seek the frills when we have the wonder in our day-to-day conscious living. As we develop our human inner capacities, do you feel that recreational drugs will begin to fade and be seen as an 'antiquated' method for accessing transcendental realities?

Yes, we do feel this will be so, for we feel that with all things they do have their time and place. But you see, as you evolve, as these internal pathways connect, reshuffle, and reconfigure, we see that it is not needed for it will be of a natural connection and therefore a catapult too. It will not be needed now. You see, you have but recognized that something natural once has now become a bit of a fad. You but - and we say this with great love - run away with the frill of the ride, of the experience. And what we would like to say is that its already here anyway, you just need to reconnect back to it - back to your roots as human beings. You need to but come back home and in this you create pathways within and therefore new viewing posts without. Is this of understanding now?

30. We feel that as part of human development our species will come to enhance its acceptance, and connection, with greater cosmic/universal relations. It will be a connection that is natural and a part of our genetic inheritance. It will be like

having natural relations amongst ourselves, yet upon differing vibrations/wavelengths. Could Abe comment upon this?

Oh yes, this is but seen for the way your species will develop, of course. But you see, it is not to be all a fancy with it; to make it but all into a cosmic show. For you see, you were never apart from it, you have just been growing, developing, enhancing your capabilities, becoming more alert, more aware. And it takes some time to root this, for with any change, with any new jump in evolutionary terms, it needs to settle in. For when there are but a few that are inclined to be this way, to find it but easy to connect, they are seen as a little mad, a little different. But you see, they are the ones that can also say 'look here - what I do is very much you too.' The big show, the big song and dance about it, really does need to be dropped now for you will then only ever bypass truth, bypass what is here and ordinary. For it will but always be simply overlooked, the same as with enlightenment - it really is only the light coming back on; it's really just someone back home. Do you so see this now? For you see, we will continue to say that it is a drive back to the bare bones for then to reach forth in a new direction now. And if truth be said, making everything into a grand show really misses the point of the even grander show that has been playing out all along right under your nose. With much Love and Light – Abe.

31. So far, we have explored various topics relating to the theme of relations with the greater universe. Is there anything else on this subject that Abe would wish to comment about? We feel that perhaps we could shift toward another subject area. Would Abe wish to indicate another subject area for discussion?

We think it has been but discussed sufficiently at present, that of relations, and see that it will be something that we do come back to later on for we see a stepping back as to step forth now. We do so feel that indeed the subject that will be of use going forward, as we previously said, would be one to allow people the tools to set a starting point of but turning around, drawing back and enabling you to find YOUR way back home. As we said, it will not resonate with all, and it is but very fine and well to adapt as seen for. For you see, these are too just the bare bones. We do not want it to be restricted in any way or form but more so a take it or leave it, or even an adapt it, to your own needs. For you see, with everything it does so have to resonate with your own being. Now, in this we would like to discuss the symbol in more depth, and also that of the exercise. We feel that for anyone to take this on, to resonate with deeply, to make it any kind of practice for themselves, they would have to but know the basis of it - the 'why' if you will. We would also like to discuss that these are but footings, they are not to be a ritual as such for we feel that you do not need attachment for anything to be seen. But we do so understand that tools are of use so long as, we have said before, they too are put down, are put aside. We do hope that this communication is to be continued with now and we do so hope that it is rooting within, this connection, within yourselves for we feel it is now - and are grateful for this time spent. We do so feel it is but time to bring this forth now. With much Love and Light – Abe.

SECTION FIVE
Consciousness, Time & Energy

S ome of these communications came from sittings without a question - a free flow of information. Later, after reading the material, some follow-on questions were asked. Where there is no specific question asked, we have included the date of the sitting, where possible.

1. Tuesday 30th April 2019

We would like to but come forth again this morning to talk a little about the next journey, the next bricks if you will - and what we feel would be a good direction now, if you are both so feeling you would like to continue? We feel that we have covered ground, but we feel to wanting to be focused now on how to find THE WAY BACK HOME - how to deep-seat this. How to but really bring it back in from a world that constantly pulls you out. It is but a tug-of-war, but it is also a worthwhile process to but have this deep-seated, rooted within to nurture this. We are in no way saying that what we say will be of resonance to all, and also will be a forever becoming, one of nurture and continuance. But what we can help with is to start this process - to help you truly find THE WAY BACK HOME. We hope this is to be continued and nurtured within this trigram of communication, of evolvement. With much Love and Light and continued communications – Abe.

2. Wednesday 1st May 2019

We would but like to come forth this morning in regards to something but important, for we see that sometimes physical confirmation and Synchronicity is confirmation of where you are at vibrationally. Not only that at which your vibrational essence is at but also that of your conscious evolution as humans. You do so like feedback. You like to know that you exist materially - you like to but strengthen this in all your endeavours. And what we would like to say - it is all in trust for it is but not physical. But you see, you feel it so at your core, but you do so want confirmation, an echo. This is why it is but good to collaborate now. You see, it is all but in relation. We would also like to add that, and we say with great love and respect for the time given already, that you could but be doing so much more with this. We feel though that given time, and as this bond strengthens, you will both be doing much more with it. Healing and nurturing will be a part of this connection too. We do so hope that now we can root this within yourselves, within this connection, and we hope that it is to continue and grow and in trust for one another. And also, of that that can guide you - it is of importance to strengthen that now. With much Love and Light – Abe.

3. Abe, you have stated, and we accept this also with love and respect, that we could be doing more with our connection. As you rightly say, we have been taking time to develop our bond

258

and relationship. We also appreciate your guidance. Could you say more and perhaps offer guidance in regards to this 'more' that we could be doing now? Thank you.

You see, we do not mean more in regards to the actual work for we are but grateful that this is now underway and should always be of flow as to get it right, if you will. We do think when we say 'more' we mean in a way to allow more, and the theme here is but healing. For healing is not just one of placing the hands upon people and allowing to see this. No, but one of all these differing levels for this is but the symbol - one of healing of relation, of but syncing back up. We feel this should be known that healing is on but so many differing levels but only ever just the one. Like the scale build up in kettle, the flow has but been contaminated and then in this the mechanism is not so effective - do you so see this now? For you see, this 'more' is that you are but both healers - you do it through this connection, you do it through your relation to one another and with your food, and your relationships and your planet. So now it does so make sense to heal yourselves. But hear this, it is not but a long drawn out process but like the vinegar that is left to do its magic within the kettle this is too this flow, for in this it will make it sparkling, as good as new. Do not think that a healer has to be one of unpacking every single thing and one of miraculous healing. No - it is but not about the show now, and you will but see this for yourselves. You just have to allow the flow to work its magic - it is but not in the doing now. But you do so see that there will be prompts and nudges and to allow this to be, for this is what we meant by more. With much Love and Light – Abe.

4. Friday 3rd May 2019

We would like to but come forth this morning to discuss something in which we would like to allow now, for we would like to underline a couple of things that do so seem unfitting. You see, we would like to state that you are but not channelling, in a sense that channelling is but made out to be, for it is not that way. For our purpose of coming forward is not to create a special few - it is but a gift that you both are able to communicate. But you see, as much as a gift to us also. But as your species evolves it will not be considered so as much for it is really a switching of a channel, an upgrade if you will, from 3 channels to 5 - do you so see this? You see, this is evolution knowing that in which you are and that in which you can truly receive. And this fountain of knowledge that you can so step into at any time, like your whole body has an order, a natural order, an intelligence. It is too of your outer world and, like the heart that beats too fast and out of rhythm, wasn't in coherence with the rest of the body and therefore caused disharmony within the body. It is but your duty now as conscious beings to take head, to rebalance. And it starts with one person at a time to truly see this simple coherence of being and the role in which you play to change the winds of time - it is but time now to readjust the sails. With much Love and Light – Abe.

We would also like to say that: do not be dismayed in old patterns coming up, patterns you feel that you had got a hold of or had suppressed. Sometimes things need to raise their heads in order for it to be seen clearly - they but have to be brought into the light to be seen. And you can see that this very much is a purging of the old patterns, the old humanity, and you see this happening in your outer world. For anything to be changed it has to be brought to light, to be allowed to move out of the

260

system - be that internally or externally. The reason we steer away from blame is because we really do see your human potential. Yes, there may be many that do so want to manipulate and in this crave power, but there are also so many, many more that do not want this - focus on those for now. For you see, the secret is there is no secret of life, for it is all there in front of you. You just need to clear the view, clear the way, re-sync, then re-adjust. If you are thinking there is but a secret to life that is but only available to a few, is kept in the dark, then you see to it that you are not human. For you see, you all have power, you all have insight, you but all have these capabilities – it's just a matter, if you will so see this now, and to what means you will use it for. With much Love and Light – Abe.

We would also like to state that moving forward now with the way back home, of finding your way back home, is where you will both really seat this, will really inhabit this. For then we feel there will be but more to the foundation in which you can then help to heal others. This is now onto the path of healing and you realise, as you heal others, you heal yourselves and all your layers of relations. But you will also see that when you see these layers and things that do so look differing, separate, are nothing more than one thing - a coherence. For you see, you are again, in regards to all that we said, you are but piecing things now back together - are seeing the full picture. For when said that you are but all one, it is not a lie; but some cannot grasp this for they see themselves on an island for one, doing their own thing. It's like the sun lying to itself that it only shines for itself – it's a myth, an old pattern that need to be rid of now. With much Love and Light and continued communication – Abe.

We would like to state something very clear at the start of this communication on discussion of the way back home, on giving some simple tools - that this is not a SELF-help book. We want you to know that it is not to embed this notion that you have of self, that is so tightly conditioned in your being - you have a body but the self is really the fundamental oneness. The body is part of a system so how could it ever be that you are but adrift – self-help can so get you caught up in a bind as to see that you need to fix something. There is nothing needed to be fixed, just rather let go of. If you think that there is but something to be fixed you are not seeing clearly the underlying truth of your magnificent, extraordinarily ordinary existence. With much Love and Light – Abe.

5. Saturday 4th May 2019

We would like to but come forth this morning in such a way as to discuss a little on time and timelines in your physical existence. You see, we stated that time is very much a human concept, in a way that it does so slice and dice. But also, we see that many a people talk about this ever present NOW; and you see that this too is a concept in such a way. For when you try to catch the present you are but chasing a ghost, a shadow, and it will always be in future tense. It could even be classed as past too, for when caught it is but gone. But you see, in this you are never NOW for you are always lagging behind a little in regards to your bodily functions. What we see it as, for truth to be seen, is not so much the NOW - not a place to settle in externally - but a place to come back to internally. Time only stands still when you gather yourselves back, back home. You could argue that this is the 'now' tense. But you see, it is not, for 'I' is suspended -

to have no time, including the ever present now, you come back home. Try it NOW, and we say this word with a loving light heart – stop, gather, come back and feel. In this, you do not have any concept of time, including now; it is really then just a constant becoming. Do not try to pull back to past; do not race ahead to future; do not try to stand still to capture the NOW - you can't. Just BE home, and in this you will be suspended between all these concepts, all these conditions - you are but a flow. With much Love and Light – Abe.

WE would say about timelines, and differing events, in a way as that: in a way an artist does not know that in which will appear upon the canvas. He trusts in the creation, in the flow - he is but suspended, if you will. It is seen as a timeline, a process, and timelines really are nothing of the sort - never a line but an interference, a reaction, a conveying between differing vibrations - an arising. Do you so see this now?

You see, when you're but back home - when you are in alignment with the whole system - you will feel these slight changes, and you do so feel that humans are at a disadvantage sometimes. But you see, in this part of your evolution it is but pure magic for you are at the levels at which you can so feel. You can feel the Earth externally, you can feel your body internally, you can then feel the cosmos; you can converse easily between these seemingly differing levels - it is an advancement. This is so achieved when synced up, when realigned. You see, we state you as you; but in the you, you see, you feel, when you aren't but synced back up. You see, it is never a self as such but, like we said, when synced up you create space - the space is the allowance for all of these to emerge, to be united. It is a gathering - in this gathering you see that it is but just a collection point and the body allows this. It is not who you are for you are but much more; and also, in this space you realise there is never a NOW. We do hope you see this. With much Love and Light – Abe.

We would also like to be given the space to come forth as to the difficult question as to what is real - is there an overall truth, a real world, in which you are amiss? And we would say no - it is not so, for real is only ever real to you, and real to you is always dependent upon the doll that you are but encased in. For you see, 'real' too is a bit of a concept; and even so the 'seeker of truth' is but a bit of a lie too in the way that you say seeker - and we say this with great love for your human experience. Let us explain: in your physical existence you can only ever work to the mechanism, for you could ask - is the toaster a toaster or the electricity that runs through it? What would be your answer? For without the current it cannot toast - this is true. So, truth is not something you see but rather something you become. You gather, you accept that your truth is but a collection, a bundle - not you but a system within a system within a system. Is this so seen now? You see, what is 'real life' as you state - is it but your day-to-day? Or is it something you feel? Why could it not be something you feel that you do so bring into your day-to-day - could that not be real? Something that spontaneously arises, and you then allow this into your physical by means of the whole? With much Love and Light – Abe.

6. Is this space, this gathering, a place to constantly reside?

You see, it is never about 'hey, I'm staying here' - for what is there to truly stay? And you could try as you might to stay put, like a stubborn mule stating this is my happy place, this is my

264

home, and I am not leaving. For you see, your home is not your prison or your capture; and although we would like you to find your way back to this, it is not so that you should stay there. It is but impossible to TRY to do anything, for you see it is in the realisation that you are but a gathering, that you are not a little 'me' caught up inside a mechanism - you are but a point of attraction of the whole show. Once you feel this, once you have made your way back home, you can then see that you do not need to stay put but allow yourself to move through all of life. For that is what you truly are - you are but the space that allows all to arise. Do not constrict with notions of this and that; it is but a falsity and will too end up keeping you trapped. For when you do truly find your way home, when you are but suspended, you realise that here you let go of it all, even us, and you allow it to just BE. Is this so seen?

7. You have said there is no secret, we only need to allow this space/access. It seems to us that people are receiving/interacting with this allowing all the time, we just don't realize it. We may call this inspiration, gut instinct, or creative ideas? It is only when we then filter this allowance through our personality-self that we de-sync – is this so?

You see, it is not so much of it being a de-sync as such - for you see, this space lends way to all. It is in the constriction of, and how far down the rabbit hole, it is so. For you see, like a Chinese whisper game, the further around the circle it goes the more it does not resemble the original whisper. Is this of understanding now? You are not to rid but to emerge, to allow, and realise that you are but it all - and all is one thing in play. And you see, like the stone that skims across the surface of the water, do not grab a hold and then take it to the depths for will it even be the original, the whisper at all? For it will be of taken into the dark and you will not see clearly that in which it is. With much Love and Light - Abe.

You see, it is in this space that you allow life to move for you are suspending yourself in a sense. And in this, you are but really just allowing yourself to merge, to piece yourself back together. Do never try to rid yourself of anything for the time is now. And the energy that is evident is not ever in ridding anything but attracting the splintered true self together - its magnetising it back together vibrationally. Is this so seen?

8. Sunday 5ᵗʰ May 2019

Good morning. We would like to but come forth this morning in regards to consciousness. For you see, in your world it is of importance for there are but many whom are seeking consciousness - are trying to capture as if they get this recipe they can play with the Gods in a sense. And like there was once a race to the moon, so now it is to but create conscious beings - to harness this life force. But you see, consciousness was to be had within it from the very first living cell - the very first living organism. It is not a thing that is floating around ready to be but captured. It is really in relation, in coherence with but everything else. Now, you see, it has been questioned but many a time upon your planet of what consciousness is - and we would like to say that it is but an interrelated intelligence, a communication, if you will, of the whole thing. One thing, but always of many. For you see, we are but the original state of consciousness. We have no space or place or continuance like yourselves who do so have a material existence. But for reason of communication we do. It is, and like we have said before, from this suspended place you can but bring forth us. It sounds very odd to many but is very much natural that this can so happen. But you see, many do get this; many think it to be themselves; many think it to be creative expression - it all depends upon the evolution of the mechanism. It really is so of but how it is going to be but filtered. If you can allow no filter; in a sense, if you are in this space, you create room for this to come in. And although not differing it is in allowing space - if you do not create so much room it is but filtered. Not in a sense as to be cut off but almost like an over-speak of your own vibrational essence. It's not to be dropped, to be rid of - it is an allowance, a clearing if you will. Is this of understanding now?

Now back to consciousness: we would like to state that consciousness is not a by-product, it is not something that is born from material existence but something that brings material existence. Material existence is born from it, from this zero-state. You see that we say about the neural pathways, the pathways within, then creating pathways without. Pathways in a sense of a differing vantage point of your human existence - do you so see this? Well, this is really also like the doll analogy, and like the Earth that has its own system, and the body has its own system, and the cosmos but all interrelating, all listening to one another – evolving, incorporating their own vantage, working with but one intelligence. For would it not make sense to work with this one intelligence from which all is born, that created all, rather than fight against it like the student who is but always over-talking the teacher? And hear this, you are but the teacher and also the student. How will you ever learn anything to then pass this intelligence on through the ages, through the levels of consciousness? You need to but listen. You see, you are but all at points from where you are at in evolutionary terms - and this is but very much vibrational. Vibrational is really just this continued conversation between all things; this intricate web of communication; this keeping connected like a child that continues to ring back home. That connection is not gone no matter where you are - unless you are not willing to listen. Listen to yourselves to connect back up. But do so hear this, there is not but hierarchy here for you are but the birther and the born, the teacher and the taught. Is this of understanding now?

See, the race is on for you to harness this life force. And that is but what it is - it is the builder of existence. But hear this, it can also be the destroyer of it too. For if you do so not see that consciousness is but an harmonious integrative system of many things, of communication, of vibrational resonance, of but building blocks that creates intricate orders of systems - then you are but missing what life is in totality. You are missing the point in which anything exists at all. For you see, if you do so sync up again, if you vibrationally allow yourselves to fall back into this integrative system, this life force, this intelligence, you know that it is but in and around everything. Life is but orchestrated and when back in rhythm, back in sync, you can allow yourselves to be both the enjoyer of it and also the conductor. With much Love and Light – Abe.

We would but like to say one more thing: that in the order of systems, in the intricacy of individual or seemingly individual complex systems, you can see that the more complex the system becomes the more segregated it seems - but actually, is pushing for integration. Do you see? It is but getting the mix right, the balance of seemingly two opposites, knowing that all the time it

268

is a whole they become. As if you want to see how far you can push the child out into the deep end to then swim back - always to swim back. Do you so see this conundrum? The question is - will humanity now sink or swim? With much Love and Light and continuance of communication, of allowance, of integration - Abe.

We would like to add that we state from the very first living cell. But you see, it goes beyond that. And like the baby that takes its first breath it is but a continuance of this - constant births, constant becomings, constant reconfiguration, restructure - do you so see this pattern, this oneness? For you see, for something to be birthed you need something to be birthed to birth - and in this you can sense that it is but a constant turning in and outside itself. Is this of understanding now? For you see, there is but never a Big Bang, a start point - and there will never be an end, just constant reconfiguration of being, of networking. With much Love and Light – Abe.

The perfect life is never created, it is always allowed. It is in trust and guidance that the next steps will follow, and the next, and the next. Your job is to but step and trust without there even being a place yet to step too. In the step forward, life meets you there; it is a correlation for perfect is not an ideal, but it is always where you are at. For it is always in relation - you just have to grow in your awareness, gather the pieces to realise that there is magic right where you are. With Love and Light – Abe.

9. We would like to return to the subject of consciousness. You have stated that if we allow no filter, we allow a space for the original field of consciousness (the Unity) to come in. This

original consciousness is what people often believe to be 'themselves' or their creative expression. Can it be said that people *allow* the expression of this original consciousness to greater or lesser degrees according to the state of their mental-body-emotional complex? So, the more a person is conditioned by their personality, the more filters they have, and the less they allow space for original, unity consciousness?

This is but true, yes. It is again like the analogy of the dolls - the tighter and tighter the filter, the constrict of your identity, the less you allow to flow. Some people doppelgänger's not want to give up this notion that there is more than just this idea that you do so hold onto so tightly, day in, day out. It's known, it has predictability, it has but predictable patterns; so therefore, to open yourselves up, to crack these dolls open, would be but a scary idea for you are at whim to what is not predictable, is not known. You see, throughout your lives you do so go back and forth into this box, this doll. You say you want more, and you decide to venture; but you see that it is not known, so you do so clamber back in and shut the doll up again. This is but fine - but at some point you need to allow the unknown, the unpredictable; for that is but what life is, is what consciousness is - what you are. You have but made yourselves small when you are but much more. But do so hear this, it is not to be rid of as if you have to chuck yourself in the bin. No, not at all - it is but in this space where all can emerge. Is this of understanding now? What we would like to say is: sometimes you but have to empty yourselves to then be full again - to allow all to flow you just do not need to be stuck on ideas of being this or that, for you are but the containment of all. When you realise this you are but full, you are but allowing life to flow. With much Love and Light – Abe.

270

We would also like to add that this unity, this space, is but Consciousness. It isn't that you switch it on and off - it is but always a flow. It's just that you get so caught up on naming it but one thing - do you see this? For if you let go of the notion - if you like, the click of the fingers - you are but snapped out of the resonance of being. Just like that, you open yourselves up. It is merely just a tie, a tag, a label, if you will - like sorting through a box of smarties stating, 'I only like the orange ones.' They may have but a differing colour, a slightly differing taste, but in the end all just smarties.

10. Can it also be said that part of our natural, evolved state as human beings is to be able to 'step aside' from our filters/personality, and allow unity consciousness to manifest through us? In other words, we stop 'speaking over the teacher' as you put it (our voice is like the student - although we are ultimately both student AND teacher). Is this not the same as what happens through genuine mystics - they have dropped their filters to allow a space for unity consciousness to be expressed through them?

This is but true - they do so allow this flow. For you have not got that overlaying, dominant resonance that does so want to continue to say, 'well, I know all this, of course.' You do, you are but always guiding yourselves back to this place. You are but all in communication with this oneness - for you are it. It is in the listening that allows it to flow unfiltered - to listen and feel and connect back up with it as if something is but taking you by the hand and stating - see here, I know the WAY BACK HOME. But hear this, you are but also evolving as a species. To enable this connection more, to allow unity - although never amiss - it is but

271

the overlying filter, the resonance of disconnection. This does so then break apart, and like the world that was seen to be all by itself in the universe, it is not so. You are but piecing it back together now, and as you evolve you will see more and more evidence to support this oneness, this unity - the pathways are being created. With much Love and Light – Abe.

11. It is said that genuine mystics recognize one another immediately, without the need for verbal communication or signs. Is this because the unity consciousness recognizes itself, like looking in a mirror? Also, that this sharing of space - between unity consciousness and our own vibrational essence - is a natural state of being?

Ahh yes, the mystic recognition - the oneness recognition is but always a mirror. But you see, not just in a mystic - you see it clear in a mystic for that mirror is clear, is spotless. This is why people are drawn to such people; they see, feel, and sense this home resonance - this space. They feel it deeply and it is like a moth to a flame. You are drawn in, not quite knowing what it is. But you see, this is magnetism - the draw to but piece it back together again. For if you stare in the mirror for long enough you do so see parts of yourselves that are good and that are bad. This is but what every person is on the planet - is a mirror, if you are willing to see clearly. And we say not even every person but everything, for you are but in conversation with oneself - it just depends on whether you are but willing to see life as such? With much Love and Light – Abe.

12. Abe has said that 'the race is on' to harness this 'life force' (unity consciousness) - a life force, which is in constant becoming, within all living cells. Does this signify that to try to 'harness' this force within artificial mechanisms (e.g., computers/machines) is not only futile but has potentially negative consequences for us?

We feel that it is but futile; in a sense that you will ever get this human mix. It will but always be a connotation of it for it is in the combination, not just in the consciousness. And this is but where they are but going wrong - they are thinking of it as a singular and it is not. And it will never be so, for oneness contains it all. It is absurd to try and but think that one could take a part and pop it in and then 'hey presto.' An artificial human life is complex - there are but complex systems. And yes, it would have negative consequences at present for you are but not coming from unity yourselves firstly. With much Love and Light – Abe.

13. Monday 6ᵗʰ May 2019

Good morning. We would but like to discuss a little more in which was given and felt yesterday. You see, the energy that was so felt was correct, that Abe communication was but differing. But you see, we never change for we are not of form and only ever a point. For what we are, and that in which you are, is purely one of unification - you but always hold the polarities. There are but differing states for that is what is within unification; you are but piecing it all back together again. You see, this means that all is there for the taking - from oneness everything is born. You see, it is not at all about choosing but allowing. In allowing, you let what is arise when need be, without the differing, of this and that. The feminine energy of the communication is rising, and this does mean that it is but time - not for the showing of things like it was so of, one would say, the masculine energy - but one of self-nurturing, of deep healing. For these energies are not to be one over the other, but a dance, if you will, of the polarities of life - of the seemingly opposites. Now this energy is abound on your planet at the moment for it is but a time of great healing, of great nurture. But you do so see that these energies are but always at play, it's just that you see in individuality, in such black and white - this is what does so throw you off balance, off course. For what you would truly see is that one is always underlining the other and, like in a dance, non-stop dancing, it's just that one becomes more focal than the other. But just a bigger part in that beat, in that rhythm, and they do so allow this grace between one another. You see, they are always of equal quantities for in the dance it does so need to be one of balance; otherwise, there is no dance at all. Is this so seen now?

This dance will be evident in this communication now for there will be times in the communication when one is more prominent than the other. And you will but see this in your connection too, and also in your outer worlds. It will though always be that of a dance of seemingly opposites - do you see this now in the physical? Do you see this in this connection? We think you will deeply feel it so. You see, you all have the unity, the masculine and feminine, and you need to realise the rhythm of that in which is in play now is but taking the hand to guide the dance now. With much Love and Light – Abe.

We would also like to add that now is but the time to follow and allow this guidance, this silent whisper, to arise - let the

274

feminine in all arise. Let it be known that it is in all and now it is time to let it speak - to let it come forth to allow it to guide and nurture. For now, let silence speak and let it do so through your heart. You will but know the next steps soon after. For you see, and what we did so communicate at the very beginning of communication, what one lacks the other makes up for. And this dance then is of complete balance, is of supporting one another rather than fighting one another - rather than favouring one over other. You will so see this in your connection, that one will always support the other and vice versa. It will but always be one of coherence - it only gets imbalanced when one does think that the other is not needed, for it is but never this way. For if one isn't centre stage it is but always behind the scenes – nurturing, prepping, and ready to join the dance again, and always in support of one another. We do so hope this is but seen now. With much Love and Light – Abe.

14. Thank you for the recent communications. Yes, this shift in the energy has been recognized - the arising of the feminine energy in the communication. As you say, it is not separate but a part of the integral whole - a dance of all energies as unity. You have said it is time for this - time for self-nurturing and deep healing upon the planet. You say these energies are abound at this time. Could you say more about this. Are these nurturing energies arising because of a natural, evolving spiral flow - or because they are now needed more than ever on this planet?

It is but a balancing act, always; and as you see now in your world there is but a bit of confusion. For you see, it is only ever rebalancing, recalibrating; and you see that yes, these energies can be felt at this time if you are but in tune. For in this you do so know these patterns and, as you say, these spirals. You see, no ONE ever wins; no ONE ever overrides the other in totality. It is about this dance, for when one does become too dominant, too over-bearing, if you will, the other will rise again to balance it out. We do so say rise in the sense that one allows the other - a constant flow, a constant becoming, not ever in a way as to overlord or push the other out of the picture but always to rebalance. For you see, if you are but in tune you can but dance, converse, and play between the two. This is balance, this is suspension - for this is life. Is this of understanding now? What we would like to say is that as humans, and we say this with great love, that you do so feel this energy and start to run with it and it is not to be so. Do not capture, either - just allow yourselves to be but the meeting point of the two. To allow both to rise and fall at whim, void of the conceptions you hold. With much Love and Light – Abe.

15. You have suggested that this silent, nurturing energy is always behind the scenes, perhaps not so centre-stage as the masculine energy. Will we now see more of this arising across the planet - and if so, in what ways?

It will be so, for it is again back to the rise and fall - the wave, the resonance. All but have this pattern - it is no longer about grabbing a hold of either one in trying to flatten it out and but neaten it up. For like we have said before, it would be void of life; for life is motion, is a flow, is but a wave. We would like to say that it is rising, and again not in a way to over-bear, to over-rule, but rebalance. It is about connecting back to the heart space - for there is a time to listen and there is a time to speak. You see,

276

as humans you fight this whisper; you do so drag it through the mud far too much. It is about meeting yourselves with an open heart, with an open mind - for then you see all can flow. It is about connecting, collaborating, and loving, but for the sake of it - never scared. For the fearful heart, the one that is but closed off, is so closed off from self, from what you are. How can you ever meet anyone in such a place if you have first not yet to of met yourselves? It is not about closing off but allowing space now for something other to move - to allow, to come forth. Listen, truly listen, and it will speak - do you so see this now? If you are but asking in which ways, we would kindly say that this does not but wear one face, one essence. It is about allowing this to express in so many ways, for you have but labelled this feminine energy and it is but time to move away from the concepts that have been but built upon. Do not now let it wear anything - see the naked truth for that is but its originality. Truly just feel - you will feel it arise within if you give space. With much Love and Light – Abe.

16. We are very open and allowing of this feminine energy to arise, as we feel it is necessary for this energy to heal and nurture. You have said that it is now time to follow and allow this guidance. Could you speak more about what you mean here?

Allow is just that – allow. Nothing more. Do not get over-bearing in such a way that you but have to fit it into any kind of concept. We say this with great love and affection – now let it rise, let it come forth within your very being. Connect with it, allow it, and let it flow free – flow, for it will merge you with all. It will gently usher you back on path, on track, on rhythm - for in this it is but truth. It is but all in the feeling now - is this of understanding? For this is but rhythm - you can allow this pattern to but emerge within. Do you so feel it? It has to be but felt. With much Love and Light – Abe.

SECTION SIX
Clarifying the Way Back Home

1. We would like to ask Abe in what direction would they like to take these communications. We have explored the topic of our relations and relationships. Are there other specific areas Abe would wish to explore and transmit in these communications? Thank you.

As we said before, we would see it fitting to clarify THE WAY BACK HOME now. What this means? For we see that people are disconnecting in such a way, are feeling that no longer modern life is not allowing you as human beings to flourish. Therefore, it is not working; but then you are left adrift. You hook onto something other, that does so look like it may know the way. But you see, it is always within, it was never in another religion, another guru, another fad. It is but always underlying and it needs to be synced up with. Therefore, we see it fitting to direct in this path as to what we truly mean in finding your way back home and how it is but accomplished in a world that does so want you to be out, involved, and always entertained. Does this so answer the question?

2. Thank you, Abe. Let us begin to focus on the subject of The Way Back Home. To start, could you describe what you mean by this phrase. What is Abe wishing to convey here?

The way back home is but a space, never a place, for in your human existence if there is space then its purpose is but to be filled. What we say is - what is the part that you do so use? The pot is but the carrier pot; the space within the pot is the use. For you see, space is never empty but full of life; so never be afraid of the space. Suspend yourselves there if only for a moment and feel this sense of fullness - not because you are filled but because you have opened to allow. This is but being back home; home from where you can see all paths meet and all things flow. And like you fill and create your physical homes, allow this place to be where nothing stays; but a space where everything only ever visits for that is but home. Home is within, and whilst you are away from that place you will only search for outer gratification in which will never sustain you for you are but always selling yourselves short. Is this of understanding of the place we call home - of the place we do so want you to find your way back too?

You see, whilst you are away you are but splintered; you are easily enticed away from this space in reach for things to fill this emptiness. But it is never so, not if you give it a moment. Allow yourselves to rest there; rest for a while and see if this place does so feel like a void - or is it full with life? For isn't the saying 'home is where the heart is,' and you see your home is always here. With much Love and Light – Abe.

3. Let us go back in history. Was there a time when humans were less disconnected from Home? And what were the major factors that instigated this disconnection – was it a growth of the human brain and the emergence of self-consciousness? Was it the rise of institutionalized religions and the decline of indigenous beliefs? The rise of urban lifestyles and the decline of pastoral living? Could Abe give some background as to why humanity became increasingly disconnected and disengaged from the Home vibration?

You could say this, yes, for they had less things to take them from themselves. But you see, as you are evolving, and have evolved as a species, there is but more to you. Those times were all well and good for then; and was in coherence to the environment, to the mechanism - the space that which was held then. It is good and well to take note of the ones in who have all along not been taken apart from themselves - in gratification, in fulfilment of outside sources. You see, life is transactional, and it is but good to be involved in life so long as you do so from this place of home. For if not, your being is weakened in a sense that it can be but pulled to and fro and never truly seated. Is this of understanding now? You see, as time went on you evolved consciously; the reason you did become disconnected and splintered is because you are forever looking outside of yourselves. And the more you look outside yourselves the more things grow to want you to look outside yourselves. This is in many a human connection - from relationships between yourselves, to the food that you consume, the things that you do, the jobs that you work. It is abundant in your modern lifestyles. There is really very little connection, whereas in times gone by you had this connection with your planet - this system in which you are a part of. But it seems that many have stepped aside of this and do not belong there. That is why you are really at loss. See, it is not about stepping back in time. You evolve, that is evident; but allowing this space, finding this way back home - this space in the chaos, a calm, a place of being, of belonging and bringing back. The recognition of the complete picture rather than frantically running around with just a part. With much Love and Light – Abe.

4. Once the disconnection from Home vibration occurred, what were the factors that sustained and further developed this disconnection? And how were these factors maintained in human societies?

Like we said, it was in this transactional resonance of creation, of material existence, that you hooked but parts of yourselves to this existence. It is well and good; but you see, sometimes it does so tip the balance and balance then needs to be restored. There is but a fine line between flourishing and thriving and in over-dominance of just one species. For whilst it is detrimental to other species it is also detrimental to yourselves - it is in the fine balance of things. But you see, the more you resonate with the outer gratifications the more you are but splintered; and the more you are but splintered, the more you feel unfulfilled - as if an itch that you just can't quite scratch so, in this, the more it is resonated to. It is really an interactional web of resonance, of communication, and for you to but cut yourselves off it is but essential to find THE WAY BACK HOME. With much Love and Light – Abe.

5. It is said that humanity has been dispossessed of its true potential. Some mythologies and spiritual teachings say that this has occurred through outside forces - whether it is false gods or deceptive spirits. Is there some truth to this? Or are such 'false gods or deceptive spirits' only projections of our own imaginations in which we delude ourselves?

We would like to say in such a way as to never discredit what has so been before, for at the time and place and space, and of your evolutionary stance and perceptual capacity, it was but meaningful. It is never to wipe the slate clean, as such, for it is a path, and only by retracing your steps do you see to find that in which you were but looking for. But you see, you have been taken apart from yourselves for you have but grown; and like anything of the animal kingdom, and indeed in your human species, there is but a time in which you are but taking off, fleeing the nest so to speak. And no matter whether it was consumerism, as it is today, that you do so get lost in and try to find the nugget of truth. Or whether it be spirituality or the Gods, or the contacting of the other side, it really does not matter in the physical manifestation of such things that do so put you off track. It is what is that does so take you back home. Is this of understanding now? For you see, life is but a mirror of that in which you hold individually, collectively, and there are but always conflict of interest to differing systems. It is in the recognition that you are but a part of it and that your physical life is but a reflection - like we say, a doll within a doll within a doll. The only thing you can do now is to not put the head on, so to speak. With much Love and Light – Abe.

6. Is all our reality a reflection/projection of our human creative imagination? Are we somehow 'vibrationally trapped' within a splintered state of our own making? Is this what is meant by the admonition for us to 'awaken from our slumber'?

It is so. It is as if, like we just stated above, you peep out of the top and then decide to put the lid back on again - or the overcoat, whichever analogy you see to be fit. For you feel this changeable, uncertainty of life and you would but much prefer the comfy slippers of certainty. Albeit it being that in this you also cage yourselves in - you cut yourselves off from the human potential you were born to enhance, to nurture, to evolve to. Is this of understanding now?

7. The human collective psyche has been greatly influenced by the idea that a 'divine intervention' will manifest into human affairs and help to save us. Are not such ideas counter-productive to the necessity for humanity to realize and activate its own innate potentials? Have not such ideas added to our dissociative state?

It is definitely as so, for you do not need to be saved. You have to but swim yourselves - there is no divine intervention unless you do so allow it to flow through you. And all the time you play the 'poor little me card' and state that something above and beyond yourselves will but save you, the more you push yourselves further from the inherent truth in that you are but the saviours that you have been waiting for. Do you so see this? This is a key factor now. And we do say this with great love - that do not play so little; do not sell yourselves short. For what we are, and what you are, are no differing. And when you do so play this game of victim and saviour, we want you to see that you are but playing both parts. With much Love and Light – Abe.

8. There are many people who do not feel at home upon the planet - a feeling of alienation from their home environment. This shows a dissonance in vibration, a de-syncing from HOME vibration. Does this not show that some of us have lost the ability to distinguish the false from the true - the pearl from the plastic, the simulation from the real? Does not modern life play upon and reinforce this lack of discernment?

It is so, yes. But to see it you have to 'see' it. And to see it, you but have to feel this dissonance - really allow it to raise its ugly head, for you spend much a time distracting yourselves from feeling it. And in this, you want a band aid fix for this deep disconnection in which you feel - it keeps you locked in and disenfranchised from that in which you truly are. Do you see this loop of vibrational communication in which you do so trap yourselves?

9. In talking about people who do not feel at home upon the planet, or alienation from their home environment, we would like to return to the subject of Gaia – our home planetary organism. What can you say about the subject of Gaia and the ancient understanding of our planet being a conscious entity?

You see, it could so be likened to that of your internal functioning. And we go but back and forth with the analogy of the dolls - an encapsulated conscious being within an encapsulated conscious being, all wanting state of harmony, albeit on differing levels but all seeking harmony within a whole network. All striving, in a sense, for balance - for equilibrium from the point of place that it is so at. You see, how you evolve your planet is but at a shift. And you see, if your planet is but at a shift it is too further and further out until you are so expanded that you are but nothing. But you then see it is but never nothing but again vibrational; there is this fractal relation, this turning of inside and out and back around again. You see, everything on some level is of evolvement - from the microscopic to the macroscopic - it is but all in relation; all so tightly intertwined. To say that your planet is not conscious, therefore placing whatever is living on it in a hierarchical form, is to be one of absurdity for it is placing importance upon one thing independent of the other. And although independent flourishing and nourishment is of importance, of course, the knowledge of this entire interconnected system upon this planet is but of great importance - of great evolutionary stance. For in this you are able to move with the subtle changes and therefore thrive. And like we said earlier, as in the dam change, if allowed to flow and not resisted, will be subtle. If not allowed - if stunted and stopped - will at some point break through and flood your material lives and will overwhelm it. Is this of understanding now?

10. Various ancient teachings consider that a wisdom vibration – which has been named *Sophia* – materialized, or emerged, as the planet we are living on. What is this ancient teaching trying to tell us – what wisdom is being transmitted in this narrative? And is part of the 'way back home' for humanity to synch up with the Gaia/Sophia vibration?

There has been many a wisdom, many a story to be told over time - this is how your human lives have but kept this undercurrent of being in flow so that it will not be lost. In this, it is never to be discredited. But what we say is that there is no longer a need, as such, for your minds to conceive of a material entity for that is what the mind will grab a hold of in this splintered state - to have something apart from yourselves. For this vibratory essence of which you speak is just a reflection of that in which you are; it is but always in relation to the place in which you stand still, in which you are but in relation to. Therefore, it is not of need as such to realise that there is an external vibration, and in this a named one, but something that is so evident within each and every one of you. There is but no need now to cast these shadows of mind. And although they are but reflections of the light mind, and what could and have been of use and good, they are but no longer needed for they will only cast shadows now, for what you are in that in which you carry. For you see, you are but splintered; and what we want you to see, in a sense, is that there is but nothing for your minds to grab a hold of externally. In this, you have but no other choice than to delve deep within your being - for, yes, if putting something apart from yourselves as a species you are but keeping your hands in. It is time to pull right back, to be seated in the depths, so that you can but come back up for air to then appreciate deeply that in which you are and not that in which you are directed to be or are told you are. Is this of understanding now? It is time for directness, not indirectness. And it will not serve this part of your evolutionary movement to keep a space between what you think you are and that in which you know you are within. With much Love and Light – Abe.

11. Thank you, Abe, for all your clarifications. We know that we may repeat ourselves in some of our questions, yet in trying

to understand these things it helps us by asking similar questions or repeating perspectives. We would like to ask you about the role of humanity. Does humanity have a specific role to play as a sentient species upon our planet? That is, are we supposed to be assisting in the evolution of our planet also – and how?

You see, we would but not like to get into falsities here in stating that humanity is above and beyond. For you see, it is also in the relation to differing species - to your planet, to the cosmos - that does so determine other factors too. This web of life is so intricate and has been but building, piecing, growing, arising, interacting, and always very much interdependent. But hear this, just like the heart has its specificities, so does the human race. It is but the beating heart of the living organism of the planet. It is the resonation that does so allow this living planet to but feel, to sense. Many think it is but the capacity to think, to create; and although this is a part of your evolutionary stance, it is not the meaning - it is but not the nugget of truth. You are but the resonators - you are the receivers, the expressers of this. You are but the heart that does so pump within the Earth. The reason you have splintered - have dispersed, have fractured - is for the reason that you but wanted to take over all the jobs. And in this you lost faith of who you are - you lost heart. Is this of understanding now? If you are but asking how, and if, regarding your evolutionary path as a whole then, but of course you are - you are but the receivers. You are what allows flow; what pumps the universal energy around. But you have become weakened and stagnant - do you so see this pattern of relation, this turning inside and out? Do you but see this fractal relation of your being to that of your outer being - it is but a mirror, is it not?

288

12. A lot has been said about humanity's free will. Some sources say it is a unique feature. As humans, we are free to make mistakes; and also, how we learn from our mistakes. How does human free will contribute to our situation, in terms of our connections to the planet, the cosmos, and to the larger evolutionary pattern?

Ahh, free will - many a people have but tried to figure out if this is but true. But you have to see, does the mirror or reflection have free will? Does it freely move? Is it not the physical manifestation that does so impress upon it? What you have to see is that it is a reverse - that for anyone to have free will at all you but have to come from within. There is but no room for surface reflections when it comes to free will, for you are as free as you allow yourselves not to be impressed upon. You have to realise this conundrum of being that you are but so intertwined with. It is not in the conscious actions; it is not about that, but in also seeing this interconnected system too. And you but can only see this when you realise you are but a part of it - and you only realise you are a part of it when you do not stare into the reflection but allow yourselves to reflect. Do you so understand this now? Hear this, free will is not about choice - and never has been. True free will is in the conscious relation to that in which you truly are; for all the other surface dances and choices are just that - a dance of polarity, a dance of games. With much Love and Light – Abe.

We would but like to come forth with a short note to that of free will and continuing that theme of such. For what we say is what truly is will - will is something that drives you to act. To have an individual will of your own it is but a desire to participate in life, to interact. And you see, that is but all you can do so - is to interact. And we say this with great love that you are but a part of this interaction, this interconnected web. Only when you put yourselves above it and beyond it are you not free, for in this you are but deluding yourselves. If you can but see - if you can but come back and truly see, truly align - to that in which you are, then that is free will for you are aligning to all that you are. You are not captured by the dancing shadows of your disillusioned minds but are free to see the grander picture of life in which you are a part of. Is this of understanding now? The will to dance with life, to participate in Life, should not be held in the sparkly, in the jazz, but in the simple - in the ordinary - for in this there is true beauty. With much Love and Light – Abe.

13. Can we say that human free will allows for great errors to be made - rather than stating this as evil – and that this learning from our errors is a strong human trait? Yet if we permit our errors to go undetected and not rectified, we fall away, or deviate, from our directed goal. As a whole, can it be said that humanity is in danger of great deviance at this time, hence the importance of finding the way back home?

Errors are but made when you are splintered for you but lose yourselves in the choices. Is it not wise to say 'to sync back up first and foremost' when you are but in this space? When you feel this internal relation do you so feel that you but have to choose at all or is it not just a flow, a natural occurrence? You have but been long lost in choice and this is where the problems come. Do you see this pattern that is so deviating you from your paths, from yourselves?

14. Can it be said that the 'way back home' represents an organic path, aligned with Nature, human nature, and in biological resonance with a living planet? If so, it would seem that the rise of artificial intelligence (AI) and machine technology would be a simulation, a replication of organic life. Would this suggest that AI is a deviance from the 'way back home? and therefore a false path, an error of direction?

We would not like to say a deviance as such for you will but evolve, and this is so. It is but when this comes from this splintered being, this un-human lost being, that it is but of issue. For in this, you see, how can one create a human-like being when you hardly know what you are yourself? For it is as if you are a mechanic trying to fix a car in which you don't even know or have never heard of what a car is or does. Do you so see this now? You do not know yourselves; you can know the mechanics of your material being but when do you know this intimate being, the one that does so feel life? Is it just in the body or is it not in the flow of life that is happening? In the relation?

15. Monday 27ᵗʰ May 2019

We would like to come forth this morning in a way that speaks of this connection, for what we see is that the more you do so open up, the more you release fear - fear of not knowing, fear of getting it right, fear of fear. And we say this with great love - that you do so go around and around; it is a tedious pursuit for your species. It is but a distraction from that in which you are; and like the dog chasing its tail, trying to but capture it, it is so with yourselves. You do not realise that it is there, and there is but nothing to capture for it is already a part of you. Is this of understanding now? We would, and if this does so feel the right way for you both too, like to discuss more on the misconceptions of spirituality and how it has but a little, and sometimes unintentionally, been captured as to sell you back something that is already belonging to yourselves. It is just as we said before; for you see, when some direction is being herded by more and more people it can so get lost in translation - lost in the language, and the tools, and the deities, and the things that do so resemble all that you already are. There is no longer a need to chase the shadows. No need to chase your own tails in hope of capturing something for it is your innate capacity now. It is your new evolutionary stance to get back to the bare bones of that in what you truly represent - in which you truly are. With much Love and Light – Abe.

16. Thank you, Abe. Yes, we would be pleased to now begin discussing more on the misconceptions of spirituality. Where would you wish to begin – further back in our human history or more recently? Would you wish to say anything about our religious traditions, and how they are functioning today?

We would but like to discuss from the beginning as we feel a good overview of how it began would be paramount to understanding this continuance, this pattern. For you see, it is but a thing that has had many a face over time, and it would be but good to sort the fact from the fiction - the misinterpreted truth, the misconceptions. For you see, like any story passed through your time, through the ages, there is but a little added. And like we said at the beginning, it is time to go back to the bare bones. Not in saying that all that has been before has been unnecessary, for everything is of relation of where you are so as a species; but you have evolved - you are but evolving. What we would like to show you is the 'simplicity of being' in which has been long lost - the nugget of truth that does so lie in all of your religious practices, in your spirituality. For you see, it is but never beyond you - and we would not state anything in hierarchical form - for there is no differing in all of life. It is but just the order is different, the pattern is differing - the mechanism. It is just that for too long you have put yourselves apart from this; and in this, something above and beyond yourselves must have created you. But you see, it is not true; for it was an emergence - it is all but one thing expressing in but many a form. This is unity, this is the true beauty of life - this is the true meaning of oneness. With much Love and Light – Abe.

Back from the very beginning of time you have but put something other governing your world. And whilst this is true, it is also a great misunderstanding - for what is governing your world is but also you. You are an interconnected governing system - a system within a system within a system - and as time has gone on you have but emerged, you have grown. And you are but still emerging, you are but still growing. But you see, to move forward now it is not within your evolutionary stance to put things outside of yourselves anymore - to be splintered anymore. For it is not a broken world that needs to be fixed now – no, not at all. It is but the parts, and you are but a significant part. You see, you are not to go about straightening out this and that but realigning and re-emerging from this space so that you can allow all the counterparts in which you are, and that of which you are but a part, realign. You see, like we have but said before, that you have wanted to state that 'I am here,' and 'I exist;' and in this, you but have adapted to life outside of yourselves. For if something was just a part, an unseen, you would of but not had the stance. And this through time has been constructed, and many a time also misconstrued, for in this wanting to of exist you had but placed the unseen, the felt, out into the physical world - out on show, pinned it onto something other. But you see, in this you did so lose yourselves. Do you see this conundrum of being - this flip side, if you will? But hear this, we are not stating that it was but wrong or disillusioned, for it did so serve its purpose. But you see clearly now that it is not so this way anymore. And sometimes, as a species, you do so have to let things just fall away that cannot carry you through to the next stages of life. We are not stating to give them up, to give any practise up that does so resonate. But you see, sometimes it is but good to look behind the curtains and see what is beyond the fancy packaging and bright lights - and see the characters without the masks. Do you so see this in which we are but trying to get across to you now?

We would but like to come forth on continuance of this spirituality theme and talk to you on what may be fitting. In conversation today we would like to bring up the notion of twin flames, for we see this so deeply embedded in your new age philosophy. And what to know here is to separate fact from fiction; this being what the mind does so cling to. Fact being the feeling and fiction being the clinginess of the mind. See, in this very connection it could be one thought of as a twin flame, for isn't everyone from this 'one flame' - this oneness split apart and apart, further and further? You have the female and the male - this is true twin archetype. But you see, it is not one of physicality, for you but all hold this energy when you feel a draw to another as such. What is said in a twin flame connection it is because one, no matter which sex, holds that in which you lack, but also that in which you are - this is the spark, if you will. Also, this one is of evolutionary resonance, and although you seem very differing in the external world you are not so for all are but connected. It is just so that you both meet upon the same path, albeit in differing themes. See, one may be more logically minded, holding more of the masculine energy; and the other but more sensitive, more feeling one - to say, more female energy. But you see, you but both show each other what it is to be balanced - this is the mirror. And what is so seen as mirror is that it is not saying for you to BE with that person - that is entirely a free choice - but more so to show what real love is. And that is but unconditional. Many a people get this attached to romantic love - and it is not so. This is definitely not the point of it for it is in the uncovering, the raising of each other - for it is so like a vibrational detox. You've had but a universal kick, and we mean this with great love, but it is an almost shove as so to speak. As to say - take the leap and stop dilly-dallying on the side lines. You can so see this for what it is, or not now. When this happens, many a people are caught up in the patterns, in the old patterns. They but try to fit what you are but wanting to expand to into a tight container that you cannot put the lid on. In this, it is caught up for such a long time, chasing and running. Allow it to be, to flow, for it will find its own space. And what we say in this triad of being - and but what life, what this is trying to show you - is this: this triad, this unification of being, that is *you*. Not in the other, but in you. This is but the home space - this is but THE WAY BACK HOME. For this triad is really a physical manifestation of that in which you are - it is but a mirror too. We hope you do so understand this for we feel it is but an important pointer upon this spiritual path. Drop twin flame altogether if you are to move on into truth and not get stuck on the merry-go-round of but chasing your own tail - for you are but already it.

Heed way of what it truly is trying to mirror back to you. With much Love and Light and continued growth - Abe.

17. Abe, you stated that back from the very beginning of time we have 'but put something other governing' our world. Do you refer here to how our major religions were established? And how we placed authority onto an externalised form of a god? In this way, we allowed hierarchical and control structures to be set-up to manage relations with these 'external gods.' Was this the case?

This is but the way, yes, for you have placed what was inherent within as to give you an echo. And we say again, it was but of interest to your species then, to where you were at, but now these systems are not serving you. Know this, you see it for you are but not flourishing as a species; for to flourish as a species it is not to have wealth and status but to be healthy - to be collectively healthy. And this means on all levels, and this is just not so now in your world, in your reality now. Do you so see this?

18. Many of our religious structures placed suffering as a central idea - that is, redemption through suffering. Some see this as a form of 'spiritual control' as the need to suffer has also led to people inflicting suffering 'in god's name.' The need to suffer does not seem to us to be a human, humane, or spiritual concept. Could you comment on this?

You see, to suffer is, and always should be seen, for what it so is - for suffering is not necessary. But it is but a part, for you only suffer if you cling to an ideal of any kind. So, to suffer is to

296

cling to one thing over another - you do not need to suffer. There will be times that if you cling to a certain construct that you inevitably suffer, for you are wanting something to be sure, to be stagnant, to be still - and this is so not life. You see, if one can control the spirit, to say that one should suffer, then you see that you are but kept in a bind. This is not getting your species anywhere at all. We see that people do suffer great hardship, great disasters, but you have to see that you are but a part of this interconnected ecosystem and not above it, trying to straighten it all out. Is this so seen?

19. We agree with you that it is time 'to sort the fact from the fiction' as you say. Which parts of our religious-spiritual understanding are particularly fiction? What are some of the most debilitating fictions that we now need to be rid of in order to evolve forward at this time?

We would say that the most debilitating one is to set yourselves apart from this creation. If there is a God that you wish to praise, realise that you too are it. It is not an ideal that you need to reach to, but a realisation that you were never apart from it - you are it. See, to evolve now you do need to find your way back home - home to this oneness. Not something governing over you, to say to you - 'poor little humans, you should be reaching a certain ideal.' This is not so now, and it will forever be taking you away from what is truth. You are not Godly but human. You have the capabilities to turn things around - grow, evolve, become and receive so much more. Why stump your growth by allowing others to lead on what is their truth, their path? Create the path from this place of unification and you will realise that the area is likened to the brain - a grand network working for a common goal, a common humanity - an Earth, a cosmos, the whole. With much Love and Light – Abe.

20. You have suggested that it is misleading to believe that something 'above us' created us. You imply that the 'Creation' story is false, and that the truth is closer to emergence. Could you say more about this?

True. It's an emergence - a resonance, a collection. For what does so happen when synapses resonate - they create a connection, a pathway. And just like this, your planet has an intelligence. It is but creating more in this sense, and like the analogy of the dolls - a consciousness within another, within another - all conscious, and it is this fractal relation. What we see is that this in which you call a natural resonance has but created new pathways, breaking it off from this central intelligence – de-syncing it. Do you so see this pattern of being?

21. Would Abe consider that many of the 'external entities' - from gods, UFOs, evil spirits, fairies, djinns, and the rest - are forms of 'spiritual control' mechanisms that distract humanity from their own internal, and innate, spiritual faculties?

We would say, not one of control but reflections of what is innate; again, this fractal relation. For you see, as a species you get too attached to the external factors and do not so realise that mostly it is projection. What is needed is a true, clear seeing - a clarity of what life is but trying to say, trying to whisper. And this is only done so by listening - you do not need the middleman anymore. You have, and are evolving to have, this direct experience, this direct connection. If you so allow, you do not need the filter as such. Do you so see this now?

22. Thursday 6th June 2019

We would but like to come forth with a note on love today, for it is said to be the foundation of truth. The love vibration is but seen to be the state of everything. The love vibration is but said to be the zero-state in which we are in - which you are. What we would like to say is that you do so take love too seriously. For you feel it is something sought out from another and that in which you give to another freely; and also, one that you can stop flowing to another. It is such a tiresome pursuit – on, off, redirect, attach. But love is not this at all. Now, many a spiritual sector say 'to love all' but there are some in your existence that seem to be not so lovable - and this is understandable for some do so cause atrocity upon others and great suffering. How can you love those that do such things? But you see, it is never about directing love to those stating 'I shall love all' - but more so in the allowance of love to flow. This doesn't mean that you do so hug and love every one thing, everyone, but you do not allow it stop flowing within your being. Love is not your definition of love. In fact, let's call it flow – let's call it allowance - for love really is movement, is unconditional. It is really a presence of no presence - a space, if you will. Sit for a moment - what does love truly *feel* like for you? It is expansive, un-constricted, it opens you up - is this not so? For you see, the word 'love' has been over-complicated, over-compensated, for the void you do so feel within - that you feel you must continuously fill. But you see, this very thing is love - is allowance, is space - and should not be susceptible to your human conditions. It is but unification; so,

299

maybe it is to be that you do so find another word for love. In this, you can somehow allow it to truly flow un-constricted, uncontaminated. For you see, you do not have to love everyone to feel love. And it is but never given by anything outside of yourselves. And why you always assume so, you will but always suffer. It is truly just an allowance - an allowance of being. It is just so that as humans you call it 'love.' With much *Allowance* and Light – Abe.

We would like to come forth with a very short note on conscious experience. And we see that we have stated as life as a mirror of your own conscious reality. And you see, we would but like to say that as you see this, and what is effectively happening, is that vibratory resonance is a mirror resonance. That is but how your existence or pathways are but built both within and without. And like the analogy of the dolls - a doll within a doll - this fractal relation is but so. Reflection grows resonation; resonation grows pathways; and pathways internal create pathways externally - is this so seen now? Can you but see what we mean by the term fractal relation in relation to consciousness?

23. Sunday 9th June 2019

You see, as human beings what you have long, long forgotten is that evolution is a vibrational match - is a call, if you will. Spirituality is just that - evolution of the vibrational signature, allowing evolution of the organism, the material things. And evolution of the organism is evolution of the vibrational signature - the meeting back up, the inside out and upside down. You do so see this, for it cannot be so easily defined as one thing or the other, for it is not so. For science to focus purely on the material evolution and not take into account the spiritual evolution, you are but missing out a large part. For these two are not separate at all, but like everything else, a dance of seemingly distinct opposites. You see, it is but never about one or the other but seeing that they are but so tightly interwoven. For someone purely focused on materiality is but half the picture; and someone focused purely on spirituality is too. You see, it is always, always, about the dance - that is what makes your very being so treasurable, so diverse, so splendid. With much Allowance and Light – Abe.

24. Monday 10th June 2019

You see, the reason you do not get anywhere is you swap one attachment for another - be it love, or money, or status, or even trying to find oneself, of spirituality. It could be in finding your purpose of being. But we would like to say - is it not your very being here purpose enough? Is there really a purpose beyond that? It is but true that you yourselves create meaning. But sometimes in the space, in the nothing, in this place where you can but not grab onto anything whatsoever, you cannot attach yourselves to anything, any belief system - any THING or ANYONE - as if you are but in the great void. What if here, in this space, in this suspension between all the noise of the world, you truly allow what you have been searching for? What if it finally finds you and you but realise it was never amiss, just drowned out by all the noise, by all the activity of your being, of your trying to find something? You see, at some point you have to get comfortable with feeling uncomfortable - without the knowing, without the structures that do so prop you up. At some point you have to not BE anything, but just to feel that freedom - if only for a nanosecond at a time. For this will be enough for you to keep dropping it all, allowing the noise to continue but just doing nothing - being still, giving space, not fretting or getting but entangled. Just being - just being human. Give yourselves a break. There is but no ideal to reach; but there is also no need to be entangled either - to be too involved. It is but time to meet yourselves again, coming back. With much Allowance and Light – Abe.

We would like to say that there is but no need to find yourselves. If you are but looking, you are constantly losing yourself to others, to outer structures. For what you do so get entangled in is this conundrum that something is outer - to be sought out. And this is but the illusion. And what is true spirituality, and this word has so been but over-used, is space - this suspended space, this unification. Don't name it, don't conceptualise it - just feel it. Allow it, albeit it being uncomfortable, being foreign to you. Do not fill this space with new beliefs, new patterns. Allow it all to meet there, undefined and unconditioned, and you will but see not a word that will fit it - just feel. With much Allowance and Light – Abe.

25. Thank you, Abe, for your recent communications. We have found it very useful to see how love is an allowance, and that it is our natural flow. Our species has got love mixed up with so much baggage and other emotional associations. Sometimes we become more blocked through love than liberated. It is the same with the idea of what is spiritual - we become blocked by all our associations. We need to strip back our ideas about what is spirituality, do we not?

This is indeed so, for you do so get lost in the language and the baggage of the association in which you have but tied your own emotional responses to things. For you see, everything is but neutral until you name it, claim it, grasp it, and you then interpret it to mean such a thing. And you see, it is but not taking the language as the definite answer to things, of the things you do so retrace it to, tie it to. But hear this, we are never saying to be a blank, to not convey, for stories are but what you are. But sometimes you have to step back and truly understand what is really trying to be conveyed. And sometimes this needs no words at all - no translation, just a direct connection to it, to allow it. Do you so see this? Do not get so mixed up in the meaning of things for it is but an interpretation - feel into it and allow it to convey something to you. Spirituality has indeed been claimed as to so have an overall notion to it. But like we said, it is but spirit-full and this is indeed in the very allowance. And in the allowing of something you do so realise it was but never amiss. With much Allowance and Light – Abe.

26. Abe, you said recently that it is not about being spiritual but rather about being spirit-full. This suggests an understanding that less is more. That is, we do not need to be striving for 'spiritual behaviour' or spiritual imaginings. Rather, we should allow the natural, genuine resonance of life to flow through us. The spiritual is in allowance and flow, not ritual or religious observances. Is this so?

This is indeed so, for it is never something apart from you. It is merely being aware of it, recognising this adamant flow of existence. For you see, you really do not need tools, and healings, and crystals, and prayers, and any other myriad of things. The wind in your hair can tell you as much as you need to know by feeling it. The Earth under your feet can feed you, can breathe into you. For you need to realise that it is but all here - you are a part of it. And when you see this, and you do so feel this, you will truly know what love is for it will flow through all that there is. It is allowance - it is life, it is love, it is creation, and it is but you. What a wondrous stance to take - truly awe-inspiring. For what else could you feel when you realise that you are a part of it all and it is but all a part of you? And you will but stop to think 'how did you but miss it for so long, it is but truly astounding.' But at the same time, so very simple and mostly always overlooked. With much Allowance and Light – Abe.

27. Abe, you say that we no longer need such spiritual tools as crystals or prayers, and that feeling into the flow of life is enough. A phrase you have used is - 'it was never about being enlightened but to light-up what was previously unseen.' Are people blocking themselves by being overly focused or concerned on 'spiritual matters' and 'finding the truth'? Is there any truth to be found, spiritually speaking?

Ahhhh. You see, what spirituality can but seem to do is make the notion of it to be very much fanciful. And you see, it is not - it is but quite ordinary, and you say it must be but more spectacular than this. But you see, spirituality is not a thing to be chased, but to be seen, to be synced-up with. And you see, it has never been amiss - it has just been overlooked because you were so wanting to find something spectacular, with fireworks and such a display. But you see, it was never lost, it was just not brought light to. You see, and we say this with much love for your species and with such great reverence, that you have been searching for truth and in the same breath also overlooking the truth. For you see, TRUTH is sometimes hard to face because it is bare and naked and always there but seemingly overlooked in favour of the opposite. You will know what is truth for when you shine light of your own perception on what was always there – underlying, never amiss - the lie that you have been telling yourselves for such a long time, and that in which has kept you going, kept you wanting and searching, will not be able to withhold the facts that it is all here and nothing was ever not. It's just that you had to grow, to see, and to evolve - that is it. It isn't extravagant; it isn't ground shaking - but it is truth, and it is here. You just need to open your eyes and but see. With much Allowance and Light – Abe.

28. Would Abe say that by allowing the flow of life, a person is also allowing the flow of spirit? Is there are tangible difference if we are, by inherent nature, spiritual beings?

This is one we do so struggle with for we see that spirit, soul, and a myriad of other terms have been but contaminated by the notion of something other. But you see, it is like the yin and yang and that which seems separating or opposing is never so. It is but a dance, a mutual arising - never one without the other. But you see, as humans you get so caught up in one or the other; and this is but true for both sides. You seem to but pick a side. You see that the material sense has not given you so what you need, so maybe I should drop that and go so down the spiritual path. But you see, the same is allowing all; never one or other - never this or that but to allow the two to finally conjoin. To see that they are but one in the same, and because your minds have to pick a side, pick and choose and decipher your existence, it is but hard now for you to let go. But you see, it is an entanglement and once you do so let go you are where you have always been searching. For this time, this evolvement of humanity, is not to pick and choose but to allow life - allow yourselves to but rhythm up, for when you do you will no longer see spirit and material but a dance of life and you are but it too. With much Allowance and Light – Abe.

29. Some people may think that by 'allowing the flow of life' we are becoming detached from life. Yet isn't allowing also another form of participating? Could Abe comment on this?

You see, it could be seen as such if you are but caught up in the polarities, and we will not say any differing for it will be a tug. But you see, it is never about attachment to one or the other; not to any one practise, any movement, any one word. Let it all go and then see - open up in the space. It is like seeing it all - allowing it all flow. Get involved, love with all your heart; cry at the loss of a loved one; marvel at the sunset or the birth of a child; love family; love life - but see that underlying current that is never amiss. Flow - allow that to but guide you. You do not need to lose who you are but allow more. You do not need to deny your parts but accept yourself wholly. There is but never anything holy, just wholly. Rest in the unease, laugh at the discomfort and know that this human experience is just that - you can feel, you can sense, and you can but transmute and transform this wonderful flow. How truly extraordinarily ordinary - what a gift. With much Allowance and Light – Abe.

30. In one way, spirituality is seen as a form of 'New Thought' whereby human consciousness can act upon external reality and influence it. This 'New Thought' has itself become a type of religion. Should such mental 'spiritual-science' be encouraged, or does it distract from allowance and flow?

You see, you have to but sense this one for yourselves to know, for New Thought is a directing and intention and it can be but practised. But you see, like any tool, you take the tool as the thing. But you see, the tool is not the table - but the tool is there to help bring the table to light. Do you so see what we are but trying to put to you? We never want to discourage or say this is but right or wrong, but you do so get caught up in the word, the tool, the process, and you miss out on the very ordinary reality that it is here. Just light it up, sync back up, and bring it forth in all you do. For you may say it is not so simple; but you see, simple or truth is but sometimes the hardest to see for it is but continually overlooked or even sometimes over-exposed as to be something much more. Do you so see? With much Allowance and Light – Abe.

31. Although we don't wish to focus on matters that may distract us, we wonder about people's use of the 'dark arts' and the 'devilish' side of religious matters. What is actually happening when people invoke and focus their conscious intention upon such 'devil/dark' aspects? Are they conjuring energies that block or work against the natural flow of life/spirit?

You see, it is so again picking a side, entangling your conscious experience to experience more of but one thing over the other, to bring forth from your own darkness. You see, you but all have this capability and it is but dependant on the mechanism that you do so filter this flow through. Like we say, it is never amiss but is transformed – overlay, if you will. You see, in all your stories going right back, the dark side has but always had or been light, but has been but changed, transformed somehow - contaminated to then become dark. It's not a flow for it is but not shining your light on it. It is the same thing; it is just that the mechanism is but disguising it. To become an opposition, to rise up against all, brought forth from your conscious experience by that in which you do so hold, it is but a fancy-dress party. Do you so see this conundrum of being?

32. We wonder if it might be useful for humanity to drop the word/vocabulary of 'spiritual/spirituality' altogether since it represents a natural, innate state of being. Could Abe foresee a future where religion and spirituality are no longer issues of concern, separate from our way of life, but a non-spoken integrated part?

It is right that this is but your human capacity - your inherent truth, if you will. But you see, you want to pull it out and see it for yourselves so you but use words. You use opposites - you disguise and transform and imitate. But you see, for the heart to beat you can't see it - you feel it, you allow it to just beat. Let things, all your parts, combine to unify and allow it - just allow it. Don't name it, don't chase it, but nurture, appreciate, and allow what is natural - what is you, what is there. Allow yourselves to be. With much Allowance and Light – Abe.

33. Abe, in an earlier communication you talked of how the Earth, or evolution upon the Earth, goes through periods of activity and periods of rest. You said that at this current time we are experiencing a period of rest where we can gather ourselves together and take this period to re-align and re-sync. Is this still the case, and is this what you mean by 'allowing' and 'going with the flow'? That is, by recognizing the energy of the time and harmonizing with that energy?

It is but always so. For you see, out-of-sync you are but that - you feel it so, you feel disharmony. This is allowing - allowing yourselves to drop back. You have been but so accustomed, or one could say overloaded, by so many differing energies through your life – teachers, parents, friends. It is but time to flow back into rhythm but express in your own way. You see, you can get caught up with others in what they do, believing it is but your choice. And you see, when you do so step away you see you were just flowing with someone else's strength. Real strength is holding this flow amidst the varying vibrations, for you have but strengthened it in you. It is your setting point - you have nurtured it. To allow to but rhythm up again, we feel there is but a time to step now. You will feel this if you are so in rhythm - step too early and you are out of rhythm; step too late and you are having to catch up or skip parts. But when you root this, seat it when you are but home. Everything is of flow because you arise with it - you allow it to take you. Do you so see this now?

34. Regarding these larger periods of activity and rest, are these also mirrored in our individual actions too? We ask this because recently you said that when we feel the flow is right in our lives, we should take the leap and jump into this change

and new activity. Is Abe saying that we should also take moments of activity and important personal change even when we are in a planetary 'rest period'? Could Abe say more about this?

Like we say, the doll within a doll - all but connected, all but a flow. And always relational to that in which you allow. It is all dependant on that in which you see and that in which you then allow. A hall of mirrors is but only realised when you realise that you are it - you so see it now? You see, if you are but a flow, when you bring it back you do so see the reflections. It's always about being aware - what is being said when not said. It is allowing you space to feel, to sync up; there may be time of rest, but it can also be a time of change. But you do so have to feel it, you see? For you see, action is within your paradigm, and although there is but planetary rest you have to be of rhythm to FEEL action arise. Sometimes it takes all the noise externally to hush a little - to realise what step next. With much Allowance and Light – Abe.

35. We would like to return to the theme of understanding what spirituality means. Is now an opportune time to readjust and recalibrate our understanding because we are in a planetary (or cosmic) period of rest? That is, by gaining a deeper understanding of our spiritual nature now, this will assist us for when we return to a period of activity and growth? Is this why there is so much activity now present in our human societies concerning the nature of consciousness and inner growth?

It is so that way - for rest is allowing and allowing you to rhythm up. And we say about this ebb and flow, you rest to flow

310

- it is but this way. What we see so much is that you are but constantly charging forth - this is not allowing. You are but on a destructive path; you need to stop, listen, and then move forward. But hear this, when all is but quiet and still you see great movement too - do you so see? Spiritual is human, and human is spiritual - there are no two parts. It is realising that you have not been allowing it; you've been but too busy, too active. Ebb is allowing your true nature rest and merge with your temporary nature, and knowing that they are but one in the same in this form. This is intertwined, interdependent; it is an internal conversation of listening, then acting. Listening and acting - not necessarily to words, or people, or situations, but to the unheard. You can but allow this to arise before the mind gets a hold on it - before it is but contaminated with other peoples' do's and don'ts. Feel into it, rhythm up, and then know when to act; when there is a nudge to do so. There is never a right time but a flow, a rhythm, a beat - follow that, resonate with that. With much Allowance and Light – Abe.

36. Abe, you have said that humans have a somewhat fixed frequency, or vibrational signature, through which we can only gain a limited perception. It also seems to us that the human frequency is being influenced, or interfered with, in an attempt to fix this frequency that then halts, or obstructs, further perceptual expansion. Could Abe comment on this?

You see, it is not so much about others - you feel it is so, but it is not. Most of the times you get yourselves caught up within yourselves – entangled, if you will, in the perception of a perception. Do you see? For it is also about the frequencies that can influence you in such a way as that you yourselves allow it to be so. You are far more than what you are told that you are; but yes, limits are put in place within your societal structures. But you see, also that these outer limits are always being pushed. For you see, there are no such boundaries - only the line of fear in which you dare not cross. Is this of understanding now? We continue with this that the key is allowance. Do not bother yourselves so much about what you are, who you are, for that too will limit your connection, your flow. With much Allowance and Light – Abe.

37. You have talked about the importance not to create 'attachments' by picking sides in terms of external events, practices, themes, or theories. By doing this we are directing or 'fixing' the flow of consciousness which then places us within a certain frequency vibration. That is, Abe has said that humans 'get stuck' in these so-called 'setting frequencies' that will in the long run govern the unconscious states.' How do these 'setting frequencies' affect the collective consciousness of humanity? Are not certain manifestations in our reality a consequence of these 'settings' within the collective frequency?

You see, this is but the conundrum. We are not saying ever to rid yourselves in anything - for yes, you are but choosing reference, one thing over the other. But it is about not being fixed, allowing all frequencies, for they can come and go. It is in the attachment to them that keeps you stagnant; and as you grow you gather more - you sift and sort and box, and contain varying vibrational resonances, almost as if you are building a house, a home. But you see, you are merely building an outer structure over a home that you already had - you are encasing yourselves in, further and further, like the dolls, like the overcoats. More and more is added until the original flow that enables you to be but connected to all - conscious of your own state of being and that of the whole - is lost. This is but the effect. It has, like we have said before, it is not so much on what is out there at all but what your own individual setting point is. This does really need to clear out now for you to see the bigger picture. Do you so see this?

38. You have rightly said that Abe does not wish to bring in anything negative, for good reason. Neither do we wish to discuss subjects of the negative frequency. As Abe has said - all is frequency. Yet it sometimes seems as if humanity is caught within a now non-advantageous frequency range, and that this is being maintained by distraction. Is this so? And by allowing flow, we can break out of this debilitating consciousness frequency?

It is so, for you have encompassed it yourselves. You have resonated with it that is so what keeps it being fed into, and fed into you like an argument back and forth, back and forth - but no resolution until someone is but proved wrong or just simply breaks the connection. You see, it is almost like a tug of war with yourselves; for yourselves it is quite delusional, in a way, to be as such. And we do not mean this at all in a dismissive way but for you to see the conundrum of your conscious efforts. If you allow, you flow. You do so know this but then you think 'I must get back in life' and start doing it, battling with it. But hear this, life is not easy sometimes; things do so take you away from this flow. But if this is but your setting point, and you but give yourself time to readjust again, see it is not about staying there -

life does so want you to participate. Its knowing that this is but what you flow back to - not to get there but to simply allow. Allow it again and again - it should never be a one-way street in any connection. And this is but so with life also. With much Allowance and Light – Abe.

39. Could Abe discuss more about the relation between individual consciousness signature and the collective human consciousness frequency. Was the psychologist CG Jung correct with his insights into archetypes and synchronicity regarding the collective consciousness?

You see, this is so. It is as if the consciousness has been but split, and the feminine and the masculine constituents of your own conscious reality. You see, this is what we mean in regards to twin flames - it is not in 'other,' like your spiritual sectors have but grabbed a hold of, and many are but stuck here trying to chase another. But you see, you are but only chasing yourselves. The mirror in which they speak is one of your own reflection in which you are to realise that you are but both male and female. You are but chasing again a ghost if you think you will be but whole when you claim another physically - it is but your conscious playing out in your reality. You see, a mirror unification is but with you. It is but sad to go a whole life and chase another when it was always but you. You were seeking you - do you see this pattern? Sync, like we say, is but synchronicity - it is a dropping back. You don't need to look for it - it is there for you know when you have dropped back into the flow. For what is synchronicity other than the natural flow - it is but you meeting life and life meeting you, is it not?

40. We would like to ask about human gatherings and their effect on vibratory frequency. When a number of people are gathered together for a shared event, this can create an intensified consciousness field. Could this consciousness field be used to alter frequency and perception? Are human gatherings sometimes utilized for this purpose - consciously and/or unconsciously?

It is so this way, yes. For you see, it is but a gathering back - a piecing back, if you will - and can be used either for fact or fiction. Either way, this is why it is but important to come back home and see that in which you are but gathering with, setting up to. You see, it is but like the hive mind - you are but all gathering inside a certain doll. The important thing is really not to be contained. Not to be identifiable but allow - do you so see this?

41. You have stated recently that it is now time to return to a direct connection to ourselves. Is this part of the 'change' that you have indicated? Must this change be a conscious effort on the part of the individual or will external events also contribute to bring about the stimulus for this change?

It is but a joint effort, and realise we use the word 'effort' loosely. And like we have always said before - one of coherence. But you see, to make use of the flow, the energies that are present, you have to allow it - to meet it. And allowing is meeting it - otherwise it will be but defaulted to your own setting, filtered through hatred down. You so see this now? Change is always motion - motion is always change. The reason you do not flow is because you do so prefer the stagnant, stale waters. Allow, and see what does come. For in this, life will meet you - and you will meet it. And in this, you are but in rhythm to yourselves; therefore, in rhythm to it all. Cut out the middleman. You have direct contact - why you do so need to see this for it is in everything you do. You light the world up in this way - you light up your own worlds. With much Allowance and Light – Abe.

42. In our last communication Abe also stated that 'This does so mean our topic of conversation is going to be one of change - it will be so to bring now the non-physical to physical.' Could you clarify more what is meant by bringing now the non-physical to physical?

It is so now a shift, a change of topic; and what we mean in this regards is bringing yourselves to the forefront - uniting yourselves, gathering your parts. This is the ebb, the allowing, the non-physical feeling - it is uniting the feminine and masculine, the black and the white, the good and the bad. And it is uniting this and having the physical manifestation of it, of flow in your physical worlds. It is now bringing this together, united in yourselves - vibrational signature, sensory body, and us, Abe - all combined. To see this wholeness, to bring it into physical, to have physical representation of this, your humanness - your true capability - has to be seen now, and you will be but representation of it, of unity. You so see this now?

43. Abe has recently suggested that many of our symbols and stories relate to the consciousness state. Would Abe say that most 'symbolic stories' are a reflection, or representation, of our state of consciousness and as such are meant as signs for

us to awaken to this understanding? Abe also suggested that the story of Adam and Eve signifies a split of consciousness - could more be said on this?

You see, all your stories are stories of where you are at consciously. You see that this conscious growth is but not a recent thing and following back stories you will see the patterns of conscious relation to your world. We say it is about the direct contact now, that you must see this as such - as patterns, as a conscious map, if you will. Yes, the Adam and Eve story, like all others, are also what you have called a 'falling from grace.' You see, the feminine energy was seen as something that was somehow deceptive, that they somehow should not need knowledge or wisdom. But you see, that is their very essence and it is but all yours too - it is something that is inherent within you all. That you have these polarities of being, they are a part of this wholeness, but it was separated. In this there was but a clear divide, within this story, and it was but reflected then in your worlds. You see, you are human - human is the gatherment of existence. But you put what is within you outside of you; and then you decipher and depict, and label one thing over another - how very exhausting is this. Do you see the patterns? We are not to say that these stories have not helped you evolve in a way, for sometimes you have to step out to then step back. It is a growth, a cycle. But hear this, to go forwards now, to evolve further, it will not serve you to be bamboozled by your own making. Is this clear now?

44. It has been said by past sages that the aim of the human condition is to allow the Unity consciousness (sacred, divine, etc) to manifest upon the physical through the human vessel.

Some have used the terms 'supramental consciousness' to reflect this. When Abe talks of 'allowing' and 'flow,' is this speaking of the same process - to allow or manifest the Unity consciousness state whilst in physicality?

It is so. But we would not see it as 'super' for it does put it above and beyond. And what you do so need to realise is that you are never apart from it - you never have been. The stories have been but stories you have been telling yourselves in order to awaken yourselves gradually and growingly. The key here is to know your humanness. We will but always state this, for in this you are but allowing all that you are and all that you have ever been. And like the child that gradually grows and becomes more aware, you have been growing in consciousness to allow and know your true nature. You so see this now? It is but time now to stop getting in your own way and have this direct contact - all of you to have direct contact to yourselves. With much Allowance and Light – Abe.

You see, what we would like to say is that it truly is this fractal relation - this inside out, this conscious 'bubble of being' that you get caught up with. And you see, it is not to be rid of but allowed. Allow this bubble to pop. You do not need such conscious containment, constriction of being, anymore. You will see that there is a relation, a growth, through all of your human stories. It is but the journey you take as a whole to then find THE WAY BACK HOME. With much Allowance and Light – Abe.

Other books by Kingsley L. Dennis

The Inversion: How We Have Been Tricked into Perceiving a False Reality

Life in the Continuum

Hijacking Reality: The Reprogramming & Reorganization of Human Life

Healing the Wounded Mind: Mass Psychosis in the Modern World & The Search for Self

The Modern Seeker: A Perennial Psychology for Contemporary Times

The Sacred Revival: Magic, Myth & the New Human

Bardo Times: hyperreality, high-velocity, simulation, automation, mutation - a hoax?

The Phoenix Generation: A New Era of Connection, Compassion and Consciousness

Dawn of the Akashic Age: New Consciousness, Quantum Resonance, and the Future of the World (co-authored with Ervin Laszlo)

Breaking the Spell: An Exploration of Human Perception

New Revolutions for a Small Planet: How the Coming Years Will Transform Our Lives & Minds

The Struggle for Your Mind: Conscious Evolution and the Battle to Control How We Think

New Consciousness for a New World

Printed in Great Britain
by Amazon

42738333R00176